HMS Hampshire: a Century of Myths and Mysteries Unravelled

HMS Hampshire: a Century of Myths and Mysteries Unravelled

by

James Irvine, Brian Budge, Jude Callister, Issy Grieve,
Kevin Heath, Andrew Hollinrake, Keith Johnson, Neil Kermode,
Michael Lowrey, Tom Muir, Emily Turton and Ben Wade.

© The individual authors copyright 2016

No part of this publication may be reproduced,
stored in any retrieval system, or transmitted
in any form or by any means, electronic, mechanical,
photocopying, recording or otherwise,
without the prior permission of the publisher.

ISBN 0-9535945-7-2

Printed in Orkney by The Orcadian, Hatston Industrial Estate, Kirkwall, Orkney KW15 1GJ

Published by the Orkney Heritage Society 30 August 2016.

The proceeds from this volume, including the authors' royalties, are being donated
to the Orkney Heritage Society for the Kitchener Memorial Refurbishment Project.

The Orkney Heritage Society, founded in 1968, is a charitable body which aims to retain all
that is best in the architecture and culture of the islands, and to encourage beneficial developments.

To join the Society, see http://www.orkneycommunities.co.uk/OHS/ > Membership.

For the previous publications of the Society, see rear inside cover.

Contents

	Foreword, by Admiral Sir Jock Slater	vi
	Preface	vii
	Map of Orkney showing track of HMS *Hampshire*	viii
1	HMS *Hampshire*, by James Irvine	1
2	The German Mining Offensive and *U 75*, by Michael Lowrey	2
3	Lord Kitchener and the Mission to Russia, by Andrew Hollinrake	5
4	The Fatal Voyage, by Andrew Hollinrake	12
5	The Rescue Efforts, by James Irvine	18
6	"If you go near the cliffs we'll shoot!", by James Irvine	33
7	Outrage, by Issy Grieve	38
8	The Conspiracy Theories, by Tom Muir	43
9	Minesweeping and the *Laurel Crown*, by Kevin Heath	48
10	The Kitchener Memorial, by Neil Kermode	51
11	The Men Lost from HMS *Hampshire*	58
12	The Survivors, by Brian Budge	62
13	Diving the Wreck, by Emily Turton and Ben Wade	69
14	The Artefacts Recovered, by Jude Callister	77
15	The Centenary Commemorations 2016, by Neil Kermode and Keith Johnson	78
	Conclusions	84
Appendix	I Roll of Honour, by Brian Budge and Andrew Hollinrake	85
	II The weather and tides, early June 1916, by Keith Johnson	96
	III Summary of surviving artefacts, compiled by Jude Callister and James Irvine	98
	IV The reliability of previous accounts, by James Irvine	99
	Acknowledgements	105
	Bibliography	106
	Index	110

Foreword

by Admiral Sir Jock Slater GCB, LVO, DL
First Sea Lord 1995-1998

I was taken up to the Kitchener Memorial on Marwick Head as a boy in 1949, exactly thirty three years after HMS *Hampshire* was sunk by a mine and Field Marshal Lord Kitchener was lost along with 736 others. To this day, gossip and rumour persist about the circumstances of the tragedy and why there were only twelve survivors on that dreadful night.

Over the years since, I have heard many views on exactly what might or might not have happened: why the ship was ordered to sail West of Orkney and not East; what, if anything, was really known about German mining activity in the area, how much was actually known of Kitchener's mission to Russia, and much else besides. This admirable book draws all the strands together and analyses in detail the events that took place on that fateful night only days after the Battle of Jutland in which HMS *Hampshire* had participated. The loss of the ship and its distinguished passenger with his staff must have been a devastating blow to the Commander-in-Chief, Admiral Sir John Jellicoe, who, that very day, had received Lord Kitchener, the Secretary of State for War, on board his flagship, HMS *Iron Duke*, in Scapa Flow.

Ten years later, in 1926, there was an impressive gathering on Marwick Head to witness the unveiling of the Kitchener Memorial by General Lord Horne, with HMS *Royal Sovereign* firing a gun salute off shore. The Memorial was generously funded by the people of Orkney. Sadly no names of those lost were recorded at the time, so the establishment of the new Memorial Wall to seaward of the restored tower is long overdue and an excellent and most moving addition to the site.

Taking stock of all the facts after a century of reflection, with reference to hitherto unpublished papers, has cast fresh light on some of the misconceptions of the disaster but revealed few additional facts. This book rightly does not apportion blame nor, indeed, add further criticism. That said, the Commander-in-Chief must accept ultimate responsibility which, I am sure, he did. Moreover, the censure for the failure to mount a speedy and effective rescue operation must lie with the shore authorities. However, in their defence, initial communication about the disaster was clearly sparse and, in retrospect, it was understandable that the military personnel were reluctant, at the outset, to involve volunteers, despite their undoubted local knowledge and experience. Thus the perception of the locals and indeed their descendants was of a mismanaged recovery in which they rightly felt that they should and could have played a greater role. Hence rumours were rife and persist to this day that, had they been swiftly co-opted, more lives might have been saved. However, I fear that conditions were such that night that, had they been allowed to participate more fully, there would still have been very few survivors.

I was honoured to be present at the Centenary Commemorations at Marwick Head on the evening of 5 June this year and to lay a wreath at the new wall on behalf of the Royal Navy and the Royal Marines, paying tribute to all those who lost their lives exactly one hundred years ago. It was a most moving ceremony with the Royal Navy's latest destroyer, HMS *Duncan*, lying in the setting sun off the coast over the *Hampshire* wreck and the NLV *Pharos* positioned where HM Drifter *Laurel Crown* was subsequently mined with the loss of a further nine lives.

The new wall, bearing the names of all those who perished, owes much to the commendable work of the Orkney Heritage Society and the Project Leader, Neil Kermode, and his team. Moreover, this book is a most welcome addition to the history of the First World War. The individual contributors deserve great credit for their chapters which called for detailed research; and a particular thanks must go to the editor, James Irvine, for his determination to see this worthy project through.

Jock Slater
Admiral
June 2016

Preface

At dusk on 5 June 1916, four days after the Battle of Jutland and four weeks before the Battle of the Somme, the cruiser HMS *Hampshire* was carrying Field Marshal Lord Kitchener of Khartoum from Scapa Flow to Russia when she suffered an explosion 1½ miles off Marwick Head in Orkney. She sank quickly, and the Field Marshal was not among the 12 men who survived. Today Kitchener is best remembered for his recruiting poster, but in 1916 he was Secretary of State for War and a Cabinet Minister with a reputation almost as great as that of Winston Churchill in World War II. The news of his death caused shock waves around the world similar to that which later followed the deaths of President Kennedy and Princess Diana. In Orkney reports of civilians' rescue attempts being thwarted led to widespread outrage that continues to this day. Censorship and the Admiralty's secretive instincts led to a wave of conspiracy theories on how and why *Hampshire* was sunk, and rumours that Kitchener had survived. Even his own family were kept in the dark:[1]

> *the reports are very trying, entirely owing to our being given no information as to where the fault lay or the cause of the disaster.*

In addition to various national initiatives to commemorate Kitchener, the people of Orkney funded a memorial on Marwick Head, unveiled in 1926. Later some diving expeditions on the wreck led to alleged damage before further diving operations were banned in 2002. To commemorate the centenary in 2016 the Kitchener Memorial has been restored and a low surrounding wall built to bear the names of the 746 men from HMS *Hampshire* and the minesweeper HM Drifter *Laurel Crown* who lost their lives off Marwick Head in June 1916.

During the past century many writers have discussed the sinking of *Hampshire* and its causes, the rescue efforts and their failings, the salvage attempts and the artefacts recovered, and the various associated myths and mysteries. In the 1920s Kitchener's secretary Sir George Arthur claimed the deaths were no accident, and the journalist Arthur Freeman, alias Frank Power, wrote a series of controversial allegations in the *Sunday Referee* and the *Orcadian* and claimed to have discovered Kitchener's body. In 1959 the journalist Donald McCormick wrote his comprehensive and hitherto well-respected *Mystery of Lord Kitchener's Death*. Alas it now transpires that McCormick, like Freeman, was a fraudster more interested in his pocket than the truth, and that few subsequent writers have made use of the extensive contemporary Admiralty files which had been closed to public scrutiny under the 50-year rule, perhaps because it was thought the most controversial material was still secret.[2] But now that all of the surviving files are available to researchers, these internal records make clear that the Admiralty had nothing substantive to hide, even if the authorities' rescue efforts were poorly coordinated and their natural reticence led to sustained suspicion. It is now clear that many of the previous interpretations of the disaster have been misleading, even those of the more pragmatic commentators, biographers and historians. The men who lost their lives in 1916, and Admiral Jellicoe who is often blamed for the tragedy, have been ill-served.

This commemorative volume draws on these hitherto little-used files of the Admiralty and the Kaiserliche Marine, and on the many contemporary first-hand accounts by survivors, rescuers and other eyewitnesses that are now available, to determine what actually happened on 5 and 6 June 1916, and why. It includes previously unpublished accounts of the mining operation by *U 75*, the sinking of the *Laurel Crown*, a complete Roll of Honour of the lives lost, the building and refurbishment of the Kitchener Memorial, and brief notes on those who survived and many who did not. It discusses the background to the outrage still felt by many Orcadians, especially in Birsay (where, ironically, no survivors or bodies came ashore), and revisits the many conspiracy theories. It describes the various diving operations on the wreck, including that of 2016, and the artefacts recovered. Finally it records the events in Orkney that were arranged to mark the Centenary.

Each chapter of this collaborative volume has been written by an individual with local knowledge who has generously summarised their specialist interests in different aspects of this emotive saga. Our objective has not been to apportion blame, or to prove or disprove any particular theory, but to seek and explain the relevant facts. In pursuing this goal a number of fresh interpretations have emerged and several widely-believed traditions have had to be challenged. These findings are summarised in the concluding chapter.

NB One of the many causes for confusion in the unfolding saga is that in Orkney in June 1916 the Royal Navy still worked on Greenwich Mean Time while the civilian population kept British Summer Time.[3] In this volume most times are as used in the source documents; those in 24 hour notation indicate GMT, those suffixed "am" or "pm" indicate BST.

---

[1] IWM Docs.10730, a letter by Kitchener's sister, Mrs Frances E Parker, 19 July 1916.
[2] The last two files concerning Kitchener held at TNA became accessible to the public in 2014 (see Appendix IV below).
[3] The confusion may have been at least in part because BST had been first introduced just three weeks earlier, on 21 May 1916.

Map of Orkney showing track of HMS *Hampshire*

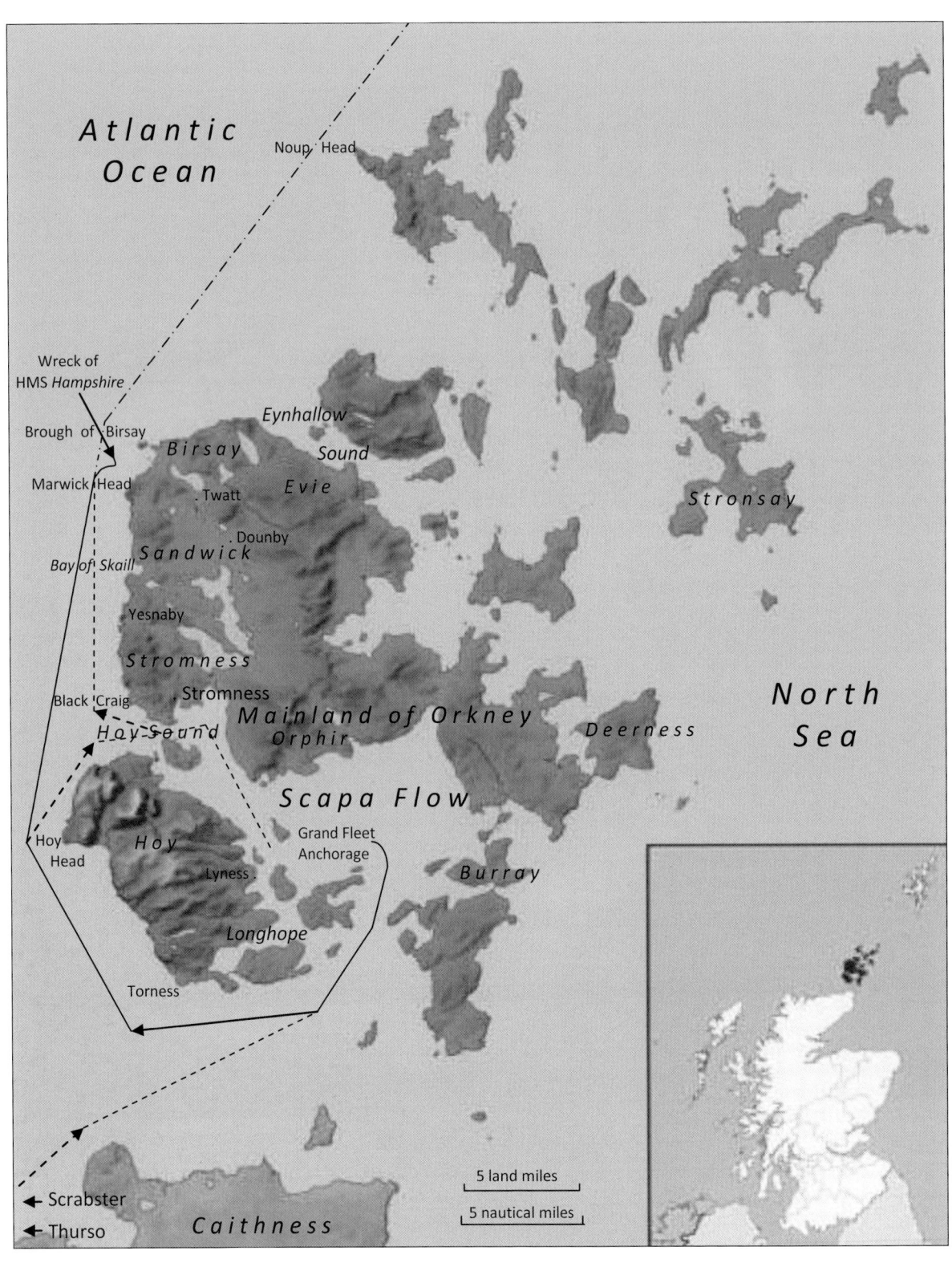

Chapter 1

HMS *Hampshire*

by James Irvine

HMS *Hampshire* (IWM Q39007).

HMS *Hampshire* was one of the six *Devonshire* class of armoured cruisers. She had an overall length of 473½ft, beam of 68½ft, draught of 25½ft, and displaced 10,850 tons (including 6,665 tons of armour plating up to 6 inches thick and 1,033 tons of coal). Twenty three boilers powered two 4-cylinder triple-expansion reciprocating steam engines which drove two propellers to give a trial speed of over 23 knots. Her armament was four 7.5-inch guns with a range of about 7 miles, six 6-inch guns, two 12-pounder guns, eighteen 3-pounder guns and two 18-inch torpedo tubes. Her peace-time complement was 610 men.

Hampshire was built by Armstrong Whitworth at Elswick on the Tyne.[4] Laid down on 1 September 1902, she was launched 24 September 1903, completed 15 July 1905, and commissioned into the Channel Fleet a month later. In December 1908 she refitted at Portsmouth and then transferred to the reserve fleet. She took part in the Coronation Fleet Review for King George V in June 1911 before joining the Mediterranean Fleet. In 1912 she carried Field Marshal Kitchener from Egypt to Malta, and later transferred to the China Fleet. Most of her final crew joined in Colombo in January 1914.

At the outbreak of war in August 1914 *Hampshire* was at Wei-hei-wei in China. While en route to destroy the German radio station on Yap she sank the German collier *Elsbeth*, but ran short of coal and returned to Hong Kong. She then searched in the South China Sea for the German light cruisers SMS *Emden* and later SMS *Königsberg*. In November she replaced HMAS *Sydney* as one of the escorts of the first convoy of ANZAC troops bound for Egypt. She returned to Devonport in January 1915, and from there joined Admiral Sir John Jellicoe's Grand Fleet, taking part in North Sea patrols from Cromarty or Scapa Flow. On 1 July 1915 while in the Moray Firth she survived an attack by *U 25*, whose torpedo failed to explode. In November she escorted shipping to Alexanddrovisk in the White Sea. After a refit in Birkenhead she was docked in Belfast from 10 January to 16 February 1916 to have the 6-inch guns that were mounted on her main deck re-sited to her upper deck to improve her seaworthiness. *Hampshire* participated in the Battle of Jutland on 31 May/1 June under Admiral Jellicoe as part of Rear-Admiral Heath's 2nd Cruiser Squadron; this squadron was tasked with reconnaissance to prevent enemy light forces from 'discovering' Jellicoe's battleships.[5]

Hampshire was a "happy ship" and Herbert John Savill, her 45 year old captain who had taken command in May 1915, was a capable, experienced and popular officer. Contrary to subsequent claims in the press[6] his ship was well suited to her next mission.

---

[4] Reports that *Hampshire* was a battle cruiser and that she was built in Chatham are incorrect.
[5] Five of the ship's company left accounts of the battle: Capt. Savill (TNA ADM137/302), Cossey (*Times*, 13 June 1916), Fellowes (IWM Docs.10969), Phillips (TNA ADM116/2324A; 1930, 25) and Tucker (*Orkney Herald*, 21 June 1916). Fellows and Phillips (and McCormick 1959, 21, Royle 1985, 382, and Paxman 2013, 175) claimed *Hampshire* sank a German cruiser and/or at least one U boat; the accounts of Savill and other historians (e.g. Campbell 1986, 321) make clear she just fired at a cruiser and collided with a U boat.
[6] *Referee* 15 Nov. 1925.

Chapter 2

The German Mining Offensive and *U 75*

By Michael Lowrey

German naval doctrine during the Great War placed much importance upon minelaying.[7] The Kaiserliche Marine's light cruisers and torpedo boats (destroyers), for example, were designed to accommodate mines. This capability was not just theoretical, as German cruisers conducted several minelaying sorties near the English east coast in 1914 and 1915, leading to the sinking of nearly 100 vessels. They also fitted many of their surface raiders to carry mines. The results were again significant, including the sinking of the battleships HMS *Audacious* and HMS *King Edward VII*, the latter off Cape Wrath in January 1916.

In late 1914 the Kaiserliche Marine decided to construct ocean-going minelaying submarines as well. As they didn't think the war would last a long time, for the type to be worth building it would have to be ready sooner rather than later. Germany's industrial capacity was finite, and U-boats in general and the diesel engines that propelled them on the surface in particular were very advanced technologies for the time: all this argued for keeping the new design as simple as possible.

The result was a rather odd submarine. Called the UEI class, they were 57 metres long and with a surface displacement of 755 tonnes. The aft portion of the hull was given over to carrying 34 type UE/150 moored mines,[8] which were released at the stern through a pair of 100cm diameter tubes via a cog drive mechanism. All this took up considerable space, leaving the engine room in the centre of the submarine with the control room and conning tower much further forward than in a more conventional design. There wasn't adequate space for internal torpedo rooms, so instead single external torpedo tubes were fitted forward and aft. Torpedo reloads, if carried, were simply lashed to the deck. A single 88 millimetre gun was fitted aft of the conning tower.

The UEI was a single hull design with a saddle tank on each side amidships to provide additional fuel oil storage. To enable faster construction the hull was made of steel cut to basic geometric shapes. A more complex hull form would have increased the surface speed. More powerful diesel engines would have helped too, as the two 450 horsepower units fitted weren't really adequate for a submarine of that size and a radius of action of up to 7,000 miles. Their top surface speed was nominally a slow 10.6 knots, and in practice they rarely cruised at more than 6 knots. In service the class met with general disapproval by their crews, being described as large and clumsy, with the sole redeeming feature of having excellent depth-keeping stability.[9]

A total of 10 UEI minelayers were built. The first four boats were ordered in January 1915 from Vulcan AG, Hamburg (*U 71* and *U 72*) and the Kaiserliche Werft Danzig (*U 73* and *U 74*). Vulcan AG received a follow-up order for an additional six boats (*U 75* - *U 80*) on 9 March 1915.

By spring 1916 the first of these UEI boats were ready for action, with *U 71* sailing in April 1916 to lay mines off Berwick. Other UEIs soon entered operational service, including *U 75*, under the command of Kapitänleutnant Curt Beitzen.

Beitzen had entered the Kaiserliche Marine as an 18-year old cadet in April 1904, and in September 1907 was commissioned as a Leutnant zur See. He was an Oberleutnant zur See on the battleship SMS *Thüringen* when the war began, and started his submarine training in June 1915. He was promoted to Kapitänleutnant based on seniority on 17 October 1915, and assumed command of *U 75* when she was commissioned on 26 March 1916.

Kapitänleutnant Curt Beitzen.

---

[7] The references used to compile this chapter were Groos 1925; Rangliste v.d.; Rössler 1981, 1997; Spindler 1933; Stoelzel 1930; TNA ADM186/628; BM KTB *U 75*.

[8] A moored mine is a buoyant explosive device secured below the sea surface by a wire attached to a sinker on the seabed.

[9] TNA ADM186/628, ADM186/629; ADM137/3903, 81a.

2 – The German Mining Offensive

U 75 to the Orkney Islands

As part of Vizeadmiral Scheer's plan which led up to the Battle of Jutland, *U 72*, *U 74* and *U 75* were dispatched to lay mines off the Firth of Forth, the Moray Firth and Orkney respectively.[10] On 21 May 1916,[11] Fregattenkapitän Hermann Bauer, the commander of all High Seas Fleet U-boats, instructed *U 75* to sail on her first mission and lay her mines off the Brough of Birsay. Beitzen's written orders can be translated thus:

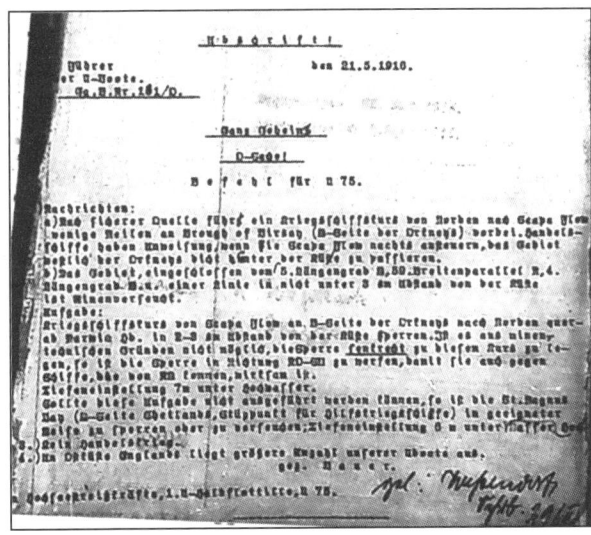

Intelligence: According to a reliable source, a warship route runs from the north to Scapa Flow a few miles off the Brough of Birsay (W side of the Orkneys). Merchant ships have instructions when approaching Scapa Flow at night to pass the area west of the Orkneys close inshore ......

Task: Mine warship route from Scapa Flow north along the W side of the Orkneys 2 to 3 nautical miles from the coast abeam Marwick Head.[12] If it is for mine technical reasons not possible to place the barrier perpendicular to the course, then lay it in direction NE-SW, so that it is also effective against ships coming from the northwest. Depth setting 7 metres under High Water.[13]

If the task could not be carried out then St.Magnus Bay (W of Shetland, base for auxiliary warships) was to be mined in a suitable manner, depth setting 6 metres below High Water. These orders, like those of the other UEI minelayers operating in 1916, also instructed *U 75* <u>not</u> to seek out and sink merchant shipping, though she could attempt to torpedo Allied warships should she come across them.

U 75 sailed from Heligoland early on 24 May 1916. The outbound trip was far from uneventful, as the submarine began taking in water through the diesels' exhaust pipework a few hours after sailing. She continued north while repairs were made, which took about a day. On the morning of the 26th they sighted the Norwegian coast, and at 2pm, off Utsire, set course for a point north of Shetland before turning southwest for Orkney.

Beitzen's challenge was to arrive off the Brough of Birsay during a narrow window when the combination of tides and darkness made minelaying at the desired depth possible. Early on the 28th he thought he could just barely make it there with both diesels at full power, giving him a speed of 9 knots. It was then discovered that the U-boat was some 17 miles from where he had thought it was, thus necessitating the submarine spending nearly 24 hours loitering off Orkney.

Overnight, while waiting, *U 75* sighted a blacked-out ship passing about 1,500 metres away. Beitzen assumed this was a large warship but refrained from making a torpedo attack due to limited visibility.

At 2.10am on the 29th *U 75* dived and was soon able to make out Noup Head despite the lighthouse being extinguished. By 7am Beitzen had worked his way to her minelaying area west of Marwick Head, having stayed well clear of land so as to avoid detection by patrols. To confirm the boat's location, he took bearings while submerged as close as 1,000 metres offshore before turning west to begin his mining run, with several of the mines being laid before the submarine made a turn to the north, then the northeast, and then back to the west. As *U 75* was preparing to discharge the 12th of the planned 17 mines from her starboard mine tube, the cog mechanism failed. While the crew were able with some effort to get that mine out, the remaining five mines had to be moved to the port tube, which took considerable time. As a result, the depth setting for the last seven mines had to be adjusted by 1 metre.

---

[10] TNA ADM186/628, 36. *U 72* aborted her mission. *U 74* was lost with all hands on 17 May 1916 through an apparent mine-handling accident while discharging her cargo off Dunbar. *U 77* disappeared in July 1916 while on a mission to lay mines off Kinnaird Head. Clearly submarine minelaying was not without its dangers.

[11] i.e. five days before Admiral Jellicoe knew of Lord Kitchener's journey.

[12] In his war diary and minefield notice Beitzen gave (misleadingly) the coordinates of the minefield in his chartlet as 59° 05'N, 59° 09'N, 03° 24½'W, 03° 28'W (BM KTB *U 75*). These coordinates were repeated in the German (Peace) Statement of Mines laid by the High Seas Fleet 1914-1918 (TNA ADM186/628, 36).

[13] The clarity of these orders shows that the Admiralty's alleged suspicion that *U 75* laid her mines in the wrong position (Admiralty 1926, 12, footnote) can perhaps be attributed to a face-saving motive. However the Admiralty were correct in criticising the German belief that large warships often passed a few miles off the Birsay coast.

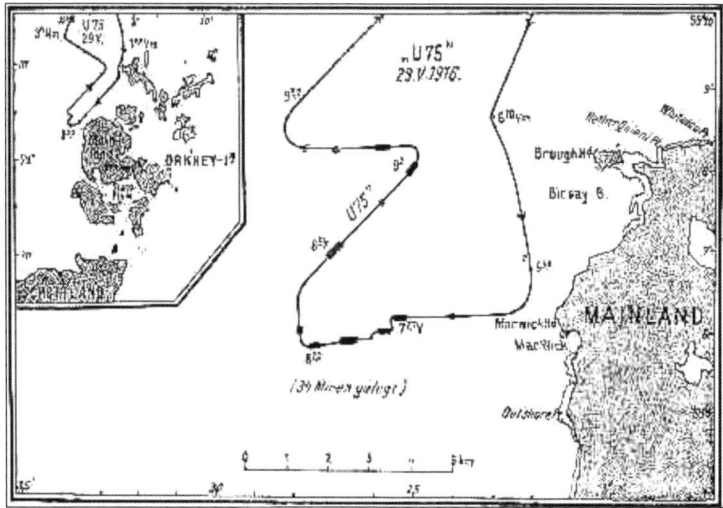

U 75's track off Orkney and the positions of her mines, 29 May 1916.

At 9.35am *U 75*'s 34th and final mine[14] was discharged and the submarine headed north on her trip back to Germany. She surfaced at 2.50pm, and was off the Norwegian coast by the morning of the 31st. She then passed through the very waters where the Battle of Jutland had been fought only hours earlier. Her war diary[15] notes an oil slick, an abundance of dead fish and seagulls, and the sea littered with debris. At 3pm on 1 June she sighted six miles away the bow section of the battle cruiser HMS *Invincible*, then still afloat, sticking 20 metres out of the water, with a British destroyer nearby.

The weather turned nasty the next day, almost causing the loss of the submarine. With very high seas, the boat was forced to close the diesel air intake, and rely upon the conning tower hatch to provide air for the diesel engines and crew. Then a large wave hit the boat, slamming the hatch shut. This meant that the still-running diesels were effectively sucking all the air out of the submarine. At the same time, it created a pressure differential between the interior of the submarine and the outside air, leaving Beitzen and other crew members standing watch on the conning tower unable to re-open the hatch, despite their desperate attempts to do so. Beitzen's banging on the conning tower hatch also failed to attract anyone's attention inside the submarine. The boat's chief engineer, Marineingenieur Hans Schmidt,[16] who had been working on repairing the gyrocompass, recognised the danger and ordered the air intake opened, thus saving the boat and its crew.[17]

Later on 2 June, near the Horns Riff off the German coast, *U 75* thrice sighted and evaded what were believed to be British submarines. She arrived back at Heligoland early on the 3rd, by coincidence the day before Kitchener left London.

Curt Beitzen was awarded the Iron Cross, First Class,[18] but neither he nor *U 75* survived the war. Beitzen remained in command of *U 75* until May 1917, when he took command of the newly-commissioned torpedo-attack boat *U 98*. He transferred to *U 102* in November 1917 but died on or about 30 September 1918 with the rest of his crew when *U 102* sank off the Orcadian island of Stronsay while homeward bound and attempting to transit the Northern Barrage, an American and British minefield designed to keep U-boats from entering and leaving the North Sea.[19] The wreck of *U 102* was located and identified in 2006, revealing the irony that after his U-boat struck an American mine, Beitzen lost his life in Orcadian waters.

U 75 hit a mine off Terschelling on 13 December 1917 while outbound to lay mines off the Dutch coast. Her commander Kapitänleutnant Fritz Schmolling and eight of his crew survived, but 23 others lost their lives.

The mines that *U 75* laid on her first sortie were to have consequences that are developed in the later chapters of this volume, but first we need to understand why HMS *Hampshire* had Lord Kitchener on board, and why she steamed into the trap set by the Kaiserliche Marine.

---

[14] Groos (1925, 202), quoted by the Admiralty (1926, 12) states *U 75* laid 22 mines, but her War Diary clearly states all 34 mines were laid, as does Groos' map and TNA ADM186/629, plate 10!

[15] BM KTB *U 75*.

[16] A Marineingenieur in the Kaiserliche Marine was the naval engineering equivalent of a Leutnant zur See.

[17] TNA ADM186/628 speculates that things might have turned out very differently if Schmidt had failed to open the vent: *U 75*'s engines would have eventually stopped for want of air and the disabled submarine might then have been captured by British warships searching for vessels damaged during the Battle of Jutland.

[18] Rangliste 1916, 37; TNA ADM137/3903. The German press report of this award alerted the Admiralty that a submarine had laid the mine.

[19] McCormick (1959, 150) believed Beitzen died off Ireland (which was from where *U 102* sent her last message stating she was starting back for home).

Chapter 3

Lord Kitchener and the Mission to Russia

by Andrew Hollinrake

Lord Kitchener in the uniform with full decorations which he would have worn when visiting the Tsar.
(courtesy of Lady Kenya Tatton-Brown)

Introduction

Field Marshal Earl Kitchener of Khartoum, Secretary of State for War since 1914, was a popular national hero and acclaimed by many as the greatest British soldier of his generation. An imposing figure at 6ft 2ins tall, with piercing blue eyes and his widely-recognised handlebar moustache, in 1916 he had already long been a household name, his victories in the Sudan and against the Boers epitomising why the British Empire was at its zenith. The most senior military man to lose his life during the Great War,[20] the shock and numbing impact of his death echoed with millions of people around the world and brought Orkney to the forefront in the newspapers. Although they were not to blame, many Orcadians felt embarrassment, perhaps even shame, that this national disaster had occurred on their doorstep. While space does not permit a comprehensive biography of Kitchener, some appreciation of his fame is key to understanding Orkney's reaction to this tragedy.[21]

Kitchener's early life[22]

Horatio Herbert Kitchener was born in Ireland on 24 June, 1850 at Ballygoghlan, just west of Limerick. He was the third child of Lieutenant Colonel Henry Horatio Kitchener and Anne Chevallier, both from Suffolk. The Lieut. Col. had served in India in the 1840s before selling his commission and, on the advice of his brother Philip, a land agent, bought a small estate in Ireland, a country still reeling in the aftermath of the Famine.

Herbert, as the family knew him, was almost thirteen when the family moved to Bex, near Geneva, on the advice of the family doctor: his mother suffered from tuberculosis, and it was hoped that the clear, dry air of the Alps would be a better climate. Herbert and his brothers attended the local school, becoming fluent in French and learning some German. Alas the Swiss air was not enough to save his mother, who died in 1864.

In 1867 Kitchener went to stay with his cousin in Rugby to prepare for the entrance exams to the Royal Military Academy at Woolwich, and he started at the Academy in early 1868. Problems with his eyesight, which he always fought hard to disguise, meant he did not excel as a sportsman or marksman, and those who knew him there saw no obvious indication that he was to lead such a prominent military and political career.

---

[20] Excepting the Tsar of Russia!
[21] Kitchener was in fact a controversial figure – for some of his less flattering features see page 43 below.
[22] Except where otherwise stated, details of Kitchener's career are taken from Arthur 1920, Pollock 2001 and ODNB 2004.

India and Egypt again

On his return home in July 1902, to another hero's welcome, Kitchener received a viscountcy, and was one of the first to become a member of the newly-formed Order of Merit. He was then made Commander-in-Chief in India, and en route to take up his new post he visited Khartoum to open the Gordon Memorial College. Kitchener set about radical reform of the Indian Army, although his plans were often resisted by the viceroy, Lord Curzon, who was wary of the military exerting too much control of the country. He improved the central administration and the machinery for mobilisation and modernised the system of training. This reaped great benefits in the Great War, when Britain relied heavily on the Indian Army and other Commonwealth troops.

On leaving India in 1909 Kitchener was promoted to Field Marshal, and after visiting the battlefields of the Russo-Japanese War, went to Australia and New Zealand to advise on organisation for defence. He returned home in 1910 and received his Field Marshal's baton from King Edward VII himself, and for eighteen months he served on the Committee of Imperial Defence. In September 1911 he was appointed British Agent and Consul-general in Egypt, enabling him to devote his time to improving Egypt's commerce and use of resources, and to carry out social reforms. He was rewarded with an Earldom, which he received in June 1914.

Secretary of State for War

Towards the end of his annual leave in 1914, with war looming, the Foreign Office instructed all those on leave to return to their overseas postings. Kitchener feared that Prime Minister Asquith would want to him to fill a lowly advisory role in the Committee of Imperial Defence, and boarded a cross-channel steamer on 3 August, hoping to sail before he could be recalled. However the ship was awaiting the boat-train, and with the train came Fitzgerald, Kitchener's personal military secretary, with a message from Asquith, asking him not to get 'beyond the reach of personal consultation and assistance'. Kitchener returned to London and met with Asquith late the following day, just hours before the expiration of Britain's ultimatum to Germany to respect Belgian neutrality. Kitchener made it plain to Asquith that he wished to return to Egypt unless he was given the full authority of Secretary of State for War. Britain's ultimatum passed at 11pm on 4 August, and Britain declared war on Germany. The next day Kitchener was formally handed the seals of office as Secretary of State for War. He insisted that although he would be a member of the Cabinet he would stay as a non-party aligned soldier. A hugely popular figure, the news of his appointment was well received:

> *No appointment could have produced a better effect upon the hearts of the British people and upon those of their Allies. The nation felt ... that Lord Kitchener was holding its hand confidently and reassuringly in one of his, while with the other he had the whole race of politicians firmly by the scruff, and would see to it that there was no nonsense or trouble in that quarter.*[23]

At the first meeting of an ad hoc war council, Kitchener stated that the war would last at least three years, to the astonishment of all present except General Haig, and would require the recruitment of a vast army. No more could the country rely on its dominance as a maritime power. Posters appealing for recruits prepared just before the start of the war were printed in most of the national newspapers, and one of Kitchener's first acts at the War Office was to order a new poster including his own name. He made it a personal appeal:

> *An addition of 100,000 men to His Majesty's regular Army is immediately necessary in the present grave National Emergency. LORD KITCHENER is confident that this appeal will be at once responded to by all those who have the safety of the Empire at heart.*

His most famous poster was printed a month later, firstly on the cover of the *London Opinion*, then later adopted by the War Office, with Kitchener's steely-eyed gaze and pointing finger. His name was not included, his image alone so well-known that it was simply followed with '... wants YOU', a powerful and direct personal invitation, painted in such a way as to give the impression of the eyes and finger following the reader. This powerful style was replicated by other countries in both world wars, for example the 'Uncle Sam' poster 'I Want You For U.S. Army.' The recruitment poster using his image has endured as one of the most familiar and iconic images associated with the Great War.

Some 2.5 million men enlisted in 1914-15, creating the second largest volunteer army in history.[24] He created the "Pals" battalions, initially famed, later notorious, and by coincidence his death coincided with the last of his 70 volunteer divisions crossing to France, no doubt en route for the Somme.

---

[23] From *Ordeal by Battle*, F.S. Oliver 1915, p 254 quoted by Pollock 2001, 374.
[24] Conscription was introduced 17 Jan. 1916, and again in 1938. The largest volunteer army was the Indian army of World War II.

The munitions crisis

At the outbreak of war, Kitchener had recognised that it would require vast new armies needing unprecedented amounts of munitions and would involve a great number of casualties on both sides. His views were not supported by his Cabinet colleagues at the time, including David Lloyd George. In late 1914 Kitchener placed huge orders for shells, rifles and other munitions with companies in the United States and Canada. But very little of this matériel had been delivered by the time of the so-called 'Shells Scandal' of 1915. Just over a year before his mission departed for Russia, responsibility for the production of munitions had been taken away from Kitchener and passed to a newly-formed Ministry of Munitions, headed by Lloyd George. Kitchener and the War Office had been blamed publicly for the shortage of shells on the Western Front, the 'Shells Scandal' sparked by reports in the national newspapers in mid-May 1915, firstly in *The Times,* then taken up by the *Daily Mail.* It was claimed that a shortage of munitions had led to the failure of an offensive in France in March 1915, and Lord Northcliffe blamed the death of his nephew firmly at the feet of Kitchener himself. Lloyd George expressed his belief that Kitchener and the War Office were not up to the task of bringing in the major improvements required to boost production, and he pressed for the creation of a government department devoted entirely to the supply of munitions. Along with the resignation of Lord Fisher as First Sea Lord[25], the scandal brought about the fall of the Liberal government, although Prime Minister Asquith managed to form a coalition which kept him as premier.[26]

In the new Cabinet formed in late May 1915 Churchill was replaced by Arthur Balfour as First Lord of the Admiralty, while Kitchener retained his post as Secretary of State for War. Asquith had considered removing him from the post, but realised Kitchener had such strong support, both from the public and the Army, that to eject him from power would have caused a great outcry and, more importantly, an adverse affect on morale. Asquith was well aware of Kitchener's value in this respect, particularly after the surge in public support following the *Daily Mail*'s headline on 21 May: "The Shells Scandal: Kitchener's Tragic Blunder". This provoked dramatic scenes such as the burning of copies of *The Times* and *Mail* at the Stock Exchange. It was clear that despite his lack of support from most of the Cabinet, he was too popular to be sacked.

Throughout the rest of 1915 and into 1916, Kitchener was not only attacked by his opponents in the Cabinet and press, but by many in the House of Commons. Efforts to have him removed from his post continued, culminating in a Commons motion raised just days before his departure for Russia. On 31 May 1916, at almost the very moment the Grand Fleet was nearing the first main engagements of the Battle of Jutland, a debate started on the motion raised to reduce Kitchener's annual salary as Secretary of State by £100, a traditionally symbolic opening to what was a censure motion and attempted vote of 'No Confidence'. Various MPs spoke in favour of the motion against Kitchener, including Winston Churchill, but a strong speech defending Kitchener, which brought cheers from the House, was made by Prime Minister Asquith. Of Kitchener, he stated:

> *There is no other man in this country, or in this Empire, who could have summoned into existence in so short a time, with so little friction, with such satisfactory, surprising, and even bewildering results, the enormous Armies which now at home and abroad are maintaining the honour of the Empire. I am certain that in history it will be regarded as one of the most remarkable achievements that has ever been accomplished; and I am bound to say, and I say it in all sincerity, for that achievement Lord Kitchener is personally entitled to the credit.*[27]

The censure motion was defeated, and Kitchener retained. But during the debate Kitchener was committed to host a meeting on 2 June at which he would answer MPs' questions. The meeting, held in a Commons Committee room, was a great success. Kitchener answered many of the accusations laid against him during the preceding months and during the debate itself. He spoke in some detail on the unfulfilled orders from American manufacturers, noting that of one order of 2 million rifles, only 480 had been delivered. A proposed vote of thanks to Kitchener for his statements and for addressing the doubts raised during the earlier debate was seconded by Sir Ivor Herbert who had just the week before brought the censure motion against him.[28]

So when Kitchener set off on the first leg of his ill-fated journey intended for Russia, he may well have breathed a sigh of relief at the prospect of getting away from London and the political wrangling of the preceding twelve months – so much for the "nonsense or trouble" he was expected to have avoided. Some of his political opponents even contemplated a permanent absence: "There is [in England] a hope and feeling that he [Kitchener] may not come back."[29]

---

[25] Fisher's unwillingness to continue working with Churchill, First Lord of the Admiralty, after the failure of the Dardanelles Campaign, resulted in his resignation 15 May 1915.
[26] This whole episode is described in depth in Pollock 2001, aptly described by Tom Muir as 'a bit of a hagiography'.
[27] Hansard 31 May 1916.
[28] Coincidentally Jane Byas, who saw *Hampshire* sink (see Chapter 5 below), visited this room a few years later (OA TA/26/3; RO7/131).
[29] Walter H Page, US Ambassador in London, quoted by Pickford 1999, 84.

Mission to Russia

It was vital to Britain that Russia's efforts on the Eastern Front continued, forcing Germany to keep significant forces in the East that would otherwise be committed to the Western Front. Since the outbreak of war, Kitchener and his staff at the War Office were engaged in procuring munitions for Russia from British, French, North American and Japanese manufacturers. They had soon recognised that Russia's manufacturing industry would be unable to supply their armies with adequate munitions, but the seriousness of this deficiency had not been fully realised until early 1915, when Russia drew attention to the fact that very little of what had been ordered had actually been delivered. The complicated and corrupt bureaucracy through which Russian armaments orders had to pass within the Tsar's army and government departments was also an obstacle.[30]

Tsar Nicholas II personally authorised Kitchener to place orders on Russia's behalf that were financed by Britain using Russian treasury bonds. Some large orders, placed in America and Canada, and to a lesser extent in Japan, were secured almost entirely on the strength of Kitchener's name. Efforts were made in America and Canada by the War Office (and later the Ministry of Munitions) representatives and inspectors to assist with the organisation and improvement in their industries and to accelerate the production of the huge orders placed. Complicated technical matters had to be addressed to co-ordinate the supply of arms and ammunition.

Communications between Britain and Russia were established using a Russian military commission in London headed by General Hermonious, while Kitchener was in regular, direct contact with Major-General Sir John Hanbury-Williams, the head of the British Military Mission in Petrograd, and with Grand Duke Nicholas Romanov, the Tsar's cousin and supreme commander of the Russian armies. A key figure in the process was Brigadier-General Wilfrid Ellershaw who travelled with Hermonious to the USA, and made visits to Russia.

Both Kitchener and the British government had desired more detailed and higher level talks between the two countries. The possibility of a diplomatic mission to Russia with Lloyd George included was discussed at Cabinet and War Council meetings in early 1916, with Kitchener expressing a desire to lead such a mission at a Cabinet meeting on 28 April. After the Easter Rising in Dublin that month, Asquith required Lloyd George's help in dealing with the situation, so he was to be sent to Ireland rather than Russia. At least a hint of this plan appears to have been passed on to the Russian Ambassador, and on 14 May a telegram arrived from the Tsar saying "Lord Kitchener's visit to Russia would be most useful and important". The Tsar had for sometime made it known that he wished Kitchener to visit Russia, but it was the first time King George V had heard word of any such plan, and when enquiries were made on the king's behalf, Kitchener admitted it had been discussed at meetings.

On 13 May Hanbury-Williams had reported to the War Office that there were rumours of Kitchener coming to Russia and that he had discussed the matter with the Tsar. The same day, a formal invitation was sent to Kitchener by the Russian Ambassador on behalf of the Tsar, who replied on the 15th:

> *Nothing would give me greater pleasure than to visit Russia, but at present the arrangements for doing so are not finally settled, and I shall have to see the King and the Prime Minister on the subject before I can let you know at what date I shall be able to avail myself of His Majesty's kind invitation.*[31]

The cabinet agreed to the mission on 26 May. The King was happy to sanction the visit, and a telegram sent the following day to Hanbury-Williams in Petrograd:[32]

> *Lord Kitchener intends to accept the gracious invitation of the Emperor. Please arrange for Nielson to meet Lord Kitchener at Archangel and to be attached to his Staff during his visit. The party will consist of Earl Kitchener, Sir Frederick Donaldson, Brig. General Ellershaw, Lieut. Col. Fitzgerald, Mr O'Beirne, F.O., Mr Robertson, Assistant to Sir F. Donaldson, 2/Lieut. McPherson[sic], one clerk, one detective-inspector, and three servants.*

A specific aspect of the mission was to discuss arrangements for further loans to Russia, and if the amount Britain was prepared to place at Russia's disposal appeared insufficient to cover the required orders, Kitchener and his staff were to discuss which orders should be given precedence. Amongst the most important matters to impress on the Russians was that the financial securities promised by Britain could not be extended without limit, and it was thought that it would require someone of Kitchener's status to convince them.

There were motives behind Kitchener's mission to Russia beyond the financial and technical aspects of the supply of arms. Such a prominent and prestigious figure at the head of the mission was expected to be a great

---

[30] Neilson 1982.
[31] TNA PRO 30/57/85/9.
[32] Arthur 1920 iii, 350. With two further servants this was the party that left on 4 June – see opposite.

3 – Kitchener and the Mission to Russia

boost to Russia's morale at a time of political upheaval and with an army struggling to maintain its efforts on the Eastern Front. Kitchener was a well-known and much revered figure in Russia, held in high regard and trust by the Tsar, his regime and the armed forces. There were plans for him to visit troops at the front. But the key aims of the mission concerned the areas of munitions manufacture, the logistics involved in supplying the matériel, and the money to finance the arms deals set up by Britain on Russia's behalf.

Members of Mission to Russia

The composition of the 14-man party[33] reflected the various motives and intentions of the military and diplomatic mission. As Secretary of State for War, now aged 65, Field Marshal the Right Honourable Horatio Herbert Earl **Kitchener** of Khartoum, KG, KP, GCB, OM, GCSI, GCMG, GCIE, Col. Cmdt. RE, Col. I Gds. carried the full authority of the British government, and as outlined above, could not have been held in higher regard and trust by the Russians. He was accompanied by his valet, Henry Walter **Surguy**, aged 35, who had evidently served his master for some years.[34]

Kitchener's Personal Military Secretary and his ADC since 1904 was Brevet Lieut. Col. Oswald **Fitzgerald** CMG, aged 40, an Irish national born in India, an Indian Army officer from the 18th Bengal Lancers, and known as 'Ozzy'. He was accompanied by his valet, William **Shields** from Birkenhead, a former Lance Corporal in the East Lancashire Regiment, who had been invalided out of the army with a wound sustained near Ypres in 1914.

Kitchener's protection officer was Detective Sergeant Matthew **McLoughlin**, aged 37. Born in Co.Tipperary, he joined the Metropolitan Police in 1900, and transferred to the Special Branch as a Detective Sergeant in 1909. He had been chosen for protection duty for both Edward VII and George V and was assigned to protect Kitchener in 1914. McLoughlin remains to this day the only officer of what is now known as the Royalty and Specialist Command and its preceding equivalents to have been killed in the line of duty.[35]

To deal specifically with the matters of finance and Anglo-Russian relations, Hugh James **O'Beirne** CVO CB, aged 49, an Irish-born Foreign Office minister, was attached to the party. Educated at Beaumont and Balliol College, Oxford, he had entered the Diplomatic Service in 1892. His experience in Russia was of great value – his first posting had been to Petrograd, and after service in America, Turkey and France, he was in Petrograd again as Councillor to the British Embassy in 1906. He returned from Russia in 1913 with the rank of minister, and was involved in negotiations with Bulgaria during a spell as Charge d'Affaires in Sofia. O'Beirne was accompanied by two members of his staff, Leonard C. **Rix**, aged 31, a shorthand clerk, and James W. **Gurney**, his valet.

Two senior civil servants from the Ministry of Munitions were given temporary army ranks. Sir Hay Frederick **Donaldson** KCB, MICE, MIMech.E, aged 59, was educated at Eton and Trinity College, Cambridge. During his career he worked at Crewe, in Goa, on the construction of the Manchester Ship Canal, at the India Docks in London, was in charge of the Woolwich Arsenal and was President of the Institution of Royal Engineers. He was appointed Chief Technical Adviser to the Ministry of Munitions in September 1915, and made a temporary Brigadier-General. His valet was Francis P. **West**, aged 30. Leslie Stephen **Robertson**, aged 52, was born in India and graduated from University College, London with a degree in Marine Engineering. He worked in Dumbarton and at Le Havre, and latterly with Donaldson who chose him as his Deputy at the Ministry, his meticulous and analytical mind proving crucial to the dramatic increase in the supply of munitions. For the mission to Russia he was assigned the temporary rank of Lieutenant Colonel.

Temporary Brigadier-General Wilfrid **Ellershaw**, aged 44, was an artillery officer who served at the Front early in the war, and an instructor at the Royal Military Academy. As a staff officer he represented Kitchener on several trips to both America and Russia, and was posthumously awarded Order of Stanislaus First Class by Russia. His valet was Driver David Cliffe **Brown**, aged 32, Royal Horse Artillery.

Second Lieutenant RD **Macpherson**, aged 19, was the youngest member of the party, but nonetheless vital. He had received his commission in the Queen's Own Cameron Highlanders[36] in late 1915. Born in Petrograd, the son of a Scottish stockbroker, he was a fluent Russian speaker and acted as translator for the party.

---

[33] TNA ADM 116/1526 *HMS Hampshire – Casualties* – copy of typed list of members of party.
[34] A misreading of his name in early press bulletins resulted in his surname being merged with that of Shields (Fitzgerald's valet), whose forename was not available to the writers of the bulletin and was replaced with a dash. Subsequent lists recorded the two individuals as 'Henry Surguy-Shields', a mistake that has been replicated ever since and features in most books and on many websites. To add to the confusion Pollock (2001, 378 etc.) called him Henry *Segar*.
[35] McLoughlin's life was researched by R. McAdam in 1996.
[36] His distinctive Glengarry, kilt and gaiters render him one of the few positively identifiable members of the party waiting to board *Mayberry* from *Iron Duke* – see page 13 below.

Chapter 4

The Fatal Voyage

By Andrew Hollinrake

London to Scapa Flow

On 26 May 1916, after the Cabinet had agreed on the mission to Russia, Kitchener went to the Admiralty to request a suitable ship. The Admiralty telegraphed Admiral Sir John Jellicoe, Commander-in-Chief of the Grand Fleet at Scapa Flow, to arrange for a cruiser to take Kitchener and his party from Scapa Flow to Archangel. Jellicoe responded the next day, suggesting HMS *Hampshire* as suitable for the voyage, and the Admiralty agreed.[37]

Kitchener's meeting with Jellicoe was not set up until 1 June, when, at a meeting of the Cabinet's War Committee, Kitchener passed a note to Lord Balfour, First Lord of the Admiralty:

> *I believe it is arranged for me to go on Sunday. Might I have a look at the fleet en passant and see Jellicoe? I should not have more than about an hour or so.*

Balfour agreed to this and so rather than proceed directly to Archangel, a ship would meet the party at Thurso and take Kitchener and the senior members of the mission to meet Jellicoe in his flagship, HMS *Iron Duke*, in Scapa Flow before setting out for Russia later in the day.[38] Until this was arranged, Kitchener appears to have expected to board *Hampshire* in Thurso Bay and proceed directly to Archangel.[39] This seems surprising, for it would have bypassed a rare opportunity for a face-to-face meeting between the Secretary of State for War and Jellicoe, "the only man on either side who could lose the war in an afternoon".

Just days before departure, Kitchener's mission was put in doubt after hearing from Hanbury-Williams that the Russian finance minister wanted the visit to be postponed. Kitchener asked Hanbury-Williams to see if the Russians still wanted him to come. Hanbury-Williams visited the Tsar, who confirmed that Kitchener's mission was still desired and expected. Kitchener received this confirmation during the afternoon of 3 June.[40]

The next day Kitchener and his staff left King's Cross at 4.40pm. Later Sir George Arthur claimed there had been a last minute hitch: O'Beirne's clerk had gone to the wrong railway station as the party prepared to board their train; O'Beirne waited for his clerk, following on a later train.[41] Shortly afterwards the Admiralty sent a coded message to Jellicoe informing him that the party would be arriving at Thurso the following morning. It was only after receipt of this message that Jellicoe issued *Hampshire*'s sailing orders.[42]

Jellicoe had decided that *Hampshire* would be at too great a risk of submarine attack while crossing the Pentland Firth to pick Kitchener up from Scrabster, and so a destroyer would be more suitable. HMS *Oak*, the flagship's tender, was dispatched just before 0700 to pick up Kitchener and the senior members of the party, delivering them alongside *Iron Duke* at 1214. Meanwhile the personal servants and baggage had been embarked in the armed steamer *Alouette* and taken directly to *Hampshire*.[43]

---

[37] Admiralty 1926, 1.

[38] Pollock, 2001, contradicting Admiralty 1926 which suggests Kitchener requested that *Hampshire* should take him from Thurso to Scapa Flow. Pollock does not give a specific source for this note.

[39] Pollock, 2001.

[40] Arthur 1920 iii, 351.

[41] Arthur 1920 iii, 353; Pollock 2001, 479. This anecdote was embellished by Power (who claimed that O'Beirne himself went to the wrong station (*Referee* 20 June 1926)) and repeated by McCormick (1959, 10) and others. Arthur added to the confusion by describing the individual as O'Beirne's cipher clerk, whereas TNA ADM116/1526 describes him as 'shorthand clerk, Ministry of Munitions. Arthur's anecdote may have been a version of a story that a Foreign Office representative arrived at King's Cross with important documents which he claimed had to catch the Kitchener special. A second special was quickly arranged which broke the speed record from Kings Cross to Doncaster and caught up with the Kitchener special at York (Nock 1972, 121-2).

[42] TNA ADM116/2323. *Hampshire* had coaled ship on 4 June and moved to a mooring next to that of *Iron Duke* the next morning.

[43] TNA ADM186/628. There was some doubt on the exact composition of these two parties, and confirmation of these details was needed later for probate purposes. The Senior Naval Officer at Inverness was asked, but had no knowledge of Kitchener and his party passing through. Responses from Rear Admiral Prendergast's office (alias 'R.A. *Cyclops*', the officer in command of shore-based personnel at Scapa) suggested that there may have been seven in the party boarding *Alouette*, whereas according to *Alouette* only six were transferred to *Hampshire* on arrival, most likely just an error rather than a man overboard or a stowaway (TNA ADM137/3621).

4 – The Fatal Voyage

The party were given a tour of *Iron Duke*, looking inside gun turrets and witnessing drills. Kitchener inspected parades of ratings on the mess decks, the flagship's crew bursting into applause as he appeared.[44]

The Flag Officers of the Grand Fleet had been invited to join them, and over lunch Kitchener discussed the forthcoming trip to Russia. Jellicoe thought he seemed pessimistic about his mission. Kitchener described the preceding two years as a great strain, and hinted that he might be unable to maintain his role much longer if such pressure continued. He seems to have seen the mission as a welcome break, and spoke of it as a 'real holiday'.[45]

After lunch Kitchener showed great interest in Jellicoe's detailed account of the Battle of Jutland, but soon made it very clear that he was eager to press on, since he had a huge programme to carry out in his planned three weeks in Russia. He repeatedly asked Jellicoe to tell him how quickly he could be conveyed to Archangel.[46] The party left *Iron Duke* on the drifter *Mayberry* bound for HMS *Hampshire* at about 1600.

The last photograph taken of Lord Kitchener, boarding *Mayberry* (main group, from right, is probably MacPherson, Jellicoe, Kitchener).

Various claims were later made that Kitchener's mission and its timing were not kept secret – see Chapter 8 below. But we now know that *U 75* had received her orders to lay mines west of Orkney and had put to sea before it was claimed that German Intelligence became aware of the mission, before the British government had agreed to Kitchener's involvement, and before Jellicoe had selected HMS *Hampshire*.[47] We also know that *U 75* had laid her mines and had arrived back in Germany before Kitchener left London and before Jellicoe had decided on *Hampshire*'s route.

Admiral Jellicoe's Routeing Instructions for HMS *Hampshire*

Jellicoe's original sailing orders dated 4 June routed HMS *Hampshire* east of Orkney,[48] but on the following afternoon, with a NE'ly gale increasing, he amended these orders and instructed her instead to proceed close inshore to the west coast of Orkney. Jellicoe reasoned[49] that this route would offer some protection to both *Hampshire* and her accompanying destroyers from the expected weather. It was a route in frequent use by other traffic,[50] and although its waters had never been swept for mines, nor, because of the weather, had the alternative eastern route been swept in the past few days. Anyway there was no cause to suspect moored mines in the area: at the time neither the Admiralty nor Jellicoe had any evidence that Germany possessed ocean-going minelaying

---

Seven were carried from the railway station at Thurso to the harbour at Scrabster, according to the 'motor car contractor', but perhaps one of the seven joined Kitchener in *Oak*. (Or, if Arthur's version is believed, and O'Beirne and his clerk Rix travelled up on a later train, they may not have travelled with the first party in *Alouette* and were picked up later. This would leave the first group of six in *Alouette* as Brown, Gurney, McLoughlin, Shields, Surguy and West. However this is suspect, as Gurney was O'Beirne's valet.)

The signal from R.A. *Cyclops* forwarded by C-in-C to Admiralty is ambiguous: "As far as can be recollected in *Alouette* six crossed over, of whom four were in khaki and two in civilian clothing. The four in khaki included Detective Sergeant McLaughlin [sic], Driver Brown, R.H.A., Lord Kitchener's personal servant, name unknown, but very tall and fair [Surguy], and the servant of one of staff, probably Sir F Donaldson's servant, name West known to have been on board, short with turned up nose." (Pollock, 2001, 480). The signal then mentions two civilians, only one remembered, wearing 'rings on 3rd and 4th finger of left hand.' The two in civilian clothes, if the other identifications are to be trusted, were most likely Shields and Gurney. However, it seems more likely that Shields would be in khaki, a former Lance-Corporal only recently invalided out of active service and valet to a serving officer, Fitzgerald, than West, valet to Donaldson, whose rank of Temporary Brigadier-General had only just been bestowed upon him.

Alternatively, if there *were* seven in the party, we can add Rix, O'Beirne's clerk, while O'Beirne travelled to *Iron Duke* with Kitchener. As the signal continues: "Thurso reports seven, not six, embarked. This is confirmed by motor car contractor at Thurso."

So there were probably two parties of seven, the party going for lunch with Jellicoe comprising Donaldson, Ellershaw, Fitzgerald, Kitchener, Macpherson, O'Beirne and Robertson, and the party taken directly to *Hampshire* comprising Brown, Gurney, McLoughlin, Rix, Shields, Surguy and West.

[44] Pollock 2001, 480.
[45] Jellicoe 1919, 422.
[46] Jellicoe 1919, 423.
[47] See page 4 above and McCormick 1959, 143.
[48] Copy in TNA ADM116/2323.
[49] Jellicoe 1919, 423; Admiralty 1926, 6; TNA ADM186/628, 27.
[50] In the eight days up to midnight on 5 June the Birsay patrol had sighted 2 cruisers (excluding *Hampshire*), 4 destroyers, 2 minelayers, 4 (steam) yachts, 6 freighters and 37 trawlers (TNA ADM116/2324A).

Most of the survivors thought the ship had struck a mine, none thought it was a torpedo. Most thought there had been a single explosion; some described it as loud, others faint; several thought it was in the foremost stoke hold, amidships or on the port side. Three of them thought they heard a second, smaller explosion that may have come from a boiler exploding or a fire in a magazine, or even a second mine; one thought there was a third explosion. Half of the survivors saw flames, one described the smoke as yellow, and some said they were nearly overcome by fumes.

Several people on the shore also witnessed the explosion. The most graphic account was recorded in April 1917 when Sub-Lieut. John Spence RNR on leave in Birsay recalled his brother-in-law, a farmer, describing it thus:[73]

I saw a red flash accompanied by black smoke and water shoot from her, and the smoke had just cleared away, when another of the same nature occurred and from the same part of the ship .... right at the foremast ... immediately the smoke of the fire had cleared away the vessel headed right inshore, but did not continue in that direction for many minutes, when she again came head to wind.

Whilst we were talking the forward turret submerged and the vessel seemed to sink more rapidly. ... smoke was belching from the four funnels and the propellers flying round then clear of the water altogether. As funnel after funnel submerged, the vessel was enveloped in a cloud of smoke, but I could see her stern was assuming a more vertical position the further she went down, until when the last funnel disappeared. I think she was nearly at 45 degrees, and I think the propellers ceased working. When the after turret submerged I am certain that her forefoot touched the bottom as she seemed to hang for a minute or two. I could distinctly see the stern move up and down with the sea and the muzzles of the after turret guns just above the water, and then she slowly sank assuming a less angle until she finally disappeared, about 9pm as near as I can say.

Many years later John Fraser of Feaval, Birsay recalled his memories as a 12 year old:[74]

Early evening we were all inside, and my father went out and returned shortly afterwards saying "Come out and see this big battleship passing in these rough seas." So we all went out and almost immediately a cloud of dark smoke arose from the water's edge, followed afterwards by a huge explosion and tongue of flame shot out round the gun turret in front of the foremast, followed by a huge cloud of smoke, yellowish coloured, that drifted over Marwick Head in the strong wind.

Immediately they steered her for land, and turned her straight in, and we thought "Oh, he's going to beach the ship", but it was no time till she turned round again, I suppose with the force of the north wind and the heavy sea, turned her end-on to the weather, and by this time her bows were down in the water and her ... propellers were clear of the water .... And she just slowly went down, and the bows slowly went down until it seemed to us to hit the bottom, and the stern just settled down in the water. In all I think there was just about 15 minutes until she disappeared beneath the water.

However according to Sweeney *Hampshire* could not be steered and her turning recounted above, if true, was not intentional. More critically, however, she quickly lost electrical power: her mess decks were plunged into darkness, no distress signal could be sent, and the ship's boats could not be lowered. The ship lost headway as she began to settle by the bow and the steam pressure in the boilers fell. Her bow soon struck the seabed; then she heeled over to starboard, her two propellers still turning slowly high above the water, and she was gone by about 2000 GMT, i.e. 9pm BST. Sweeney claimed it was all over in about ten minutes but Bennett claimed it took longer, as he had time to first help extinguish a fire in the forward magazine and then attempt to operate some valves to flood some tanks aft before leaving the engine room at about 2002.[75]

There was no panic. The ship's company went to their "Abandon Ship" stations. Those below decks moved aft to the one open hatch. Soon those on deck opened a second hatch to enable the men below to escape more quickly, and later a third hatch was opened by those still below. Wesson saw Kitchener in the gun room flat and heard Lieut. Matthews, the Gunnery Officer, shout "Make a gangway for Lord Kitchener". Others took up the cry "Make way for Lord Kitchener". Simpson and Bowman both heard the Captain calling for Kitchener to board his galley. Some of the survivors saw some military figures in khaki on deck, including a tall officer with a stoop. Contrary to later claims, none could confirm they saw Kitchener on deck after the explosion. All the survivors were confident that he was not on one of the rafts, and that no one got away from the ship on a boat.[76]

---

[73] TNA ADM116/2323. The brother-in-law was probably Andrew Cumloquoy of Cleatborrows, aged 48 in 1916.
[74] OA TA/26/4. John Fraser died in 1988 aged 85. Other eye witnesses included Joe Angus (OA D31/TR113) from Stromness, who was aged 20 in 1916 and died in 1976 aged 81; the Postmistress Jessie Anne Cumloquoy (ADM TNA 116/2324A) who was aged 53 in 1916; James Gaudie in Netherskaill, Marwick who later claimed (uniquely) to have heard the explosion (OA D31/TR/111), and who was aged 32 in 1916 and died in 1970 aged 87; Mrs Jane Hunter née Byas of Flaws, Birsay Be-north who was aged 26 in 1916 and died in 1987 aged 97 (OA TA/26/3); Sub. Lieut., later Capt. John Spence RNR (TNA ADM116/2323), a merchant navy officer on sick leave staying at his wife's house in Palace, Birsay, who was aged 37 in 1916; and Peter Brass in Sandwick (OA TA/401, /402) who was aged 13 in 1916 and died in 1983 aged 80.
[75] Preliminary statement, TNA ADM116/2323; handwritten report June 1926 (ADM116/2324A).
[76] Following Power's claims to the contrary in 1926, later repeated by many commentators, the Admiralty double-checked the survivors' statements of 6 and 8 June to this effect (TNA ADM116/2324A; ADM186/828, 30).

4 – The Fatal Voyage

Raising the alarm

Although HMS *Hampshire* sent no distress message, her plight was quickly reported. Territorial soldiers ("Terriers") from the Orkney Royal Garrison Artillery based in Kirkwall maintained a continuous lookout from Marwick Head and from the ruins of the 16th century Earl's Palace in Birsay.[77] On duty that night were Corporal James Drever and Gunners Angus and Norn. Many years later Joe Angus recalled:[78]

> *I hadn't been very long out on my beat, and looking out to the sea I saw this cruiser coming past Marwick Head. I hadn't watched for very long until I saw a volume of smoke and flame immediately behind the bridge, and thought to myself there's something seriously wrong there. So I ran in to contact the corporal in charge, and he came out and saw the situation of the ship, and he immediately ran in and reported it, and informed to Kirkwall and also to Longhope. And they all came out, and by that time there was quite a few of the local people about the parish there watching the scene. And some of the women folk were really in tears. In fact it was a sad sight to behold, but we could do nothing very much about it, very stormy night and the sea was running high, and the wind was blowing down along the coast, causing anything that could leave the ship to go away from our direction.*

There was no telephone in Birsay in 1916,[79] so messages had to be by telegram. The postmistress at Birsay, Jessie Ann Cumloquoy, sister-in-law of John Spence, had seen the ship sinking and was already standing by to send Drever's first message. Later there was some confusion over exactly when the telegrams were handed in, sent, received and delivered. The details are thus:[80]

From Birsay to Commander Western Patrol, Stromness (Capt. FM Walker) and Officer Commanding Troops, Kirkwall ("Artillery", Col. Gerald NA Harris) for Vice Admiral Commanding Orkney and Shetlands (Sir Frederick Brock), Longhope, handed in at 1945, transmitted 1949.

> *Battle cruiser seems in distress between Marwick Head and the Brough of Birsay – Corporal Drever.*

This telegram was received by Stromness Post Office at 1950 and handed to Walker at 1954, who telephoned Brock at 2000,[81] i.e. about the time *Hampshire* sank! While it was being sent Drever rushed back to the Post Office and asked if the words "Vessel down" could be added to the message. Assured by Kirkwall Post Office that they could be, the postmistress relaxed, but in fact the two words were not added to the message passed to Walker and Harris. After some confusion a second telegram for Western Patrol was "handed in" at 2020:

> *Vessel down. Corporal Drever.*

This message was received at Stromness at 2031 and telephoned by Walker to Brock at 2035. A third telegram was sent at 2035 from Palace, Birsay to Artillery, Kirkwall, Western Patrol, Stromness and Vice Admiral, Longhope, and received at Stromness and Longhope at 2050:

> *Four-funnelled cruiser sank 20 minutes ago. No assistance arrived yet. Send ship to pick up bodies. Gunner Norn, Palace, Birsay.*

Corporal Drever handed in a fourth telegram that was sent to Stromness at 2050 and received at 2108:

> *Four boat loads of men off Marwick Head reported by Robertson Quockquoy, Birsay.*

Following a request for more information a fifth telegram was handed in by Norn at 2120 and received at 2125:

> *Ship 1½ miles from shore. Two explosions observed.*

Gunner Norn handed in a sixth telegram that was sent to Stromness at 2207 and received at 2209:

> *Wind N.N.W. along the shore boats could land Bay of Skaill or Stromness sea rough.*

Thus the authorities at both Stromness and Longhope were aware at 2000, i.e. about the same time that *Hampshire* disappeared beneath the waves, that an unknown warship seemed to be in distress, but it was not until half an hour later that they first learnt that the vessel, identity still unknown, had sunk.

The responses to these telegrams are addressed in the next chapter.

---

[77] The territorials had a billet in the village, possibly in the tailor's shop (TNA ADM 116/2324A).
[78] OA D31/TR113. Joe Angus was then a grocer in Stromness.
[79] Contrary to claims by Power (*Referee* 24 Jan. 1926).
[80] The times here are GMT, although the telegrams were originally annotated in BST. Details are from original messages in POST 33/1821A and copies in TNA ADM116/2324A; ADM186/628, 31-32; Admiralty 1926, 14-15. An investigation by the postal authorities dated 5 July 1926 (POST 33/1821A) noted the discrepancy between the "vessel down" addendum of about 1949 and the "sank 20 minutes ago" message of 2035, but recommended that it was "undesirable to resuscitate the matter after such a lapse of time".
[81] Brock received the written telegram at 2010 (TNA ADM116/2324A).

Chapter 5

The Rescue Efforts

by James Irvine

"The Sinking of HMS *Hampshire*": impression by the artist Charles Pears[82] based on information provided by survivors.
(*Orcadian* 1 July 1926, from *Illustrated London News* 24 June 1916.)

Of the 749 men on HMS *Hampshire* only 12 survived. Quite apart from the issues of how and why she was sunk, the loss of life on this scale was clearly a disaster. Much has since been written on what transpired that night and the following day, what more could and should have been done, and how many more lives might have been saved. Most of these accounts were written on the basis of fragmentary evidence, before the publication of the Admiralty Narrative in 1926 and before the availability since 1967 of copious interviews and reports of survivors and other eyewitnesses.[83] These previous analyses are thus ill-informed and speculative. Although the extensive records now available don't answer all the issues arising unambiguously, they do enable the preparation of a much more objective account of what probably happened than has been published hitherto.

1. On-scene loss of life

For lifesaving the crew of HMS *Hampshire* had been provided with lifejackets, three Carley Floats – two large and one small[84] – and several work boats: at least six, and probably ten.[85] Loss of the ship's electrical power supply and the heavy weather frustrated attempts to launch the boats: one whaler, overloaded, broke in two; another capsized; a third boat with about 50 men on board was launched but was smashed to pieces against the ship's hull by a wave; the captain's small galley was upset; one of the pinnaces was unseaworthy, undergoing

---

[82] Charles Pears (1873-1958) was a prolific war artist, and also the artist of the advertisements for Pears Soap.
[83] See Appendix IV below.
[84] The Carley Float was a form of rigid liferaft supplied to naval vessels in World Wars I and II. The largest Carley Floats were formed from a length of copper tubing 20 inches in diameter bent into an oval ring, 14ft x 9ft, surrounded by a buoyant mass of cork that was covered by a layer of canvas; a wooden platform was suspended about 4ft below the ring by rope netting. They were designed to carry about 45 men, either sitting on the ring or standing on the platform in water up to chest height, with another 22 clinging to rope loops strung around the ring. Carley Floats were easy to launch, but their users were exposed to hypothermia. *Hampshire's* Carley Floats were referred to as rafts by the rescuers.
[85] *Hampshire's* nominal complement of boats and Carley Floats was thus (TNA ADM116/2324A, note of 19 Feb.1926):

1 56ft steam pinnace	80 men	1 30ft cutter	49 men		
1 40ft "	50 men	1 26ft "	30 men	11 boats	613 men
1 42ft sailing launch	140 men	1 30ft gig	26 men	2 Carley Floats pattern 18	134 men
1 36ft sailing pinnace	86 men	1 27ft whaler	24 men	1 Carley Float pattern 19	18 men
2 32ft cutters	118 men	1 16ft skiff/dinghy	10 men	Total carrying capacity	765 men

repairs; and a picket boat also remained unlaunched. Four craft were seen to leave the scene, and eventually the three Carley Floats and the remains of a dinghy, a pinnace, a whaler and a cutter reached the shore. However, of these craft only the three Floats carried survivors.

Careful study of the survivors' contemporary accounts which became available many years later suggest it was unlikely that more than 200 men managed to reach a boat or Carley Float.[86] So what happened to the remainder? Some men were killed by the mine explosion, others burnt by the flames or scalded by a boiler explosion. Many who survived these initial events and remained aboard *Hampshire* in the unlaunched boats were taken down by the vortex when she sank, as were many already in the water who had not managed to swim clear.[87] The ship remained afloat for such a short time that few men had been able to get their lifejackets, and of those that did some wore a bladder vest that proved ineffective in the very rough seas,[88] while others were found later with broken necks, probably having been killed when they jumped overboard and their life support belts snapped up under their chins.[89] Of the remainder who wore a buoyant waistcoat[90] or who managed to reach a Carley Float, the combination of cold weather, rain, strong winds giving a wind-chill equivalent temperature of 0°C, very rough seas and a sea temperature probably less than 9°C (48°F) meant that most were quickly exhausted and soon succumbed to hypothermia.[91] In the words of the Admiralty Narrative:[92]

the bitter coldness of the sea and the violence of the waves must have brought death with merciful quickness.

At least 500 men must have died on-scene, and most of these probably within an hour of the sinking.

2. The at-sea searches

Until the Admiralty published its Narrative in 1926 many believed the claim of Frank Power that no search vessels were despatched until 7am the following morning.[93] However the Narrative showed that some 16 vessels were on the scene by then.[94] At Longhope Vice Admiral Brock learnt of a battle cruiser in distress at 2010 and sought more information, suspecting that if this report did refer to *Hampshire* she had eased up to secure something as she was losing the lee of the land.[95] After hearing "Vessel Down" at 2035 he ordered Capt. Walker to hire motor cars and send "everything out" to Birsay, and then to embark himself. Two minutes later he ordered the steam yacht *Zaza* and the trawler *City of Selby* in Kirkwall to proceed to the scene, and at 2100 he ordered Col. Harris in Kirkwall to go to Birsay. Walker had already ordered the steam yacht *Jason II* and the trawler *Cambodia* to the scene at 2031, and he embarked on the tender *Flying Kestrel*[96] which sailed with the trawlers *Northward* and *Renzo* at 2045. *Zaza* and *City of Selby* were underway by 2125, reporting wind force 9 and waves over 25ft. In Scapa Flow the Commander-in-Chief, Admiral Jellicoe, ordered four destroyers to sail at 20 knots; HMS *Unity* and *Victor* (which had returned from accompanying *Hampshire* until 1830) and *Midge* left at between 2100 and 2110, and *Owl* left at 2120. So within an hour and a half of the sinking eleven rescue vessels were underway. Five further destroyers (HMS *Oak*, *Opal*, *Munster*, *Menace* and *Napier*) left at 0110. The trawler *Mafeking* was also sent out. But because of the wind and sea it was not until two and a half hours after the sinking that the first vessels arrived on the scene, *Unity* sighting wreckage at 2230.[97] Twenty minutes

---

[86] Power claimed that "at least 200 men must have got safely off the vessel, and reached the shore" (*Referee* 22 Nov. 1925), attributing this to Wesson. In fact Wesson's account (*Daily Mail*, 11 June 1926) does not include this statement, which seems more likely to be a corruption of MacKay's account OA D1/1204/45: "several rafts were discovered, each raft containing about forty bodies .... About two hundred bodies in all were washed ashore on rafts". Other accounts suggest that probably only about 60-70 bodies were washed ashore on rafts (see the reconciliation on page 32 below).

[87] Rogerson in *Daily Mail* 11 June 1916.

[88] Admiralty 1926; TNA ADM116/2323.

[89] Liddle 1985, 103.

[90] Although the buoyant waistcoats kept bodies afloat, only 2 (Bennett and Farnden) of the 12 survivors were wearing one. This was in part because some men with waistcoats surrendered their places on the rafts and some decided to swim for the shore (TNA ADM116/2323; Phillips 1930, 35-6).

[91] See Appendix II; also http://www.usps.org/national/ensign/uspscompass/compassarchive/compassv1n1/hypothermia.htm, retrieved 1 Dec. 2015:

Sea water temp.	Unconsciousness	Death
40-50F	30-60 minutes	1-3 hours

The shorter of these times would be relevant in the prevailing conditions. Data of this sort was not available in the 1920s.

[92] Admiralty 1926, 18.

[93] *Referee* 17 Jan., 4 Mar., 25 Apr. 1926.

[94] The Narrative's details can now be confirmed and amplified by the relevant ships' logs (TNA ADM53/.....), signals and senior officers' reports (ADM 116/2323, 2324A, /2324B and 137/3621).

[95] TNA ADM116/2324A, Vice Admiral Brock, 5th at 2200.

[96] *Flying Kestrel* had been a Cunard tender. In 1919 she carried the Stromness children who witnessed the scuttling of the German Fleet.

[97] Signal Log, Admiralty 1926. *Flying Kestrel* arrived off Marwick Head at 2230, after the first destroyers. Despite rain and spray restricting the visibility, Gunner Norn was able to send a telegram confirming that two destroyers had arrived by 2325 (TNA ADM116/2324A). McCormick (1959, 59 anecdotal evidence) claimed the first rescue vessels did not arrive till after 2300.

later, about three hours after *Hampshire* sank, *Owl* "stopped to pick up bodies", although curiously it was another hour before she reported "much wreckage off Marwick Head".[98]

The rescue vessels spent many hours looking for boats and rafts, using their searchlights.[99] They found wreckage and many bodies but "did not effect the rescue of a solitary soul". Nor, crucially, did they find the rafts, which had evidently drifted clear of the wreckage. Regardless of whether or not the rafts carried lights,[100] the co-ordination of the rescue vessels seems to have been poor, for the next report of bodies being found was not until 0330, when *Jason II* recovered those of a petty officer and a marine off the Bay of Skaill, six miles south of where *Hampshire* had sunk; it was then still too rough to recover more of the floating corpses she had found.[101] At 0400, just as dawn was breaking, a crew-member of one of the destroyers, probably *Oak*, heard a shout "Black object on the port side, sir", and almost immediately they were surrounded by floating bodies. It was realised these were from *Hampshire*: boats were lowered and tugs, trawlers and auxiliary craft were soon on the scene. The quarter-deck became strewn with bodies, including that of a Surgeon Lieutenant.[102] *Flying Kestrel* started finding bodies shortly after 0400 and eventually recovered 31, including those of Commander Dasent and Lieut. Cdr. Stewart.[103] *Owl* recovered 2 bodies at 0425, *Victor* 4 at 0500, *Oak* 14 at 0500, *Opal* "some" at 0558, and *Napier* 1 at 0700.[104] *Oak* recovered the body of 2nd Lieut. Macpherson at 0732. All these bodies were later taken direct to HM Hospital Ship *Soudan* in Scapa Flow.[105]

What then were the failings of the at-sea rescue efforts? Clearly there was some delay in mobilising the rescue vessels and, perhaps more seriously, apparently some lack of co-ordination of their search patterns.[106] However it seems likely that the main causes of the loss of life was due to the majority of the men being trapped on board *Hampshire*, to drowning, and above all to rapid hypothermia. It follows that more prompt mobilisation of the rescue vessels, even if accompanied by better co-ordination of their search, would not have had a significant impact on the scale of the disaster.

One of the most controversial features of the response was the failure, even refusal,[107] of Walker to deploy the Stromness lifeboat *John A Hay*, a 40ft self-righting auxiliary motor-boat with a 30bhp engine capable of 7.5 knots in fine weather, and able to carry up to 60 survivors.[108]

Two questions arise. First, were the boat's crew aware of the crisis before Walker left Stromness and, if so, did he refuse their request to put out? And second, if the lifeboat had been launched, how useful could it have been?

The Stromness lifeboat *John A Hay*. (OA RHR4747)

In 1917 it was claimed that "The Stromness lifeboat offered their services early in the evening when they only knew it was a steamer in distress. They were insultingly told to mind their own business."[109] In 1926 Frank Power claimed that when George L Thomson, Honorary Secretary of the Stromness lifeboat, offered his services

---

[98] TNA ADM53/54247; ADM116/2323.
[99] The *Orcadian* stated that the lights of rescue ships were seen to seaward, but the rafts were steadily driven away from the area which was being searched ("5th June 1916", 1 July 1926). MacKay (*Orcadian* 1 July 1926) and Phillips of Garson (RO TA/402) also reported seeing lights. McCormick's claim (1959, 70) that searchlights were not used is incorrect – Jellicoe gave orders on this at midnight, and Capt. Davies recollected seeing searchlights (TNA ADM 116/2324A).
[100] *Orcadian* 1 July 1926.
[101] W Forbes, 2 June 1926, in TNA ADM116/2324A. Shipwright Phillips also recollected "thinking while he was on the Carley Raft that if any rescue ship – destroyer or otherwise – was to come alongside he was quite certain they would have been able to do nothing in that sea" (Interview, 6 Mar. 1926, TNA ADM 116/2324A).
[102] TNA ADM116/3621; Brown 2008, 119. This was either Temporary Surgeon Harold Chaplin or Fleet Surgeon Penry Williams.
[103] Davies' later claim that he recovered 56 bodies, the first at 0230, seems unreliable (TNA ADM116/2324A).
[104] TNA ADM116/2324A, ADM116/3621; OA D31/36/1/2; Royle 1985, 375.
[105] Formerly the P&O passenger-cargo line SS *Soudan*, 6680 gross registered tons, built 1901, was one of 29 vessels requisitioned by the government to serve as hospital ships during the Great War. She was used for the reception, treatment and movement of casualties during the Gallipoli Campaign of 1915-1916. She was scrapped in 1925. Surgeon CJG Taylor RNVR left a graphic description of his service on *Soudan* (IWM Docs.12018).
[106] HMS *Oak* searched as far away as Costa Head (TNA ADM 186/628, 35).
[107] Admiralty 1926, 19.
[108] Morris 1999, 7; Leach 2007, 32-9. The *John A Hay* served as the Stromness lifeboat from 1909 to 1928.
[109] TNA ADM116/2323. The provenance of this anonymous letter, found in Birsay, is poor, but it shows the tradition pre-dated Power's articles. Curiously in his letter of 9 June 1916 criticising the authorities' responses, S Baikie of Stromness asked why the Stromness lifeboat had not been launched, but did not allege its launching had been refused (same file).

5 – The Rescue Efforts

he was told to "mind his own b—y business".[110] Later McCormick claimed that Walker talked of "mutiny" and threatened to have Thomson and his crew locked up.[111]

In fact Walker had many other issues to address during the three quarters of an hour that elapsed between his learning of a ship in distress and his leaving Stromness. And in the words of Thomson:[112]

> *I understand that news of the disaster reached Naval or Military Authorities here at about 9.45pm (Summer time). Neither the Coxswain of the Life-Boat nor myself received any information from any source, nor any request for the services of the Life-Boat. Stromness is certainly the nearest Life-Boat Station and the scene of the catastrophe is well within the radius of our operations, on former occasions our boat has gone much further to vessels in distress. We would certainly have sent out the Life-Boat to render whatever assistance was possible if we had been informed of what happened.*

In a later note criticising the response by the naval authorities Major John MacKay ORGA(T) wrote:[113]

> *It should be borne in mind that the whole of Orkney during the war period constituted a naval area, and the naval control there was complete, even the Royal Garrison Artillery (Territorials) being under Admiralty command. ... The Stromness lifeboat [was] kept in the dark as to the nature of this information; they could only conjecture that a wreck, presumably of a naval ship, had taken place somewhere on the coast, and they were unable to take action without the necessary information and sanction to leave their stations. It is amply clear, therefore, that they were prevented by their enforced inaction by Naval authorities from co-operating in a work for which they alone were efficiently equipped. ... The Stromness motor lifeboat, a fine vessel of its class, could easily have weathered this breeze. Had it been called upon, it would have reached the scene of the disaster at 11pm summer time under its own power, and probably half an hour earlier if towed. .... [It] is manned by fishermen who prosecute their calling – lobster fishing – up and down the coast, inshore, at all hours of the day and night and their intimate knowledge of every rock and inlet goes without question. Is it not reasonable, therefore, to assume that these men, in a modern powerful motor lifeboat, could search a lee shore, where larger craft dare not venture?*

The Admiralty Narrative speculated that Walker felt he had no need of this additional vessel, that it would be unable to face the sea conditions then existing, that it could never have reached the scene except under tow, and that even then it would not have arrived at Marwick Head in time to save any lives. Or perhaps in the heat of the moment Walker simply forgot about the lifeboat. In fact, for reasons unknown, the Stromness lifeboat didn't respond to any distress calls between 17 December 1914 and 27 January 1920.[114]

From all these considerations three distinct points emerge:
- the claim that Walker did not <u>allow</u> the lifeboat to be put out is fictional;
- it is possible that if the lifeboat had been launched it could have kept closer inshore than the naval vessels, and it <u>might</u> have reached the Bay of Skaill before the rafts foundered;[115]
- by then there were probably only 33 men still alive (see summary at the end of this chapter), and so even <u>if</u> the lifeboat had managed to rescue all these survivors it could not have saved "a large number of the crew".

It may thus be concluded that the lifeboat should have been launched (for no one was to know how many lives it might be able to save), but as things turned out it probably wouldn't have been able to save many more lives.[116]

The naval authorities also failed to mobilise the Stromness Board of Trade Rocket Apparatus Brigade.[117] MacKay claimed these men could have reached Marwick Head by motor car, fully equipped with cliff ladders etc., before 10pm. There is little doubt that this brigade had been trained in cliff rescues, and would have been of considerable assistance if they had known exactly where they should deploy, especially if appropriate motor transport had been available. How significant these caveats were that June night is speculative.

---

[110] *Referee* 3, 17 Jan. 1926; letter by Power to Admiralty 14 Jan. 1926 (TNA ADM116/2324A).
[111] McCormick (1959, 56-60). Marwick (1967) gave a less speculative version.
[112] In fact at 9.45pm Walker was already embarking on *Flying Kestrel*. Thomson was responding to a letter of 15 June 1916 from the RNLI in London asking if his lifeboat had been called out on 5 June (TNA ADM116/2323). Power and McCormick were unaware that this correspondence had survived. Curiously the RNLI's brief covering letter of 7 July when they forwarded Thomson's letter to the Admiralty (same file) did <u>not</u> contain the text quoted by Marwick 1967: "It is the belief of the people of Stromness that if their life-boat had been called out the large number of crew of the *Hampshire* would have been saved."
[113] OA D1/1204/45. ORGA(T): Orkney Royal Garrison Artillery (Territorials). MacKay's family owned the Stromness Hotel. The supposition of MacKay and others that the lifeboat could have arrived earlier if it had been towed in such conditions is dubious.
[114] Extant notice in old lifeboat station; McCormick 1959, 56; Marwick 1967.
[115] If the lifeboat had left Stromness at, say, 2030 and covered the 10 nautical miles to arrive at Nebbi Geo at, say, 2330 she would have had to be able to make good 3½ knots into the adverse wind, seas and tidal stream. In fact in 1922 the same boat made good 6 knots in "heavy seas and strong winds" to reach a vessel in distress off Costa Head (Leach 2007, 39); see also TNA ADM186/628, 38.
[116] This conclusion is contrary to those of Morris 1999, 7 and Leach 2007, 39.
[117] TNA ADM116/2323. During the late 19th century Volunteer Life Brigades, also known as Rocket Brigades, were established around the UK to enable the use of the "breeches buoy", a crude rope-based rescue device that could be deployed using a rocket, a zip-line and a personal flotation ring with a leg harness attached.

3. The accounts of the survivors

It is now possible to ascertain reliably which survivors were on which raft, and this in turn enables the various accounts of the survivors to be combined into descriptions of what happened on each raft.[118] It is convenient to identify each raft by the name of the man who took charge.

The Survivors (William Bennett is missing):
back, l-r: Wilfred Wesson, Walter Farnden, Alfred Read, Fred Sims (bandaged), Jack Bowman, William Phillips.
front, l-r: Horace Buerdsell, Charles Rogerson, Dick Simpson, Samuel Sweeney, William Cashman.
(*Daily Mirror* 14 June 1916).

Warrant Mechanician Bennett's raft:[119]

Six men survived: Bennett, Bowman, Cashman, Phillips, Rogerson and Simpson.[120] Bowman, Cashman and Simpson helped to launch the raft. Phillips jumped into the water and was hauled into the raft before *Hampshire* sank. They picked up men as they went, but the raft became so overcrowded – numbers were estimated between 40 and 100 – that 18 men wearing lifejackets were asked to leave. Bennett himself had fallen overboard from the ship and swum away, but even so had been sucked under when she sank. He swam for about 15 minutes before finding a raft, and then drifted alongside it for another 15 minutes until four men decided to swim for the shore and there was room for him to get aboard the raft and take charge. He took one of the paddles and paddled vigorously, encouraging others to do likewise.

The raft is supplied with four paddles, but two of these had been lost after leaving the ship, so with the remaining two we kept the raft heading shorewards as best we could, until eventually the seas being so terrific made it impossible to use them.[121]

Bennett got the men singing, but they kept dropping off the raft, one by one, including men of fine physique. To keep sleep away they thumped each other on the back. Phillips was one of the many standing in four feet of the icy cold water. Standing next to him was a soldier, a servant on Kitchener's staff, who asked pitifully if they would ever reach the cliffs. Phillips was optimistic, but the soldier replied "I don't think so, mate" and died almost immediately. Another man died in Rogerson's arms. A big butcher about six feet tall died in the arms of Bennett. A lad aged 17, the smallest in the ship, sang and helped to brighten them up, but he died an hour later from exhaustion.

As the night drew on the wind and rain eased a little, but the men were buffeted by rough seas, soaked by the spray and thick drizzle, and numbed by the piercing cold. More died: some lost heart and dropped off as if going to sleep; some fought very hard to live but eventually succumbed; some poor fellows lost their reason. The more fortunate could offer little help as releasing their hold meant being pitched out of the raft. Later Phillips found himself lying across the dead bodies, his arms and legs completely numbed, his voice gone and sleepiness gradually overtaking him. He thought only 14 remained alive and "it was plain to see we couldn't last out much longer" when he heard the sound of breakers beating on a rocky coast.

A large wave swooped us against a very high cliff, only to recede on the crest of the wave ... the suspense of waiting for the second drive into those rugged cliffs was terrible, but the course of the raft had evidently been diverted and this time it did not reach the cliff, but caught and hung for a while on some low rocks. This proved a saviour to the six of us alive, who, together with the dead, were ejected on to the rocks by the force of the impact. I remember lying on a rock watching the raft go back again, of scrambling up and falling, then with the sound of voices in my ears and the feeling of hands pulling me up over the cliffs I lost consciousness.

---

[118] The accounts in the following paragraphs largely use the wording of the survivors' statements made under oath to the Admiralty Court of Enquiry held on 7 June 1916 (TNA ADM116/2323) and in contemporary letters and statements to the press. There are some inconsistencies, the more significant of which are addressed in this text or in footnotes.

[119] This was probably No.1 Float.

[120] TNA ADM116/2324; ADM116/2324A; Simpson's letter of 6 June 1916; *Daily Mail* 11 June 1916; Phillips 1930, 36; OA D31/TR115.

[121] Phillips wrote the first version of his account four or five weeks after the sinking (TNA ADM 116/2324A).

Bennett's account differed slightly:

the only place where we got out of the float was in one little corner, five yards wide. First three left the float, then the other three. I was numbed and fell down, the surface being a slippery one. I fought the tide for three consecutive times.

This was about 1am.[122] Rogerson claimed that many were killed when the sea dashed their raft against the rocks. Bowman was the first to reach a farmhouse unaided, followed by Simpson who had climbed the cliff unaided after falling three or four times, as apparently did Rogerson, who took shelter in a cowshed until he was found at 1.15am. A doctor, some marines and some farmers hauled three more of the men up over the cliffs (see below): these were evidently Bennett, Cashman and Phillips.[123] Philips recovered consciousness in bed with another survivor, his arms and legs still completely numbed. Later in the night he dressed and went out again to seek his shipmates.

Petty Officer Wesson's raft:[124]
Four men survived: Wesson, Buerdsell, Farnden and Sims.[125] Wesson put some men who had been wounded by the explosion on the grating in the bottom of the raft which he then launched, with Farnden and Sims helping.[126] There were then about 40 men. Buerdsell jumped into the water and boarded the raft later. Wesson took charge, telling them first to paddle clear of the ship and then to use the paddles on one side to keep the raft beam on to the wind. They picked many men from the water, dragging them on board, and after about an hour there were 50. However many men died, dropping off exhausted, though Wesson believed there were still 15 alive and 43 dead on the raft when they reached the shore, including the assistant paymaster, the gunner and the carpenter. They could see other men sinking as they swam for the shore. Wesson continued:[127]

The seas were terrible. They overran us and swamped the raft. The cold was bitter. We suffered greatly from it, as some of the men were only half clothed, and were thoroughly exhausted when we reached the shore. As the raft grounded I jumped off and waited until the next sea took me farther in. Then somehow I scrambled [up] the cliff. When I reached the top of the cliff my feet would not support me, and I fell again. Seeing a house in the distance I crawled towards it and tried to wake up the occupants. After shouting for ten minutes I got an answer. ... I tried to explain to them what had happened, but could not. They took me inside, wrapped me in blankets, and put me in bed with hot-water bottles. Meanwhile I had managed to make them understand something about my companions, and rescue parties of the crofters[128] living round about got ropes and went to the cliffs and saved all they could.

When he came to it was 1.15am. Buerdsell heard a dog bark and climbed up the cliff; like Wesson and Farnden, he reached a farm and found shelter. Sims crawled up the rocks and was found by a farm labourer.

Petty Officer Sweeney's raft:[129]
Two men survived, Sweeney and Read.[130] Sweeney later wrote:[131]

I ordered the boys to launch her, and then we got into the float and cast off ... everything was carried out without any panic, just routine. We were hardly fifty yards astern of the ship when her bows went down and she took her final plunge. Then our troubles started. Our two ship-stokers that were injured, died ... then the soldier. Not long after this our raft turned turtle, only six of us getting into it again. We got turned out three times altogether. Eventually four saturated, weary souls crawled ashore out of the float. We lay on the beach for four hours before we were picked up by some of the people on the island, but before help arrived two out of the four of us had died, lying on the beach. We were taken to a farmhouse, and treated with kindness.

Read recollected:[132]

---

[122] Although Rogerson claimed he was in the water for five hours, Phillips, Simpson, the farmer (David Brass) (Phillips 1930, 41) and the Admiralty (1926, 22) all agreed they came ashore at about 1am.
[123] In a contemporary note Phillips agreed Simpson was at the top of the cliff while he, Bennett and Cashman were at the bottom. Bennett endorsed this in 1926 (TNA ADM116/2324A). Later Cashman claimed he climbed the cliff unaided. Power claimed two men climbed Blossom Head, a 300ft high cliff (*Referee* 24 Jan. 1926): in fact there is no such place in Orkney; the cliffs at Rivna Geo are about 50ft high, at Nebbi Geo about 40ft high.
[124] This was probably No.2 Float, though Wesson claimed it was No.1.
[125] TNA ADM116/2323; ADM116/2324A; Sims' letters of 31 Aug. 1916 and 22 Nov. 1917; *Daily Mail* 11 June 1916.
[126] Sims later contradicted this, claiming he dived overboard (London Bus Company Magazine 1960; Royle 1985, 372).
[127] *Daily Mail* 11 June 1916. *Sunday Express* 8 July 1934 published a consistent but longer account by Wesson.
[128] Although some of the local farmers were "crofters", others such as the William Phillips of Garson were owner-occupiers.
[129] This was the "small" Carley Float.
[130] TNA ADM116/2323; ADM116/2324A; *News of the World* 14 June 1925.
[131] *Referee* 28 Mar. 1926. Sweeney claimed he was unable to swim (OA TA/401).
[132] *Newcastle Daily Journal* 23 June 1916.

We placed our injured mate in the float and threw it overboard, and then we jumped over to it. I had a jump of about 15 feet. ... It was impossible for us to see what had befallen the other floats or boats. One moment we were high up on the crest of a wave and the next moment we were deep down in the trough of the sea, and it seemed scarcely possible that we could ever rise again. Four times the float turned upside down, and once I was right underneath, but just managed to climb up and over. The poor chap who was burnt was very far gone, and after about an hour he said, 'Mates, I'm done,' and sank into the bottom of the float. Another man gave up absolutely exhausted. We drifted south. It was about 7.45 when we took to the float, and after about six hours in the water we touched shore at a place called Sandwick, ... I carried an E.R.A.[133] on to the beach and got another man out, both terribly exhausted, and then I became exhausted myself. Somehow or other two of us got into a kind of boathouse out of the wind, and there we were found about 3 o'clock in the morning by the fisherfolk, who were very kind to us. Two others of the party seemed to have got up as far as some railings, but there they were found in the morning, dead from exhaustion and cold.

Earlier Sweeney had testified he had been capsized twice, the two on the beach had died of exposure, and he was found in a hut about 3am, so weak that for a long time he couldn't speak. Power said they were a Marine and a mere boy.[134] The ruins of the boathouse below Garricot on the Bay of Skaill can still be seen today.[135]

The ship's boats

Although none of HMS *Hampshire*'s boats carried any survivors it is convenient to summarise what is known of the fate of four of them:[136]

A 16ft square sterned, clinker-built dinghy was picked up off Hoy Head by the patrol trawler *Arisino* on 6 June with the body of a sailor in the bow.[137] It lay for many years in Stanger's Yard, Stromness before being bought by Frank Power, who had it shipped south and exhibited it in Kensington and later in a shop window at 315 Oxford Street in February, March and April 1926.[138]

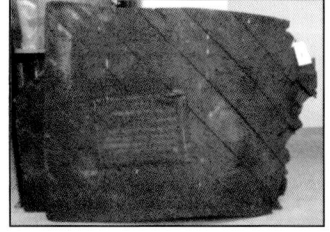

HMS *Hampshire*'s dinghy, displayed in London.

The steam-driven, carvel-built pinnace[139] had had its tailshaft removed and was not launched, but evidently floated off. It was sighted off Stromness by the *Flying Kestrel* at 0800 on 6 June, came to land on Hoy, and was taken to Longhope. Five large sawn sections of her hull were later sent to the Imperial War Museum.

Sections of the hull of HMS *Hampshire*'s pinnace. (courtesy of Imperial War Museum)

A 27ft or 30ft whaler was washed ashore at Burnside in Thurso Bay 48 hours after the disaster; it had three oars but its bow, stern and bottom boards were missing.[140]

Fragment of boat found in Thurso. (courtesy of IWM)

A smashed cutter was found empty in Skaill Bay by MacKay's party in the early morning of 6 June.[141]

---

[133] The identity of this Engine Room Artificer is unclear; *Hampshire* had two ERAs, Cuthbert Fincken and Matthew Hobson, but neither is buried at Lyness; maybe it was Warrant Electrician George Hunter.

[134] *Referee* 15 Nov. 1925; later corroborated by Willie Harvey and Peter Brass (OA TA/401, /402).

[135] Brooke's report (TNA ADM116/2324B; Admiralty 1926, 20) claimed MacKay "discovered two survivors lying in grass ... (just above the beach and) 2 bodies nearly in the same place." A detailed but inconsistent version (19 July 1916, in TNA ADM1/8468/226 misquoted by Power, *Referee* 15 Nov. 1925), by Mrs Mary Watt (1839-1924) read: "The first thing Bina (Robina Watt) saw (from Skaill House), as she was dressing on Tuesday morning, was two dead bodies lying on the grass near the Mill (of Skaill). One was an Officer of Marines. ... Two poor fellows, one a mere boy, managed to crawl up to our Boathouse but were found dead in the morning from exposure [incorrect]. James Marwick ... found two men still alive. They were carried to his cottage ....". Later Power made an unattributed reference to two men who had crawled to the lawn in front of Skaill House and died there (*Referee*, 24 Jan. 1926), while years later Peter Brass recalled finding "a big Marine and a young chap" who were both "too far gone" (OA TA/102).

[136] *Referee* 31 Jan., 21 Feb., 4 Mar. 1926; *Orcadian* 11 Feb 1926; Admiralty 1926, 25; TNA ADM186/628, 38. The fate of the Carley Floats is also unclear; on 12 July 1916 Harris reported that Bennett's raft was salved by James Whitelaw Jnr. and James Linklater of the Mill of Skaill on 10 July and broken into three pieces, while Wesson's raft had been taken to HMS *Cyclops*, Kirkwall on 11 July (TNA ADM116/2324A). A portion of Sweeney's raft may be at IWM Duxford (MAR544) but there is no supporting provenance.

[137] *Orcadian* 2 Nov. 1925; *Referee* 31 Jan., 14, 21 Feb., 3 Mar. 1926. Records clearly show that Power's claim that the boat had contained the body of Fitzgerald (*Referee* 21 Feb. 1926) was incorrect (TNA ADM116/2323, 116/2324B).

[138] *Referee* 21 Feb., 16 Mar., 4 Apr. 1926. Although Shipwright Phillips inspected the dinghy in London and found no reason to disagree with the Admiralty's claim that it had not come from *Hampshire* (TNA ADM 116/2323, /2324A, /2324B), this claim is not convincing and seems, on balance, more like a crude attempt by the Admiralty to keep clear of Power's shenanigans.

[139] Illustrated on page 1 above.

[140] TNA ADM116/2324A; *Times* 10 June 1916.

[141] TNA ADM116/2324B.

4. The military searches of the coastline

Military search parties were deployed from Birsay, Stromness and Kirkwall.[142]

The Birsay party comprised some Territorials and some local inhabitants. After reporting the cruiser had sunk, Corporal Drever[143]

> *proceeded south to Marwick Head, searching the coast on the way with some of the inhabitants. He did not go further south than Marwick Head, but some of the inhabitants did.*

In the short time before he sailed from Stromness Capt. Walker tried to find some motor cars and telephoned the Fire Commander Western Defences, Lieut. Col. Charles L Brooke RMA,[144] instructing him to organise a search party from the Ness Batteries, Stromness. Two hired cars, all that were available,[145] arrived at Ness at 2115 and a party comprising Lieut. Boissier RMA, Temporary Surgeon Lieut. WH Pickup RN,[146] a Sergeant and 11 marines with ropes and blankets immediately left for Marwick Head.

On arrival Boissier split his party into two, the main party searching the cliffs southwards from Outshore Point. This party reached Rivna Geo,[147] a narrow inlet between precipitous cliffs. There they heard answering voices, found one survivor near the top of the cliff, and with the help of some local inhabitants, pulled up three more survivors from the bottom. The four survivors were taken to a farmhouse nearby. The raft from which they had escaped was being hurled at the cliffs and eventually became jammed. Gunner Worrell and Private Read descended and a fifth man was hauled up the cliff with great difficulty but was found to have succumbed. The remainder on this raft were dead.

Marines party from Ness Battery, Stromness:
back, l-r: Gunner R Holloway, Gnr. P Scattergood,
Pte. J Read, Gnr. T Dredge,
Gnr. J Worrell, Gnr. J Otter.
front, l-r: Pte. J Wileman, Pte. S Smith, Lt. Bossier,
Sergt. Eastman, Gnr. Gill, Pte. J Henry.
(OA D1/933/4)

---

[142] TNA ADM116/2323; Admiralty 1926, 19-21.
[143] TNA ADM116/2324A. This was later confirmed independently by Sub. Lieut. J Spence RNR, writing in a private capacity, 6 Apr. 1917: "Immediately she sank, men proceeded along the shore to render what assistance they could to any survivor that might be driven ashore." (TNA ADM116/2323).
[144] RMA: Royal Marine Artillery. Col. Charles Brooke (1968-1938) was i/c The Ness Batteries July 1915 - Dec. 1916.
[145] TNA ADM116/2324A. Curiously in 1926 the Admiralty avoided discussion of the local officers' claims that they lacked transport.
[146] Both Lieut. Boissier and Surgeon Lieut. Pickup RN had died by 1926.
[147] TNA ADM116/2324A and Admiralty 1926, 20 say Nebbi Geo, but to make sense of all the reports this must have been where the second raft came ashore. Claims that rafts came ashore at Long Geo (30 yards south of Nebbi Geo)(anecdotal) or at Point of Howana Geo (300 yards south of Nebbi Geo)(OA TK956; MacDonald 2011, 72) are probably erroneous. A geo is an Orcadian term for a deep cleft in the cliffs, often extending a considerable distance inland.

Rivna Geo in 2015, looking north
(note the Kitchener Memorial on the skyline).

Nebbi Geo in 2015, looking west.

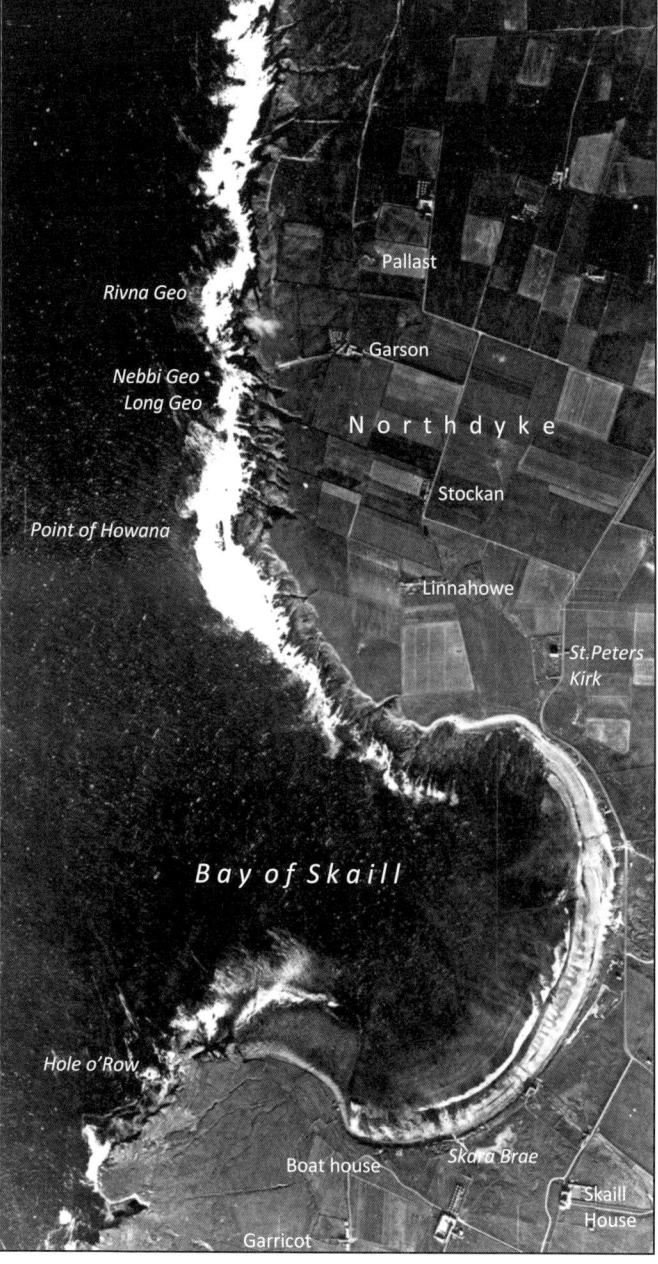

Aerial view of Northdyke and Bay of Skaill in 1951.
(NCAP SCOT 58 0802 # 4034, 4036)

Meanwhile the cars of Boissier's party went south to Skaill Bay and two men worked thence northwards to meet the main party. At about 1am they heard an unusual noise above the roar of the waves and found it was caused by a raft approaching the cliff. They met a farm labourer who told them he had seen a survivor making towards a farmhouse and the latter directed them to Nebbi Geo (300 yards south of Rivna Geo) where they found (Wesson's) raft resting between ledges of rock. In this raft or nearby were 42 or 43 bodies, all beyond medical aid.[148] Boissier's party worked through the night to move these bodies clear of the tide. Many years later Holloway recorded his memories:[149]

> *I'd been doing a spot of courting (chuckle). When I came back to where I were stationed they asked for volunteers, and of course being young .... I decided to volunteer and we went out to these rocks and dropped the lightest persons over the cliff tops .... there was one raft alone with 43 dead in it another raft had 18, [all] died from exposure. We got the chaps out of the rafts when it got daylight and put them at the side of a wall.*

Mr David F Linnie, chauffeur to what MacKay described as the Stromness advance party of officers, gave a somewhat different account:[150]

---

[148] The surgeon had to retire to a nearby farmhouse "owing to nervous breakdown" (*News of World* 14 June 1916).
[149] OA D1/933/2.
[150] TNA ADM116/2324A; OA D1/1204/45. Power quoted a version of Linnie's account (*Referee* 22 Nov. 1925, 28 Mar. 1926), while MacKay recorded two versions (see page 99 below). The discrepancies between the accounts of the Admiralty and those attributed to Linnie suggest the truth lay somewhere between the two.

5 – The Rescue Efforts

We proceeded outward, and on arriving at the junction of the Kirkwall-Birsay roads I enquired from my passengers "Where am I driving to?" and the reply was "Birsay". I then asked "What part of Birsay?" Dr. [Pickup] told the marine officer that as I knew the country well, I might be of assistance ..... They then told me that there was a ship was in distress off Marwick Head, and that they were going to effect a rescue if possible. I replied that owing to the direction of the wind then blowing, and the nature of the coast, there were only two possible landing places, viz. Skaill Bay and Marwick Bay, and Skaill Bay being the nearer, we proceeded there, but we saw nothing either ashore or afloat. ..... I went along the coast a considerable distance when I fancied I heard something in a deep geo (or gully). I clambered out on the rock as far as I dare go, accompanied by the farmer, and we came to the conclusion that a raft was there, but owing to the darkness, the height of the cliffs, and the lack of any suitable tackle, it was found impossible to get down to the water's edge. We proceeded still further, and at a little distance off I noticed a man standing at the foot of a stone wall. On seeing us he came forward to meet us, but he fell to the ground before reaching our party. We rushed up to him and discovered him to be one of the survivors of the Hampshire, and he had by some means or other succeeded in scaling the cliff. We took him to a house in the vicinity and treated him as best we could.

On the other hand Lieut. Bossier told his commanding officer Capt. J.W. Jones RMA that:[151]

Some of the survivors were on the beach when the rescue parties arrived. As soon as they found that there were some on the Rafts still alive, men were lowered down the face of the cliffs, who then had to swim through a very heavy sea to reach the Raft. The Raft in question was almost unapproachable. Two men nearly losing their lives during the operation.

Six RMA/RGA Officers;
(JC MacKay front left, CL Brooke front centre back).
(*Referee* 28 Feb 1926)

Search party of Territorials (probably that led by JC MacKay); l-r: Charles Langskaill, ?, Bill Macleod, Johnny Thomson, Rackwick; front: ?, Jimmy Oag, Dounby, ?   (OA L4829-3)

At 2230 a third car arrived at Ness Battery, from Kirkwall, enabling Capt. JC MacKay to take a small party of Territorials from there to Skaill Bay.[152] Two men were dropped on the way to search northwards from Yesnaby to Skaill Bay; the remainder searched all round Skaill Bay and on the south side found a small raft overturned on the beach. Searching again, at about 0300, when it began to grow light, they found two survivors from this raft "lying in the grass just above the beach."[153]

In the early morning other parties from Stromness searched the coast northwards from Black Craig to Skaill Bay, and southwards from Black Craig to Stromness, without success.[154]

When another car became available in Stromness at 0630 Capt. Jones led a party to relieve the parties of Boissier and MacKay. Brooke recorded that from 6.30am to 12.30pm the "new party ably assisted by 6 trawler

---

[151] Interview of 24 May 1926 (TNA ADM116/2324A).
[152] Power claimed that Brooke was reluctant to accede to this initiative by MacKay (*Referee* 24 Jan. 1926. The relationship between Marines and the RGA Territorials who manned the Ness Battery were not harmonious (Hewison 1990, 191, 247; Stell 2010, 29).
[153] Admiralty 1926, 21.
[154] Power (*Referee* 24 Jan. 1926) claimed these parties had been despatched by MacKay.

men and 3 inhabitants brought up dead bodies and identified them".[155] Capt. Jones later recalled things somewhat differently:[156]

> On personally arriving on the scene I found that everything had been done to save those alive, so I set to work on the two Rafts with an augmented Party – all Marines – to secure the dead bodies before the tide turned. The work was very difficult at the Northern one (raft) as only two men could stand on a small ledge of cliff to make fast the bodies, as two others brought them from the Raft.

Private William Calvert, a member of Jones's party, later wrote:[157]

> We took a rope with us and we went on our way in a motor-lorry to where the bodies were. We were met half-way by the party that had gone out overnight. They told us that it was a terrible sight. When we got there I saw only a few men who were getting bodies from some rocks and laying them in a field. Our little party went to a place called Rivna Gorge – a nasty looking place. A raft was suspended in the air – I should say fifteen to twenty feet from the bottom; so Captain Jones asked me if I would be lowered down the cliffs. I said 'Yes,' and down I went. I saw two men, unable to do anything because they had no help. I started on my work as best I could. Some of the men were dead, and some were, in my mind, unconscious. I could not render any form of first aid, as I was sending them up as fast as ever I could. But to my idea there were a lot of men [who] died that could have recovered, if they had first-aid on reaching the top of the cliff. I only saw one doctor the time I was there, and he could not be in three places at once.

Meanwhile two of Jones' party searched northwards from Yesnaby, arriving at Skaill Bay at 1100.[158]

Two parties were despatched from Kirkwall. At about 2100 Vice-Admiral Brock directed the Officer Commanding Troops, Kirkwall, Col. GNA Harris RMA, to proceed to Birsay by car to obtain information and to organise any assistance required. Offers of assistance and local knowledge from Col. Slater and one of his officers were declined.[159] Instead, accompanied by the Officer Commanding the Northern Patrol, Commander Bertram WL Nicholson RN, and another senior officer, an Englishman, and clad in oilskins and seaboots, Harris reached Birsay at 2345 having "struggled against the gale".[160] After telegraphing the Vice Admiral he drove to Skaill Bay, arriving there at about 0145 where he met the party from Stromness and gained the impression that no further survivors were to be expected.[161] He returned to Kirkwall at 0400.

A second party of 45 men left Kirkwall at 0800. Company Sergeant Major Robert Shearer RGA later recalled:[162]

> We soon knew something was "on," and we were dismissed and ordered not to leave the hall. After waiting for some considerable time, we were ordered to billets and to be ready to turn out at short notice. Early next morning the guard on duty was sent round to warn everybody to parade earlier than usual, and very shortly every available man was told off to proceed to Birsay. We were conveyed in two lorries and one Crossley tender supplied by the Royal Naval Air Service at Scapa. On arrival at the North side of the Bay of Skaill we were marched down to the beach, and there we saw the [Ness] battery party who had been out all night had a great number of bodies carried up off the beach and laid in rows on a field.

A later account read:[163]

> Altogether 75 bodies were collected. .... The work was very hard as no stretchers were available, and oilskins were stripped off for substitutes ... the bodies [were loaded] on a light lorry to convey them to the large naval conveyances waiting on the road. Fields and rutty cart tracks had to be traversed [and] the

---

[155] 6 June 1916 (TNA ADM116/2324B).
[156] 24 May 1926 (TNA ADM116/2324A).
[157] *Referee* 4 Apr. 1926, *Orcadian* 8, 15 Apr. 1926. Calvert was a member of Hoy Battery at The Ness, Stromness.
[158] JC Linnie, son of the chauffeur, was also in one of the search parties from Stromness, but it is not clear which, as Power's two versions of Linnie's letter to him (*Referee* 28 Mar. 1926, *Orcadian* 8 Apr. 1926) are inconsistent.
[159] *Referee* 9 May 1926; *Orcadian* 1 July 1926 "5th June 1916". Colonel James Slater VD, ORGA, Second in Command of the Orkney troops, had been Harris's predecessor. Allegedly posted to the Far East (*Referee* 9 May 1926), he died in Kirkwall before 1926.
[160] TNA ADM116/2324A; Admiralty 1926, 20; *News of the World* 14 June 1925. MacKay gave a less charitable version (*Orcadian* 1 July 1926): "Three senior officers had previously set out from Kirkwall by motor car, but they neglected to enlist the aid of a local guide, with the result that they lost their way hopelessly and did not reach the region of Marwick Head until dawn the following morning." (A classic example of gossip: Sub. Lieut. Spence independently confirmed Harris' claim that he reached Birsay at 2330/12.30am.) Some Birsay residents thought they had come via Evie (TNA ADM116/2323; OA TA26/3, D31/36/1/2). Joe Gaudie, a "Terrier" from Stromness, one of the RGA patrol at Birsay, later gave yet another version, claiming the three officers arrived after midnight, took him as a guide to Skaill Bay where they wandered round the beach for a bit. One of the officers said "Oh there's nothing here, I can't see anything". They then drove with Gaudie to Stromness (OA D31/TR113).
[161] This assumption was premature, as the last two survivors were apparently not found till about 3am. Col. Harris did not talk to any of the local inhabitants or the survivors (TNA ADM116/2324A; Spence in TNA ADM116/2323).
[162] *Orcadian* 1 July 1926: 'A Gruesome Task'.
[163] *News of the World* 14 June 1925.

light lorries sank in the yielding ground .... farmer's carts were requisitioned to convey the rest of the dead to the road. Eleven bodies were placed at one time on a cart, the tailboard being taken out to make room.

Shearer continued:

We conveyed the bodies to the road and put them on lorries as reverently as possible ... one lorry went twice to Stromness fully laden, and the other once. Next day, a smaller party was sent out to search the coast ... they remained on duty for some weeks, recovering several more bodies.

The bodies recovered by the shore parties were taken to HMHS *China* at Longhope for identification.[164] Two more bodies were found at Skaill on the evening of 6 June,[165] two more near Thurso about 8 June and about 26 June,[166] one was found on a cliff 21 days after *Hampshire* sank,[167] and a further seven bodies were recovered 3-13 July.[168] Most of the bodies initially recovered were buried at what was then known as the Naval Cemetery at Lyness, Hoy on 8 June, and those found subsequently within a day or two of their recovery.[169]

The failings of the military responses are considered at the end of this chapter.

5. Reports of civilian assistance

There are several reports of Birsay folk searching along the coast, both with the Territorials and independently. James Robertson rode down on his horse to Birsay Post Office to report seeing four craft drifting south of Marwick Head at 2050.[170] Corporal Drever later told Col. Harris:

Natives were all along the coast to Marwick Head but went to bed about midnight. Some went south of Marwick Head, but [he did] not know how far or who they were, Marwick people.

It was quite impractical to put out any of the small boats kept in Birsay.[171] No survivors came ashore there, nor are there any reports of bodies being found there. So apart from searches there was little the inhabitants of Birsay and Marwick could do.

On 15 June 1916 Vice Admiral Brock wrote "the inhabitants of Birsay and the neighbourhood showed considerable zeal in endeavouring to assist in any way they could".[172] The 1926 Narrative said:[173]

As soon as those living in the vicinity of Skaill Bay realised that there was an opportunity for rendering assistance, many ... gave valuable aid and the survivors ... received the greatest kindness at the farms.[174]

In Sandwick several accounts survive of civilians providing assistance. Many years later Mina Sabiston née Phillips, then 20 years old and living at Garson with her parents, recalled:[175]

It was a wild and stormy night. It was midnight when the rap came to the front door. We were all in bed. A voice shouted that their ship had got mined. So of course everybody got up. Jack Bowman was the first one to arrive. And by the time we got on the fire and looked for clothes for him the second [Simpson] arrived. We got them both dry clothes and got a breakfast ready and they were quite comfortable and quite happy. There were that many folk coming, I made them tea the whole night.

---

[164] TNA ADM116/2324A.
[165] TNA ADM116/2324A.
[166] TNA ADM116/2324A; *Times* 13 June 1916.
[167] OA TA/26/1. They were found by George Sabiston and Doddie Spence; the latter was probably from Garricot.
[168] TNA ADM116/2323, /3621; ADM1/8468/226.
[169] TNA ADM116/3621.
[170] TNA ADM116/2323; ADM116/2324A. James Robertson of Quockquoy, Marwick, was aged 39 in 1916.
[171] OA TA/26/3; Spence in TNA ADM116/2323.
[172] In his official report (TNA ADM116/2324A).
[173] Admiralty 1926, 20.
[174] Uniquely Capt. Jones painted a contrary picture. Writing in 1926, smarting at criticism of the response for which he had been responsible, he lavishly exonerated himself and voiced his own criticisms: "In the course of a short conversation with one of the natives from the village at Marwick Head ... I asked why they did not follow the Rafts down and try and save some of those who were still alive: 'We thought the Rafts were making for the North of Scotland and, in any case, it was no concern of theirs [sic].'" (qv Admiralty 1926, 22). He quoted the late Lieut. Bossier having complained bitterly to him "that not a soul could be seen at the time to direct them, although the natives saw the Rafts leave the ship, and must have seen they were making for the shore. This unfortunately delayed them in their operations." He continued "I should like to add here that many reports were emanated to the effect that assistance offered by the natives was refused by me. This untrue, as no one ever came near until all the bodies were brought on to the top of the cliff and then it was with the greatest difficulty that the natives, men and women, could be kept away from the bodies." Jones later sought the Admiralty's permission to instruct his solicitors to demand an apology from the *Referee* (TNA ADM 116/2324A).
[175] This quote is a composite of interviews of her by Ernest Marwick (OA D31/TR115, 1966) and Howie Firth (OA TA26/2, 1977). Mina Sabiston née Philips died 1982 aged 85.

Thus nine of the survivors were able to get ashore from their rafts unaided: five (Bowman, Simpson, Wesson, Buerdsell and Farnden) reached shelter themselves, two (Cashman and Sims) were found by local inhabitants, and two (Sweeney and Read) were found by locals or by Territorials. Three men (Rogerson, Bennett and Phillips) were rescued by Marines assisted by local farmers. Contrary to the claims of Power and McCormick, both local inhabitants and Marines probably arrived at the cliff tops about the same time as the first raft came ashore. There were by then only 33 men left alive. Of these 21 perished, of whom 3 died after getting ashore.

The most likely fate of those on board HMS *Hampshire* on 5 June 1916 was thus:

farms to which survivors were taken)	large raft (Bennett) Rivna Geo Garson, Pallast	large raft (Wesson) Nebbi Geo Stockan, Linnahowe	small raft (Sweeney) Skaill Bay Garricot	recovered ashore later/ elsewhere	totals recovered ashore	at sea	HMS *Hampshire* ship's company	Lord Kitchener's party	Total	
Alive when raft landed	14	15	4							
Scrambled ashore but died	0	1	2							
Survived	6	4	2				12	0	12	1.5%
Lyness, named grave							122	1	123	
Lyness, unnamed grave							44c	0	44	
Buried elsewhere							0d	1	1	
Bodies recovered & buried	18	43	2	>19	82-116	52-86	166	2	168	22.5%
Lost at sea, not recovered							557	12	569b	76%
Total lives lost							723	14	737	98.5%
Total on board							735a	14	749	
a: of these 735, 581 were RN, 85 were RMLI, 45 were RNR, 20 were RNVR, and 4 were civilian canteen staff.		b: of these at least 500 died on-scene, and most probably within one hour. c: 6 in single graves, 20 in double graves and 18 sharing with known bodies. d: 2 were buried in St.Olaf's cemetery but later moved to Lyness.								

Against this background it is relevant to consider the failings of the military responses and their impact on the loss of life. We now know that, contrary to rumours, 16 vessels were mobilised that night, albeit not quite as promptly as they might have been nor as well co-ordinated, but even a more zealous response would have been too late for most of those who died. Little could be done in Birsay, nor was there any need, as nothing came ashore there. Although the Marines did help to rescue some of the survivors, the scale of the Stromness response was too small, and although the reports of the officers concerned blamed the lack of motorised transport, there does seem to have been a failure to consider requisitioning even one or two additional vehicles. A few more lives might have been saved if more medical help had been mobilised. The failures to mobilise the Stromness lifeboat and the Rocket Brigade have been discussed in detail above. The advance party from Kirkwall failed to take a local guide, left the scene before the survivors from the third raft had been found, and were slow in mobilising the first party of troops from Kirkwall, who only arrived in time to recover bodies rather than search for survivors.

This analysis of the responses of the military authorities suggest several serious shortcomings. Power was thus justified in suspecting that the Admiralty had not released all the details. However there are three important caveats to this conclusion:
- the criticisms above are made with the benefit of hindsight, and it is difficult today to appreciate the challenges of organising a response when so little was known about where any survivors might come ashore and when there were no telephones or radios, let alone mobile phones, to modify or query the initial instructions, of necessity made in haste;
- the disaster occurred in wartime, just days after thousands died at Jutland and not long before tens of thousands died at the Somme: both these events were even more calamitous, with implications that demanded the undivided attention from senior officers if many more lives were not to be put in jeopardy;
- the survivors' accounts suggest that even if there had been no failings in the military responses, so many men died soon after the sinking and so few were still alive when the rafts reached the shore that the additional number who could have been recovered alive would have been small.

So it is now clear that a more prompt, larger scale and better co-ordinated response might well have saved a few more lives, each of which was of course precious to the next-of-kin. And had the circumstances been just slightly different, the inadequacies of the military responses could have turned out to be much more critical.

On the other hand it is also now clear that the claims of MacKay, Power, McCormick and others that these failings, either separately or together, contributed significantly to the scale of the loss of life are not justified. The vast majority of the men aboard *Hampshire* who managed to get clear of the sinking vessel succumbed to hypothermia, most of them probably very quickly. Even if all the shortcomings had been avoided it now seems likely that less than two dozen additional lives could have been saved. Neither in 1916, nor in 1926, nor even more recently was there any likelihood of the Admiralty holding another enquiry.

Chapter 6

"If you go near the cliffs we'll shoot!"

by James Irvine

In addition to the terrible loss of life, the *Hampshire* disaster left a deep sense of indignation and outrage across Orkney. These feelings linger on as traditions that many Orcadians today sincerely believe to be based on fact. The strength and persistence of these feelings, particularly in Birsay, are discussed in Chapter 7 below, but it is first appropriate to consider the evidence that initially gave rise to them. It has already been shown in Chapter 5 that there were several failings in the responses by the authorities. The resulting lack of respect for these authorities was compounded by rumours that local folk were ordered not to assist with the rescue efforts, that they were not allowed to go near the cliffs, and that they were not to talk about the affair. It was even said that firearms might be used if these orders were disobeyed. Censorship of the local press and restrictions on travel added to the unease. This chapter investigates the extent to which these rumours and perceptions were justified.

Little contemporary evidence of these issues has survived. The earliest surviving written reference to such orders seems to be in an anonymous letter found in a muddy condition "on the road to Birsay", "nearly a year, perhaps more" before the date it was copied to the Admiralty, 26 June 1918 by KF Kennedy Laurie:[184]

> But most emphatically the Birsay people were not to blame, they had been threatened that if they went near the cliffs that evening they would be shot.

The next reference comes in the widely-read national newspaper the *Sunday Referee* of 17 January 1926, when Power published the text of a letter allegedly written to him by a Mr D Forker from the Royal Hotel, Thurso:

> Your articles have raised intense interest here in the Orkneys, for there has always been deep resentment in the hearts of Orcadians over the manner in which they were treated at the time of the Hampshire tragedy. Not only did the Stromness lifeboat crew suffer a rebuff from the authorities when they offered their assistance, but there were many others, including the captain of the s.s. St.Ola,[185] who was very anxious to help. The captain has had over twenty years of experience of these waters ... He was not allowed to do anything at all ... a raft with over forty men from the ill-fated ship was lodged between the precipitous rocks, men whose lives the Orcadians are certain they could have saved had they been allowed to assist ... most of those locally who had seen things and knew things were told to hold their tongues.

A week later, in the same newspaper, Power embellished his claim, though this time without attribution:

> [it] can be proved that no boats were put off to the rescue and that all the inhabitants of the west side of Orkneys [sic] were told to remain in their houses and not to continue near the shore on pain of being fired on. The patrol had to drive would-be rescue parties back literally at the point of their rifles.

Power's later versions were more muted but again unattributed: "Other rescue work was also definitely hindered, if not actually prevented";[186] and the "Orcadians['] enthusiasm was checked".[187] He also cited JC Linnie in Canada who claimed "the civilians who lived right there [were not] allowed to assist ... My own father [David Linnie] was on the scene, but wasn't allowed near".[188]

All these accounts include factual errors: it has been shown in Chapter 5 that the Navy despatched at least 16 vessels to the scene that night, albeit with some delay, and that civilians in Birsay were allowed, indeed encouraged, to search for survivors even though, as it transpired, nothing from *Hampshire* came ashore in the parish. Similarly in Sandwick it is well documented that civilians did assist in the rescue of men from the three rafts that came ashore there. And the claim attributed to Linnie conflicts with Capt. MacKay's account.[189]

Notwithstanding Power's public disgrace in 1926 following the "Kitchener's Coffin" debacle,[190] many of his claims remained widely accepted, and it becomes difficult to determine whether subsequently recorded

---

[184] TNA ADM116/2323. This perfidious letter has many defects in both provenance and factual content, but its early date exonerates Power from having originated the claim.
[185] This was Captain Swanson.
[186] *Referee* 31 Jan., and similar wording 14 and 21 Mar., 1 Aug. 1926.
[187] *Orcadian* of 18 Feb. 1926.
[188] *Referee* 28 Mar. 1926.
[189] *Orcadian* 1 July 1926.
[190] See Chapter 8 below.

the presence of members of the public who, for example, had cycled over from Birsay, motivated by a sense of curiosity, helplessness or even some sense of guilt by association. In these circumstances some form of altercation would not have been surprising, and it would have been quite logical for the officer in charge to ask, or even order, members of the public to return to their homes. Perhaps Capt. Jones, tired after being up all night and embarrassed at having had to resort to the use of farm carts to carry the corpses, lost his temper with one or two individuals and did threaten to order his men to use force if their grim work was being impeded. This possibility is compatible with the unprovoked claim by Jones in May 1926 that after all the bodies had been brought to the top of the cliff "it was with the greatest difficulty that the natives, men and women, could be kept away from the bodies".[207] This claim is reflected in the Admiralty Narrative:[208]

> *On the following morning, when large numbers of bodies were being collected ..., ordinary police measures had to be taken to prevent the tendencies of members of the public to crowd upon and impede the operations. This appears to be the only foundation for the allegation that local inhabitants were prevented from engaging in rescue work.*

These two possible incidents above have several features in common: both relate to specific activities in a particular location and at a particular time, i.e. neither were general prohibitions, nor were they on-going; both, ironically, were motivated by concern for the safety or feelings of local folk rather than in pursuit of security considerations or some other high-level policy; both were probably triggered by a non-Orcadian (the first by Lieut. Bossier, the second by Capt. Jones); both, perhaps significantly, originated in Sandwick, where the rescue efforts occurred, rather than in Birsay, where no survivors or bodies were found; and, most significantly, both had no material impact on the number of lives saved. But it is also significant that both incidents would have been recounted by the individuals involved to their friends, perhaps with some bitterness, and in successive re-telling of the tale both could easily and quickly become exaggerated and taken out of context, and their local and temporary relevance easily become generalised. This could readily happen even if there had been no lack of respect for "the authorities". However with respect for the authorities already low because of their perceived arrogance and ineptitude/incompetence, such exaggerations were to be expected. It was probably only a matter of hours before second-hand versions were claiming that the authorities had banned all rescue-related initiatives and forbidden anyone to approach the coastline in either Sandwick or Birsay, with the threat of firearms in case of disobedience! Such anecdotes were in turn readily exploited later by Power and McCormick, and innocently endorsed by Marwick. It is thus not surprising that many, then and now, having seen the tales in print and heard them told and re-told in all sincerity, genuinely believed them to be factual.

Or perhaps, as Mrs Watt of Skaill House later believed, the local inhabitants were "warned not to go to the shore as they were destroying mines off the shore."[209]

However these possible explanations, be they right or wrong, in no way belittle the passion that is discussed in Chapter 7 below. First, however, it is relevant to address some other factors that may also have contributed to these feelings.

Censorship

Margaret Tait in Kirkwall recorded in her journal:[210]

> *Just as I was preparing for bed last night, word came by wireless that a cruiser was blown up off Marwick Head. ... This morning we heard it was the Hampshire, and later that Lord Kitchener was aboard.*

The next morning the *Glasgow Herald* and the *Scotsman* carried articles, and that afternoon the Admiralty issued a press release confirming HMS *Hampshire* and Lord Kitchener had been lost en route to Russia, "due to either a mine or a torpedo". The Admiralty issued further releases on 9, 10 and 16 June,[211] and the *Times* carried reports daily from 7 to 13 June. The *Daily Mail* carried detailed interviews with Rogerson and Wesson on 11 June, even though they had been reminded that the Official Secrets Act forbade them from discussing the matter. After checking with the Admiralty Censor Office, the *Times* reprinted these articles, largely unaltered, on 16 June.[212]

The authorities in London thus clearly made no attempt to keep secret either the event itself or many of the associated details. However in contrast Col. Harris, acting in the name of the Commander-in-Chief, Grand Fleet, issued an instruction to Kirkwall Post Office "to censor letters posted in Kirkwall on 3 and 4 June",[213]

---

[207] TNA ADM116/2324A.
[208] Admiralty 1926, 22.
[209] TNA ADM1/8468/226.
[210] OA D1/525. The entry is dated 5 June but was evidently written on 6 or 7 June.
[211] The texts of the four Admiralty Press releases were reprinted in Admiralty 1926, 27-8.
[212] TNA ADM116/2324A.
[213] Kirkwall Post Office Records held as OA D1/87/3, 94, undated entry (the preceding entry was dated 7 June).

although the instruction made clear this censorship only applied to letters appearing to have been posted ashore by ratings serving on HM ships.[214] In fact general censorship of mail passing through Kirkwall was not introduced until 20 July 1916.[215]

More significantly, in the same instruction Col. Harris ordered that a special edition of the *Orcadian* be withdrawn.[216] Thereafter the *Orcadian* and the *Orkney Herald* restricted their reporting of the disaster to reprinting the official Admiralty press releases.[217] This de-facto local censorship created a void and did nothing to quell the "them and us" sentiment that contributed to the outrage felt by many Orcadians and the fuelling of the many locally sourced conspiracy theories. This failing was compounded again in 1925/6 by the reluctance of the authorities to respond to Power's accusations, or to release more details or to explain, at least for many months, why they would not publish the Court of Enquiry held on 7 June, or hold a Public Enquiry. All this further fuelled the suspicion of Orcadians, and later of Power, that the authorities had something significant to hide.

Perusal of the copious Admiralty files kept secret until 1967 under the 50 year rule shows that the authorities did take seriously the many criticisms and scare-mongering in the press, the frequent Parliamentary Questions, and the many conspiracy theories, particularly in 1926. Clearly they found Power's campaign embarrassing. However it is clear that making these checks simply increased the self-confidence of the Admiralty staff that the criticisms by Power and the conspiracy theories were largely groundless. Two specific examples illustrate this interpretation: first, an internal Admiralty note "In the case of the *Hampshire* there is nothing in the minutes of the Court [of Inquiry] which need be kept secret for its own sake but it would be very objectionable if a practice were allowed to grow up of laying such minutes on the table of the House [of Commons]"; and second, a letter by Admiral Jellicoe himself criticising a draft of the 1926 Narrative for it having omitted reference to one of the submarine sightings in early June that he had been accused of ignoring![218]

It is only since 2014 that historians have been able to access the last of the many surviving internal Admiralty files to be released by the National Archives, and see for themselves that the authorities had nothing substantive to hide over the *Hampshire*/Kitchener debacle. It is now clear that over the past century the authorities' de-facto "drip, drip" modus operandi on releasing information to the public has itself contributed to many of the conspiracy theories. On the other hand it is also important to recognise that it is easy today to be wise after the event, and to overlook the responsibility of national authorities to protect the country from spies and other forms of "ungentlemanly warfare" such as were successfully practised by the Allies in World War II.

Travel Restrictions

Amongst the early reactions to the tragedy was an initiative taken by the authorities to order that no one was to be allowed to land from the many neutral vessels that stopped at sea and taken to Kirkwall for inspection.[219] This is an example of the paranoia that gripped the authorities about the possibility of enemy spies. There is also a widespread belief that the authorities acted very quickly to restrict travel to Orkney:[220]

> *The London Gazette of June 6 [1916] announced new restrictions on passengers landing at ports in Orkney: 'no passenger shall land in Orkney without permission of the Competent Naval Authority at Kirkwall.'*

It transpires that the order triggering this announcement had been made on 28 May, and was in fact simply a renewal of a similar order made in May 1915.[221] It is thus wholly co-incidental that this notice appeared the day after *Hampshire* sank – not that such subtleties need impede the conspiracy theorists!

There is no doubt that following the loss of HMS *Hampshire* and the death of Lord Kitchener, at the time when the Navy was already struggling with the sobering implications of the Battle of Jutland, not least concerns that the German intelligence service might have been better informed than had been recognised hitherto, many naval staff were "rattled"; this no doubt led to some unnecessary and inappropriate reactions. Although calm quickly returned and common sense prevailed, in Orkney confidence in the authorities had been seriously compromised, with consequences that are discussed in the next chapter.

---

[214] OA D1/87/3, 96, 97, 98. This censorship apparently related to sensitivities over the Battle of Jutland rather than to HMS *Hampshire*.
[215] OA D187/3, 104. This is contrary to some reports (e.g. www.hmshampshire.co.uk > Newspapers > The Sunday Times).
[216] At this time the *Orcadian* occasionally issued special editions – one was issued on 3 June 1916 to mark the Battle of Jutland. The *Orcadian* published the text of their special edition on the loss of HMS *Hampshire* on 1 July 1926 under the title "5th June 1916".
[217] In addition on 21 June the *Orkney Herald* carried an abbreviated version of the article by Rogerson that had already appeared in the *Daily Mail* and the *Times*.
[218] Letter by Admiral Jellicoe 4 July 1926 in TNA ADM116/2324A.
[219] TNA ADM116/2324A.
[220] TNA ADM116/2323; McCormick 1959, 197.
[221] The 1915 order was slightly more stringent, prohibiting passengers from leaving Orkney without permission as well as from landing in Orkney. It was to help enforce this security precaution that Detective Inspector Vance had been seconded from the Glasgow police in 1915 and given the honorary rank of Lieutenant – see page 46 below.

Chapter 7

Outrage

by Issy Grieve

The traditions that the authorities deterred local people from assisting in the rescue of the survivors from HMS *Hampshire*, that these people were ordered not to approach the cliff-tops, or to even talk about the matter, that the authorities' attempts to organise rescue responses were a failure, and ultimately that the authorities were incompetent, have become a long-held belief of the people in both Birsay and Sandwick who were most directly affected by the tragedy.

These traditions have been passed on verbally from generation to generation, and are still very evident today in the descendants of the locals who were alive at the time. Parishioners in Birsay can and still do, even in 2016, recount the tales of what did and did not happen and what should and should not have been done. These tales have become emboldened statements of how lives were lost and how lives could have been saved; they are shared in tones of anguish, disgust and anger, aimed mainly at what was perceived to be the overbearing and incompetent individuals who by all accounts should have known better.

What we have to ask ourselves are uncomfortable questions. Is it possible that these traditions are neither based on fact nor eyewitness accounts, but are instead symptoms of the frustration felt by a community that had been unable to save any lives? Or did the media at the time sensationalise the event, leading to traditions born from inaccuracies? Or did the authorities fail in their duties to mobilise a willing and able community? Why is the sense of injustice apparently felt more in Birsay than in Sandwick? And why has this outrage lingered on so that it is as strong today as it was a century ago?

How reliable all these traditions may or may not be is an issue which has been explored in both Chapters 5 and 6 above, but immaterial of their veracity there is no doubting that they have caused deep and lingering outrage, particularly in Birsay. It is thus relevant to explore the community in Birsay in 1916 and the background to these feelings of outrage and injustice.

Indigenous Orcadians are said to be born with "salt i' the bluid".[222] Effectively this means they have a deep affinity with the sea, and this is clearly evident in the generations of men from the wider parish of Birsay, in which the area of Marwick resides. Throughout the centuries, men from this area have gone to work at sea, particularly when there was little employment on the small farms. Many emigrated to the diasporas in Canada, USA, Australia and New Zealand, leaving behind the eldest son, in general, to maintain the farm, to supplement their diets with some local fishing, and provide for the next generation. In June 1916 most of the farmers and crofters in Marwick shared ownership in various yoles[223] which they launched from 'Boat Geo' near the south end of the rocky barrier known as 'The Choin' in Marwick Bay. They later moved these boats to the south of Marwick Bay to a geo known as 'Sand Geo', where they built the fisherman's huts. Launching from Boat Geo had become increasingly difficult as winter tides continued to erode the coastline and place huge boulders in the landing strip. Hence they decided to move further south to a more sheltered but steep geo, which had a channel from which they could safely access open water. My grandfather, James Moar was one of those men. These men knew the coast, shoreline and tides around both Marwick Bay and Marwick Head intimately. They could name each part of the shore and tell you where the cross currents would move your creels[224] in a westerly gale. They had local fishing marks, which were only known to local fishermen, and were in themselves a language which only local people understood. One I can recall from my father was 'coopers on the craig'. This meant the boat had to be far enough out at sea and far enough north so that it appeared as if the house known as Cooperhouse was sitting atop the craig at Marwick Head: this was always a good spot for catching haddock.

---

[222] Orcadian term meaning 'salt in the blood', from a poem of that name (Rendall 2012, 82) by Robert Rendall (1898-1967), the poet, and amateur naturalist who spent much of his leisure time on holiday in Birsay.
[223] Yole: a small open sailing boat of the Shetland and Orkney Islands.
[224] Crab pots.

7 – Outrage

After a fishing trip they would share the catch equally amongst themselves, but they also gave some of their catch to households whom they felt would benefit from additional provisions. This 'pairting o the fish' was a joy to behold and one which even in my lifetime I have witnessed. One man would divide the fish into equal piles, each pile having haddock, ling, mackerel etc., and then the owner of the boat would turn his back whilst another pointed to each pile and asked 'Whar's this?' and the owner would randomly say either 'Thine', 'Mine' or 'His', depending on how many men had been in the boat. They had a strong sense of equality, justness and fairness.

They were equally skilled as farmers and fishermen, and it was in these in-shore waters that these men supplemented their daily fare by both line and creel fishing. They also freely gathered 'ebb maet'. These are the fruits of the deep rock pools along the coast, including whelks and hand fishing from rocky outcrops using wands (long bamboo poles) for sillocks and lythe. They were not alarmed by the occasional practice of dangling each other on ropes, over the cliff edges, when seeking to gather kittiwake eggs. In previous decades, in the not infrequent years when harvests failed, ebb maet and birds' eggs were sometimes all that prevented starvation.

These men knew their environment extremely well. They also worked tirelessly in support of each other, whether that was at various times in the farming calendar when together they could collectively assist one another, or in undertaking a fishing trip. They were also men of strong religious faith, attending church regularly and applying their faith in their daily working lives. They cared for their elderly at home, and they said grace before each meal, thanking God for their daily lives and the bread on their table. They were familiar with death, as elderly family members died in the home and it was often from these homes that their funerals took place. To these men and others in the community at that time, life was hard but life in itself was sacrosanct. They were humble, hardworking people.

These men had personal experience of loss through emigration and death, but they had not experienced the loss of so many lives in a manner so unexpected. On 5 June 1916 they found themselves in a position which they could never have envisioned or planned for, and in a situation which challenged their instincts. By all accounts their knowledge and skills were ignored, and this treatment fundamentally belittled their faith in humanity.

So we have a community of well-informed, skilled, knowledgeable and kind people who would, could and did help the authorities on the night of 5 June. However, they were also rumored to have been

---

Where rock-piles form a vast Titanic wall,
Built by the Almighty, not by man's device:
Where Ocean's waves with ceaseless rise and fall
Lave this ruge fortress, and each fortalice,
Whose frowning grandeur might their hearts entice,
When tempest-toss'd to Greenland and the Polar ice,
Lay a world of heaving billows fleck'd with foam:
Hard by this northern rampart of our island home.

A gallant chief of gallant British men,
A modern Baynard sans reproach or fear!
On whom stern Duty never called in vain,
He with his gallant comrades perish'd here!
And in her darkest tome her bitterest tear
Albion has shed for him, who led the van,
When allied nations grasped the sword and spear
To fight for Freedom and the Rights of Man!
And liberate the Race from black Teutonic ban!

And Nature wept for them in stormiest guise,
Refusing to be comforted. The sun
Veil'd his fair face in sorrow and surprise
What time the dark and dreadful deed was done!
And when their last, their fiercest fight was won,
And, more than conquerors, they sank down to rest,
The sighing Winds o'er them made the mournful moan;
And Ocean's torn and darkly-heaving breast
Was for his favourite sons distracted and distressed!

Britannia weeps for him. Hibernia wails,
All desolate, and seated on the ground!
And oft-renewing grief her heart assails,
Opening afresh the deep and cruel wound.
In this sad time when evil deeds abound,
"This was the most unkindest cut of all";
Where shall we turn? where shall his like be found?
Who spake, and millions answered to his call!

With high, with holy aim to free the world from thrall!
Toll for the brave! who perished in our sight,
Who died the martyr's death that we might live!
Toll for the brave! fordone through Teutons' spite.
With whom they late victoriously did strive.
At their last port with honour they arrive,
Their brows encinctur'd with the laurel wreath.
While Britain's famed sea-glory shall survive,
Their names shall be told o'er with bated breath –

Victorious to the last, Victorious over Death!
Oh! Vale, vale, now great Kitchener!
With sea-kings old he lies in Ocean grave!
But his high spirit dwells in realms afar
In the Valhalla of the True and Brave!
He warr'd to end all warfare, and to save;
Respecting not each cruel tyrant's frown,
A Christian Viking sleeps beneath the wave!
With his compeers he rests in depths adown
Farewell, farewell again! our chief of high renown.

J.S.*

West Mainland, July, 1916. (OA D1/692, 67)

* The identity of "J.S." is unknown, but could be the Memorial trustee JG Stanger of Boardhouse. This elegy has little poetic merit, nor would its author have been representative of most Orcadians, but it does illustrate well the passion that Kitchener's death aroused locally.

thwarted in that process. Had they been summoned to help in the plight of so many, they would have been able and willing. These men knew where the tide and sea currents would take bodies ashore. They were instinctively driven to help their fellow mankind. Some maintain that they were prevented from this task; the Admiralty Narrative argues otherwise. What evidence is there to support either view? Does this uncertainty over what actually happened mean that we today have to choose to ignore or disbelieve either one version or the other? This would indeed be a folly, as social history sometimes only exists through the passing on of oral stories, regardless of the intervening decades of embroidery.

My father was born in 1921, and it is his recounting of the events which his father (James Moar) shared with him and the reports of eyewitnesses that has led me to describe the overwhelming sense of injustice and perceived inhumanity which prevailed across the community in June 1916. My recollection of my father's retelling included these statements: "The army lined up with their guns and held us back as the bodies came ashore." "We were told to stay inside and not to venture out". The few who knew of the disaster, who wanted to help, were in some cases "forcibly prevented under dire threats". One man was told by a soldier "that all civilians were to remain in their houses and not to venture near the shore or we should be fired on". I do not believe that my father thought these 'stories' to be untrue, but I also appreciate that he was repeating what had been told to him by his father. The events having taken place in 1916 and my father being born in 1921, I can only assume that the stories would have been told to him as a boy in the 1930s or even later, so already we have a time lapse of memories.

I do not discount that these words may have echoed across the generations, but these recollections were by all accounts only a fragment of the 'stories' which contributed to the sense of indignation which remained within the community for an entire generation or longer. My own recollection of hearing these events retold related to 1983, when it was evident that an unsolicited ship was plundering the wreck of HMS *Hampshire*. We watched in awe at night as the crane was lit, and activity was evident. My father was one of a number of locals including Randolph Hay of East Howe, Robert Gaudie of Netherskaill, James Taylor of Flaws and others, who reported what they perceived to be happening, but were all told 'it is a survey ship'. Indeed it was a survey ship, but a ship whose crew were more intent on plundering than surveying. This was evident to all in Birsay who witnessed the late night activities. So history appeared to be repeating itself, for yet again locals were seemingly being ignored. They could see that a war grave was being violated, and they were distressed at the actions which were taking place, but they were not listened to, nor believed by those in authority. They doubted that their concerns were even recorded. Later the ship docked in Peterhead, where one of the propeller shafts and other items from *Hampshire* were recovered. Did these men take any pleasure from being proved right? Pleasure is far too subjective a description of their responses, but I was twenty-five years old at that time, and I can distinctly recall the conversations of the Marwick men about history repeating itself. In their view, the authorities were again ignoring the local knowledge, ignoring those who knew their environment and those who could actually see what was unfolding before them. It is entirely understandable how this incident reinforced the long-held beliefs that those in authority repeatedly decline to engage with those who live and work in communities where local knowledge is paramount.

It is important to explore this oral history from two perspectives, the eye witness accounts and the orders issued by the authorities at the time. These two perspectives were no doubt clouded by those who penned articles to the press, based on accounts which may been embroidered. Regardless of the level of embroidery, the media may very well have unknowingly contributed to the sense of indignation.

Therefore, it is imperative to assess all the factual information that survives, in particular the claims that the local community were ordered not to assist in the rescue efforts. Tradition suggests this was the key catalyst to the strength of feeling and level of outrage which was reported at the time.

The eye witness accounts of James Gaudie of Netherskaill[225] and Mina Sabiston of Skidge[226] as recorded by Ernest Marwick in 1966, begin to provide some insight. Mina was living at Garson in Northdyke in Sandwick at the time, and it was here in her parental home that they took in some of the survivors.

When asked by Ernest Marwick "And was anything done in the neighbourhood to see if any more people could be found?" she replied "Well I think some of the neighbouring houses seemed to go down there, you see, down to the cliff where the other [ones] may be, you see but there was so much people about at the time".

The subsequent question was not actually a query but more of statement from Ernest: "They were prevented". Mina replied "They were prevented I think, but of course I wasn't there myself."

---

[225] James Gaudie, interviewed by EW Marwick 1966 (OA D31/TR111).
[226] Mina Sabiston, interviewed by EW Marwick 1966 (OA D31/TR115).

7 – Outrage

In Ernest's recorded interview with James Gaudie, James describes the scene, in particular the sinking:

Well it was lying right head to sea, and still breaking over it. The boats as we thought at the time was leaving the ship. We found eventually that it was rafts, so we stayed there for quite a while but it was nothing, it was not possible for anything to land or come near the cliffs where we were. The direction of the wind and weather was drifting it off of the land as far as we were concerned.

Ernest follows this with another question, "Were you able to keep the rafts in view for any length of time?", to which James replies (and I summarise here) "Only a very short time. They were going south. Darkness was coming down and it was no use to stay there any longer, for there was nothing had to come ashore there. ... We didn't reckon there would be any survivors."

This was confirmed by Mrs Hunter[227] when she was interviewed by Brian Flett in 1981: "Was there many washed ashore from the boat?" "Nobody" she replied, "nobody at all, no. No, nobody came in to Birsay."

Two Carley Rafts reached the cliffs below Northdyke and one entered Skaill Bay. Those coming ashore below Northdyke in a rough sea on jagged rocks had little hope of survival, but that would not have meant that the community would not wish to try to save lives. Indeed, there is an account of a man being lowered on rope in Northdyke and then being dragged back by the authorities as they felt his own life was in danger. The retelling of this event would suggest more than one local attempted to rescue men by lowering themselves on ropes on the morning of the 6 June, only to be prevented by the authorities. It could have been considered a fruitless task, given the sea conditions and the time that had lapsed, or it could have been in order to save the local people from witnessing the mutilated bodies. Some locals recount this "as they (the authorities) didn't want Kitchener saved".

So we know the bodies came ashore in Sandwick and we begin to learn that it was likely that the people of Birsay, and of Marwick in particular, could have done nothing to help, as there was no one there to help: they could only watch helplessly as the rafts drifted south. Joe Angus of Stromness, who was duty in Birsay on that fateful night, confirms this in his interview with Ernest Marwick in 1964:

And they all came out, and by that time there was quite a few of the local people about the parish there watching the scene. And some of the women folk were really in tears. In fact it was a sad sight to behold, but we could do nothing very much about it, very stormy night and the sea was running high, and the wind was blowing down along the coast.

Could these skilled Marwick and Birsay men have launched their own small boats to have gone to assist? We already know that the appalling and unseasonal sea conditions at the time would have prevented them from doing this. John Spence, a merchant navy officer staying in Palace on sick leave and who witnessed the sinking, wrote:[228]

There was no use launching a boat as there were none large enough to live outside the run of the Headlands, especially as the flood tide was forming a nasty sea outside.

He went on to say:

About 1230am a car from Kirkwall arrived at Birsay post office with [Harris and Nicholson]. They were met by the N.C.O. of the Artillery Patrol but did not speak to anyone else. I should like to have made a statement to them but they did not seem anxious to speak to any civilian.

He must have felt ignored, and it is again understandable that there were accusations of ignoring the locals.

So if the people in Birsay could not assist with the rescue at sea, then we have to ask where the claims of their prevention to assistance come from? Possible answers to this question have been developed in Chapter 6 above, but such explanations, whether accepted or not, and important as they may be from a historical point of view, are only part of the oral tapestry which was woven around the events of June 1916. These events happened in a relatively short space of time and from then onwards their retelling would have been repeatedly described and shared in homes, at church, in the local shops, standing in the post office or passing each other on the road. During those descriptions it would have been entirely natural to have talked about how people felt about the event, the circumstances surrounding it, the shock of the sheer numbers of dead, including the apparent death of such a high profile commander as Kitchener.

To have witnessed the sinking of such a large ship, and to have observed the rafts at sea which were not approaching the shore as they headed south, must have created an overwhelming feeling of helplessness to a

---

[227] Mrs Jane Hunter née Byas, of Flaws, Birsay Be-North, interviewed by Brian Flett for Radio Orkney with Ann Manson, 23 Dec 1981 (OA TA/26/3).
[228] TNA ADM116/2323.

community in Birsay whose members were anxious to assist in any way they could. Death brings with it grief; grief can manifest itself in numerous ways: denial, sadness, and often before acceptance, the anger over the needless loss of so many lives, and in the case of *Hampshire* of so many young lives. Couple these feelings with those of helplessness and we have a community bereft and confused. Add to that confusion their discussions and interpretations of the events, the responses and the non-responses, and we have an angry community saddened in disbelief.

Could the local community have done any more than they did? Probably not. Could the authorities have sought to include the community more comprehensively? Probably yes. Could those who reported the incidents in the press used less conjecture? Probably yes. Was the community at the time rational in their prevailing vexation? Undoubtedly yes.

It is probably no coincidence that one manifestation of the sense of impotence felt by the Birsay folk is that it was they who initiated the fund-raising response to the tragedy that eventually led to the erection of the Kitchener Memorial (see Chapter 10 below).

We can consider the passing of oral history as being fundamental to the sustained outrage, and hopefully this analysis begins to explain the sense of prevailing outrage in 1916. It is more difficult to analyse why this outrage has endured for so many generations, and with such passion and sincerity. Clearly the feelings and beliefs have been rekindled over the years by a succession of inflammatory articles in the press, by the perception of the Admiralty Narrative of 1926 being a "whitewash", by the publication of McCormick's book in 1959, and by the salvage activities in 1983. Nor should we dismiss the visual reminder which sits atop Marwick Head: the Memorial reminds us daily of the aftermath of the *Hampshire* tragedy and the loss of so many lives. Ironically the rededication of the memorial and the other commemorative events of June 2016 are again refuelling the passion. Whatever its origins, whatever its cause, the outrage is now an oral history that shows no signs of disappearing, and may endure for many generations to come.

Today we are the current generation of storytellers and this is a tale worth telling. So tell it to your children and encourage them to pass it on, accepting the embroidery and slight alterations as signs of good story telling. But remember too those people in Birsay in June 1916 and how grief-stricken and helpless they felt as they watched their fellow mankind succumb to the seas west of Marwick Head.

Chapter 8

The Conspiracy Theories

by Tom Muir

Horatio Herbert Kitchener was a divisive and controversial character when he set off on his ill-fated voyage to Russia and died off the coast of Birsay in a summer storm a century ago. Even today his reputation invokes the strongest passions among those who revere him and those who revile him.

Although still a member of the Cabinet, to the government and indeed to much of the British establishment he was a thorn in their flesh – a relic of an age of Empire that was being swept away by German machine guns and high explosives in the killing fields of France and Belgium. He was difficult to get along with, intransigent in his views, and had a reputation of being a bully. His brutal crushing of the Boers in South Africa by introducing a scorched-earth policy and rounding up civilians, predominantly women and children, into concentration camps where the death toll was truly appalling, made him enemies at both home and abroad. He was also implicated in Winston Churchill's disastrous Gallipoli campaign. His political opponents thought him arrogant and aloof. But the public loved him. To them he was a national hero, a demigod who had brought victory to the Empire in the Sudan and the Boer War. It was his famous recruiting poster as much as anything that had focussed the public's support for the war effort.

It is hard for us in the early 21st century to imagine that a soldier could be so universally famous and so popular with so many, just as our ancestors would struggle to understand the qualities of some of our modern day 'celebrities'. It is unwise to judge others by our own standards, especially if they lived in another era.

The nearest comparison to the loss of Lord Kitchener would be the death of Diana, Princess of Wales, an event which produced a wave of media-fed grief and a succession of fascinating conspiracy theories and accusations. His sudden death came as such a shock to the nation that questions were bound to be asked. How could this happen? Who was responsible for this catastrophe? Someone must be to blame – but who? The Admiralty's on-going reluctance to address the many issues that arose added to the disquiet.

So the conspiracy theories started to grow, nesting in the imagination of the public who were only too ready to believe a series of theories that opportunistic journalists and authors were happy to offer them. Kitchener was barely cold in his watery grave when the stories started to be woven around his fate. The rumour-mongering started in London less than 24 hours after the sinking,[229] and has been rekindled in the media and by word-of-mouth from time to time ever since. As a boy in the 1970s I remember one of my elder brothers, a crane driver employed on a construction site in Birsay, coming home with stories that he had been told of how the survivors from HMS *Hampshire* who had climbed to the top of the lofty cliffs were kicked back over the edge by British soldiers. They didn't want to take the risk of Kitchener being saved or sensitive documents falling into the wrong hands. But who were these 'they' who could act with such callous cruelty? Well – where do we begin?

As soon as the local authorities became aware that *Hampshire* had sunk, soldiers were sent out to rescue any survivors. Initially it seems that these men welcomed help from local people to try to help any survivors who had escaped the wreck and the raging ocean. But later other soldiers were apparently not so grateful for such help, seeing their task as purely a military operation with no need for civilian assistance. There are claims that some turned their bayonets towards their would-be helpers and who knows, that might have happened. But by the time the story had done the rounds for a while it had grown in the telling. It was even claimed that the military authorities had mistaken the identity of *Hampshire* and thought that it was an enemy ship, so the soldiers were ordered to shoot any survivors rather than being burdened with prisoners.

But the stories got more and more bizarre. Lord Alfred Douglas, son of the Marquis of Queensbury of boxing rules fame, was the man who had, along with his pugilistic parent, destroyed Oscar Wilde's life and reputation. Known as 'Bosie', Douglas had in his later life turned against his former lover, Wilde, embraced Catholicism and turned extremely right wing and anti-Semitic. He had edited the publication *Plain English* during 1920-21,

---

[229] Royle 1985, 377. On 7 June the *Daily Mail* carried a story of spies (TNA ADM 116/2324A), while the *Evening News* claimed the sinking to be the work of German secret agents (Paxman 2014a).

in which he claimed that Winston Churchill was in the pay of Jewish bankers and had been given a large sum of money to put out a statement overstating British losses at the Battle of Jutland in order to cause fluctuations in the American Stock Exchange, thus making his Jewish paymasters lots of money. He revived the claims, along with new ones, in a speech in London[230] in which he claimed that Kitchener was killed by Bolshevik Jews who had planted a bomb on board the ship in order to prevent Kitchener's mission as this would have led to the end of the proposed Jewish backed Russian Revolution. He claimed that *Hampshire* "… floated for some considerable time after" but that the crew had simply vanished: "No trace or sign of them has been seen since". Churchill went on the attack: he sued Douglas for libel, for which he was found guilty and sentenced to six months imprisonment.

A few years later an opportunistic journalist was making a fast buck out of Kitchener conspiracy theories in newspaper articles, speeches, two books and a film. His name seemed too good to be true, Frank Power; it was: his real name Arthur Freeman. Not all his claims were without some foundation. For example, he contested the official position that Kitchener's mission had been kept a very close secret. Although the Admiralty Narrative of August 1926 was adamant that there had been no "leak" by the Navy, and no communication with the press,[231] eight months earlier Sir George Arthur, Kitchener's private secretary, lifelong friend and biographer, advised the First Lord of the Admiralty that he received a telegram nearly a week beforehand from a Russian asking if he was joining the mission.[232] Four months earlier Fox-Davies, a barrister who had worked in the Admiralty from 1916 to 1920, had declared that it had been known in Fleet Street eight days beforehand that Lord Kitchener was going to Russia.[233] Power claimed the visit and its dates were a common topic in Petrograd in early May, and that the Czarina told Rasputin of the visit,[234] who in turn passed it to a German secret agent.[235] Even the German press seem to have been aware of Kitchener's intended visit.[236] In another version he claimed a German woman living in London called Elbe Boecker had not been interred as she was married to an Englishman who was later killed at Gallipoli.[237] She was recruited as a German spy and was said to possess "siren charms" and to have "voluptuous beauty and witchery of manner". She used her social contacts to meet officers and to wine and dine with them so that she could pass on any useful information to Germany. Then she hit the jackpot. There was another German woman whom she knew and recruited as a spy. One of this woman's male friends was on Kitchener's staff; as the wine flowed and the woman flirted, the unwitting officer revealed the plan for Kitchener to go to Russia. Later he carelessly gave her the name of the ship and the route that was to be taken. Boecker passed this information back to Germany and U-boats were dispatched to sow a minefield in the cruiser's path, with fatal consequences for the loose lipped officer and the rest of those on board.[238]

Another group of revolutionaries whom Power gave the distinction of sinking *Hampshire* was the IRA.[239] It was said that while the ship was in Belfast in February 1916 her ammunition was tampered with, wiring in a magazine was tinkered with, and bombs with delayed time fuses were hidden on board the ship.[240] I can only assume that instead of using an alarm clock as a timer they used a calendar with the 5th June circled instead.

---

[230] Douglas, 1923.
[231] Admiralty 1926, 4.
[232] TNA ADM116/2324A.
[233] Various claims have been made that the German Secret Service and even the German press were aware of Kitchener's visit (*Referee* 8 Nov., 27 Dec. 1925, 21 Feb. 1926; McCormick 1959, 88, 98, 100, 115, 118, 120, 123, 143-54, 157; Royle 1985, 357, 377, 379). Although it has not been possible to check these claims, it is now clear that none of them contributed to *U 75*'s minelaying voyage. There was a suggestion, however, not taken up by subsequent conspiracy theorists, that if HMS *Hampshire* had not been sunk off Orkney she might have sustained U-boat torpedo attacks in the White Sea (Warrant Officer Frank Parker RN, *Referee* 21 Feb. 1926).
[234] *Referee* 6 Dec. 1925; 21 Feb. 1926.
[235] TNA ADM116/2324A; *Liverpool Courier* 19 Apr. 1926. McCormick speculated on the source of this leak (1959, 115-6), but made no suggestion that the leak was published in the press.
[236] McCormick 1959, 98.
[237] *Times* 10 June 1916.
[238] *Referee* 8, 29 Nov. 1925, 11 Apr. 1926. In fact Boecker had been detained as a suspect in Holloway Prison on 8 May 1916. She was interred for two months without trial and then deported, returning to Berlin (TNA ADM116/2324A). For other versions of the claim that Kitchener's death was attributable to the German Secret Service see Phillips 1930, 53; McCormick 1959, 164-5, 168, 210; Hewison 1985, 106; Royle 1985, 377, 384; Paxman 2013, 178.
[239] *Referee* 13, 27 Dec. 1925, 3, 10 Jan., 7 Mar. 1926.
[240] Suspicions of untoward events having occurred in Belfast had been raised as early as July 1916. On 22 Dec. 1925 the First Lord of the Admiralty described as "a ridiculous and wicked fabrication" a report in the *Belfast Evening News* that the ship was surrounded by soldiers with bayonets fixed, with two electricians being summarily executed and two more imprisoned (TNA ADM116/2323, /2324A; Admiralty 1926, 3). These anecdotes were developed into a book by the German spy Carl Ernst who collaborated with two Irish Sinn Fein confederates (Ernst 1935). McCormick later expanded on these stories (1959, 19, 127-8, 167, 171-6, 195-201, 207, 211-4, 377, 385).

Power made many other allegations: he claimed that earlier in the war Kitchener was aboard HMS *Hampshire* when a German submarine attempted to torpedo her, and a spy on *Hampshire* was shot;[241] that *Hampshire* was in poor condition and unfit for the voyage to Russia;[242] that *Hampshire*'s navigation was faulty and she struck a reef;[243] and that while *Hampshire* may have struck a mine, there were two further explosions inside the ship which could only have been caused by bombs planted by a German spy, or by a Boer in retaliation for Kitchener's policy of concentration camps during the Second Boer War.[244] In another version spies were found on board *Hampshire* and were shot.[245] In one of Power's thrilling tales, Kitchener was seen leaving the sinking ship in a small wooden boat, battling against the huge waves until he and the boat were washed ashore on a flat shelving rock beneath the cliffs. Exhausted, Kitchener was safe – but not for long. After a struggle he was shot by an agent of the British Secret Service, acting on behalf of a Government who wanted him dead.[246]

Kitchener's Coffin. (OA TK960)

In 1926 Power pulled off what was to be his master-stroke – almost. He claimed that Kitchener's body had indeed been found, by a fisherman off the shores of Norway, and had been taken ashore and buried.[247] Power bought Kitchener's Coffin in Orkney,[248] travelled to Norway to have the body disinterred, and brought it home for a state funeral in St.Paul's Cathedral. He arrived at Waterloo Station with the coffin that was said to contain Kitchener's body. The coffin was placed in a chapel for the night, draped in the Union Flag and with candles burning at each corner. The only fly in Power's ointment was the Westminster Coroner. In the case of an unexplained death there had to be an inquest and a death certificate had to be issued. In the full glare of the national press the lid of the coffin was prised open to reveal, not the body of the great warlord of Empire, but a layer of tar which gave the coffin some weight. Power was interviewed by the police but no charges were made. No more money was made either.

The conspiracy theories of this period did not only originate in Britain. In Canada a spiritualist claimed submarines had been following *Hampshire* for hours.[249] In Perth, Australia a paper claimed Kitchener never embarked on *Hampshire*,[250] and another in New York claimed Kitchener had been killed some days before he was alleged to have joined *Hampshire*.[251]

Move on thirty years and another journalist, Donald McCormick, addressed the conspiracy theories once more. He poured cold water on many of Power's claims, but added several of his own. He recounts anecdotes of British Secret Service eavesdropping in a Turkish baths establishment in London, of leaks to the German intelligence service, and of interceptions of British naval signals by the same organisation. He also argued that

---

[241] *Referee* 31 Jan. 1926; Admiralty 1926, 3.
[242] *Referee* 15 Nov., 31 Dec. 1925, 31 Jan. 1926.
[243] *Referee* 24 Jan. 1925.
[244] *Referee* 6 Dec. 1925; TNA ADM116/2324A. See also the claim by Duquesne on page 46 below.
[245] *Liverpool Post* 7 Jan. 1926.
[246] *Referee* 22, 29 Nov., 6, 13 Dec. 1925, 14 Feb. 1926.
[247] *Referee* 28 Feb. 1926.
[248] More details of Kitchener's Coffin are given on page 99 below.
[249] Ala Mana 1922; McCormick 1959, 124.
[250] *Sunday Times*, Perth, 27 May 1926.
[251] *Orcadian* 5 August 1926.

Detective-Inspector Vance[252] had investigated reports that a Dutch fishing vessel had been seen in the vicinity of Marwick Head, and that a mysterious Irishman had been loitering in Kirkwall, and then submitted a report whose contents have never been revealed.[253]

Rightly or wrongly, Kitchener's sexuality has been in question from his own time to the present day. He never married, was a great supporter of the Boy Scouts Movement, was fond of fine porcelain, orchids, flower arranging, interior furnishings, and had a pet poodle and statues of boys in his garden. Not a hanging offence, granted, but homosexuality was still a court marshalling offence in the British Army at the time and, like 'Bosie's' former lover Oscar Wilde, it could bring about the end of your career, reputation and life, leaving you an outcast of society. He gathered around him a staff of handsome young men, all unmarried and unattached (they had to agree to remain so for at least two years after signing up) who came to be known as 'Kitchener's band of boys' or 'Kitchener's cubs'. When one of them married without asking permission Kitchener flew into a rage. You were no longer one of the 'cubs' if you found a lady friend. One writer claimed that Kitchener's aide-de-camp, Captain Oswald FitzGerald, who was with him for nine years before suffering the same fate on *Hampshire*, had been 'living openly' with Kitchener as a couple for three years before their deaths. Many years later the gay rights activist, Peter Tatchell, wrote in *The Guardian* that they "...died in each other's arms",[254] but unless you were actually there how could you possibly know? Another writer claimed that the British Government were worried about the potential embarrassment that Kitchener could cause them if he was found out to be homosexual and so a plot was hatched. It was alleged claims that a British secret agent made a death-bed confession that he and a senior officer went to Kitchener's cabin on board *Hampshire* soon before she sailed from Scapa Flow. The senior officer told him to wait outside while he went in and spoke to Kitchener. The young man put his ear to the door and heard his superior saying to Kitchener: "*I am going to leave you my pistol with one bullet, I will wait outside and you will do the honourable thing.*" The officer came out, a single shot was heard, and he went back in to retrieve his gun. Then they disembarked before the ship sailed, leaving a bomb on board to sink her and so leave no trace of what had happened.[255] But later claims that Kitchener was a homosexual have not been substantiated – even the last two Admiralty files to be released to the public make no hint of this.

The fact that David Lloyd George, who had taken over responsibility for the Ministry of Munitions from Kitchener, had been expected to sail on the *Hampshire* as well, but had cancelled at the last minute because of the situation in Ireland following the Easter Uprising, also led to stories of a Government plot. Another version says that the Freemasons arranged a bomb to be placed on board and spirited their fellow Mason Kitchener away to safety in order to protect his reputation.

In another tale of daring do, a German spy called Captain Fritz Joubert Duquesne claimed that he had killed Kitchener in retaliation for the deaths of family members during the Second Boer War. He had fought in the conflict and had once tried to assassinate Kitchener in Cape Town, but failed. He had been captured, imprisoned in Bermuda, escaped to the USA where he became an adviser on big game hunting to President Theodore Roosevelt and proposed a scheme to introduce hippopotamuses into the Louisiana bayous in an attempt to solve a shortage of meat in the country. Recruited by the Germans as a spy in World War I, he claimed to have met Kitchener in Scotland on his way north to Scapa Flow when he was disguised as a Russian nobleman calling himself Duke Boris Zakrevsky. Befriending Kitchener, he joined his party to Russia and while on the *Hampshire* he signalled to a waiting German submarine, which torpedoed the ship and rescued Duquesne who had made good his escape in a small boat. For this he was awarded the Iron Cross. He was later captured as the leader of a Nazi spy ring in New York in 1932 and imprisoned there. Another version has it that the U-boat that sank *Hampshire* picked up Kitchener, who was in a small boat, and took him back to Germany where he was a held as a prisoner.[256] The story of Duquesne became the subject of a whole book.[257]

Perhaps the most enduring conspiracy theory is that HMS *Hampshire* was carrying gold to Russia. There is no evidence to support this claim, as the timing of the ship's movements would prohibit the transfer of gold bullion

---

[252] In 1926 Power claimed that Vance had prepared a secret report on issues arising from the *Hampshire* sinking (*Referee* 21 Feb., 4, 14, 23 Mar., 18 Apr., 2 May, 13 June 1926; Admiralty 1926, 23; McCormick 1959 ,191-201, 204, 207, 214). However Admiralty records (TNA ADM116/2324A, ADM116/2324B) show that Vance was interviewed and signed a statement: "I was not called upon to make any investigation of any matters arising out of the loss of HMS *Hampshire* on June 5th 1916, and consequently I furnished no report re the same. All reports furnished by me during my service on Orkney were forwarded to the Admiral Commanding the Orkneys and Shetlands at Longhope". The issue is thus one of weighing the relative credibility of a carefully worded statement signed by a police officer and against the speculative hypotheses and unsubstantiated anecdotes of a fraudster.
[253] McCormick 1959, 105-121, 143-54, 157-161, 212.
[254] http://www.ft.com/cms/s/2/f3760af0-6545-11e4-91b1-00144feabdc0.html; Paxman 2014a.
[255] TNA ADM116/2323; http://www.thetruthseeker.co.uk/?p=4202.
[256] Cassar 1977, 480.
[257] Wood 1932; McCormick 1959, 169-71.

into the ship's strong-room without it being noticed by the crew.[258] No representative from the Bank of England was on board the ship, which would be expected if gold was being shipped. Also, Britain was on the back-foot in the war and simply didn't have such wealth to spare for the fabulously wealthy Czar of Russia. In fact one of the objectives of Kitchener's mission was to secure Russian payment for the war materials that Britain was supplying, which conceivably might have led to gold being carried on *Hampshire*'s return trip.[259] But what if it wasn't British gold on board but Russian gold, loaded clandestinely to bolster the Romanov regime? That would not need a Bank of England official travelling with it, but it would still need more time and effort than the Royal Navy had to transfer such a heavy and precious cargo. All this has not stopped speculation that there was gold on board. Claims of diving expeditions in the 1930s, although written up in detail, are regarded by most as fanciful. However, it would seem that the speculation did lead to a salvage vessel starting to blast the wreck to pieces on the seabed while claiming they were making a film in 1983. It must have been over the wreck site for quite some time, and they are said to have seriously damaged the bow section of the ship. It has been suggested that they were looking for the strong-room where gold would have been stored. Certainly they removed random pieces of the ship, like guns, portholes, bottles and one of the ship's two propellers and shafts, but this was said to be a ruse to put people off the scent of what they were really after.[260] These pieces were recovered in Peterhead, but it is claimed that there were two container units landed but only one was returned to Orkney, where the looted artefacts were put into the Scapa Flow Visitor Centre and Museum at Lyness, while the second container was taken away by the authorities. Another suggestion from a local "in the know" is that when British gold bullion was recovered from the wreck of HMS *Edinburgh* in 1981 in Russian waters, the Russian Government laid claim to a large portion of it as the gold had been on its way to the Soviet Union. The UK Government got a smaller share than expected, so could this be the Thatcher government's attempt to get their own back? Jonathan Aitken, a senior Tory politician of the time, was indirectly involved with the company who illegally salvaged the wreck – or is that a conspiracy too far?[261]

Many more fantastical legends grew up around Lord Kitchener over the years. He wasn't killed in the sinking as his sister had tried unsuccessfully to contact him via a clairvoyant. He was replaced by a double and made his way to Russia where he was still alive and in command of the Czar's army, or the Russian Revolutionaries (depending on whose version you listen to).[262] He has turned up in India, Egypt and the United States of America, he was seen in the corridors of Whitehall, he is even said to have become a potentate in China.[263] My favourite of all the Kitchener conspiracy theories is that he made it to Russia alive, took over the Bolshevik Party and changed his name to Joseph Stalin. If Kitchener and Stalin were one and the same person then he lived to the ripe old age of 102.

But we don't have to look as far afield as that for sightings of Kitchener. He has been spotted alive and well in the North Isles of Orkney, working on some great plan, rumoured to be a much improved version of the Treaty of Versailles in 1919. Some even said that he survived the sinking and lived as a hermit in a cave by the shore.[264] Possibly the most romantic of all the Kitchener legends is that he is not dead, but lies sleeping in a sea cave in a secret place in Orkney, waiting for a time when his country is in great need of him again; then he will awake, and, like King Arthur or Rip Van Winkle, become the saviour of his nation once more. If that is the case, I have only this to say: "You're late!"

---

[258] See also pages 70 and 71 below.
[259] One such shipment of gold, from Vladivostok to Canada, had already been undertaken in 1916 (Pickford 1999, 91).
[260] *Referee* 29 Nov. 1925.
[261] *Orcadian* 18 Aug. 1983. The gold conspiracy theory was given further life in an article in the *Sunday Times* in Aug. 1998.
[262] Royle 1985, 377; Cassar 1977, 480; Harris 1990, 117; Paxman 2013, 178. Fresh variations on this theme are still emerging – one was included in a Fereday Prize entry by Tom Flett in 2013 (OA D70/16/29).
[263] Paxman 2013, 178.
[264] McCormick 1959, 125.

Chapter 9

Minesweeping and the *Laurel Crown*

by Kevin Heath[265]

HMS *Hampshire* was not the only vessel to strike one of the mines laid by *U 75*: just over a fortnight later HM Drifter *Laurel Crown* struck another mine and sank with the loss of all nine of her crew.

Minesweeping west of Orkney in 1916

In April 1916 Admiral Jellicoe issued orders for the areas that his minesweeping forces were to keep cleared. Amongst these was "Area 2", a channel that led NW from Hoy past Sule Skerry and passed about 12-25 miles SW of the Brough of Birsay.[266] The waters close to the west Mainland were not included in these designated Areas, it being thought (at that time correctly) that Germany did not to possess submarines capable of laying mines that far north, and that with the short Orkney nights any minelaying by surface vessels would be sighted and reported by the Territorial coast watchers. The loss of *Hampshire* promptly triggered minesweeping close to the Birsay coast. Few records of this operation have been found,[267] but three of *U 75*'s mines had been swept and exploded by the Scapa minesweeping trawlers by the evening of 8 June. These mines were found to have been laid 15ft below the surface at Low Water.[268] Thirteen had been swept by 15 June.[269]

A week later Commander BW Nicholson RN was ordered to have Area 2 swept for mines; he delegated this to Lieut. Cdr. SR Lane RNR with his steam yacht *Evening Star*, accompanied by the steam drifter *Pitgaveny* and six steam drifters which had been converted into minesweepers, including *Laurel Crown*. Lane's fleet left Kirkwall early on 22 June, proceeding via Eynhallow Sound because this was a more direct route than using the Pentland Firth. Nicholson assumed that the mines that sank *Hampshire* had been cleared,[270] and anyway, at 15ft below Low Water, were too deep to endanger Lane's fleet. Lane claimed to be unaware he would be passing over a minefield when he set course WSW from the Brough at a speed of 8 or 9 knots. The weather was fine, it was an hour after Low Water at Birsay, and there was a swell, variously described as "heavy" and "5 to 6 feet".

At 0805 there was a big explosion. *Laurel Crown*, about five miles SW of the Brough,[271] was leading the starboard column of drifters when she disappeared in a column of water and cloud of smoke. Her stern disintegrated, her bow sank within seconds. All that remained were splinters of wood and one body which was quickly recovered by a small boat launched from *Pitgaveny*. But the men in the rescue boat also sighted another mine moored 3 or 4 feet below the surface, almost breaking in the swell. The mine was towed into shallow water and sunk by gunfire.[272]

The next day Nicholson was ordered to have his drifters sweep for mines in a rectangular area from 1½ to 5 miles from the shore, from Black Craig to NW of the Brough of Birsay.[273] By 30 June, 15 of the mines had been accounted for: 2 had sunk ships, 7 had been exploded by sweeps, 3 exploded by gunfire, and 3 sunk by gunfire. The Admiralty had learned that these mines were four-horned, painted red, and were smaller and held less explosive than other German mines; they suspected these features implied the mines had been laid by a submarine, but remained unaware of which U-boat was responsible.[274]

---

[265] With input by Brian Budge, James Irvine and Michael Lowrey.
[266] TNA ADM116/2324A.
[267] Lt. RH Clements DSC RNR later claimed a 4 mile wide channel was swept by minesweepers based in Kirkwall (*Orcadian* 1 July 1926).
[268] TNA ADM116/2323, Court of Enquiry; ADM137/3138. This depth correlates well with Beitzen's orders that they be laid 7 metres below the surface at High Water, the average rise of tide in Orkney being about 2 metres (see Appendix II below).
[269] TNA ADM116/1515; ADM137/1209, 69; ADM186/628, 38.
[270] The Admiralty Narrative claims that 13 of the mines off Marwick Head had by then been swept up, though this is hardly compatible with the statement of 30 June in TNA ADM116/1515.
[271] The report of her sinking at 59° 08'N 3° 22'W, i.e. 1 mile WSW of the Brough of Birsay (TNA ADM116/1515) is incorrect. So too was the report that *Laurel Crown* was sunk on 2 June (see page 15 above).
[272] TNA ADM116/2323.
[273] TNA ADM116/2323, Court of Enquiry, ADM137/3138.
[274] TNA ADM116/1515. Eventually 16 of the mines were accounted for (TNA ADM 2324A, letter by Preston 15 June 1926). This implies that 18 mines were "lost", but in the exposed sea conditions this is perhaps not surprising.

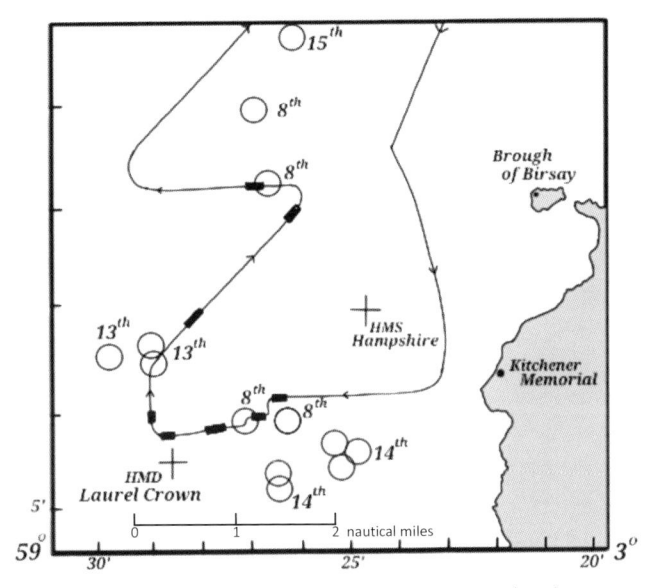

Composite chartlet (courtesy of Bertrand Taylor) showing
(1) the track of *U 75*, with rectangles marking where she claimed to have laid her mines on 29 May 1916,
(2) circles with dates in June 1916 marking reported positions of the mines swept (TNA ADM137/1209, 69), and
(3) crosses marking the positions of the wrecks of *Hampshire* and *Laurel Crown*.

Given the many inexactitudes involved, the chartlet above shows a surprisingly good correlation between the positions where Beitzen claimed to have laid his mines, the positions reported for most of the mines subsequently swept by the Royal Navy, and the position where *Laurel Crown* sank: typically these discrepancies are less than a mile.[275] In contrast, the *Hampshire* wreck lies about 1 mile NE from the nearest of Beitzen's reported positions. This larger discrepancy can be readily explained: when she struck the mine *Hampshire* was steering N30°E,[276] making good 13½ knots, and her engines did not stop immediately. Although the mine explosion itself would not have slowed her, she quickly trimmed by the head, her boilers lost steam pressure, and within about 10 minutes she had stopped with her bow on the seabed.[277] So during this period she probably made a further 1 or 2 miles of headway after striking the mine. Her heading during this time is unclear as her steering gear failed immediately and her two screws would not necessarily have lost power at the same rate, but a net NE'ly direction is consistent with witness reports.[278] These considerations suggest she could have struck any of *U 75*'s mines, but perhaps one of those laid in the first two or three batches is the most likely.

The acceptance that *U 75*'s mines had been found 15 feet below Low Water (i.e. 10 feet less than *Hampshire*'s draught), the loss of *Laurel Crown* with a draught of 9 feet, and the finding of a mine 3 or 4 feet below the surface show the weakness of the Admiralty's claim[279] that *Hampshire* had been unlucky to strike these mines.

Laurel Crown

Laurel Crown was an 81-ton wooden drifter, 88.4ft long, 18.8ft beam, 8.9ft draught, powered by a triple expansion reciprocating steam engine. She was built in 1912 at Fraserburgh in Aberdeenshire by Scott and Yule, and registered as FR506, with George Walker as her managing owner. In December 1914 she was requisitioned by the Admiralty to serve as a minesweeper, No.2050.

Typical steam drifter of the period. (OA L7868-1)

This chapter concludes with brief biographies of the nine crew members of HM Drifter *Laurel Crown* who lost their lives on 22 June 1916 and whose names are now inscribed on the new wall around the Kitchener Memorial.

---

[275] This weakens the claim by the Admiralty (1926, 13) that the mine struck by *Laurel Crown* "had been dragged by the sweeps into shallower water". It may be significant that the last mine to be swept, on 15 June, had drifted so far north.

[276] This was probably her course to steer by magnetic compass, rather than her true course, but this ambiguity is irrelevant here.

[277] TNA ADM116/2323 Court of Enquiry; ADM137/3138; Sub. Lieut. Spence's letter in ADM 116/2323.

[278] TNA ADM116/2323 Court of Enquiry. Two young eye-witnesses ashore remembered many years later that *Hampshire* turned towards the shore before her bow struck the seabed (OA TA/26/3; TA/26/4). Wind, tide and the north westerly orientation of the wreck are probably secondary considerations.

[279] Admiralty 1926, 12.

Thomas James Baker, Engineman RNR 739ES.[280]
Thomas Baker was born in Yarmouth, Norfolk on 9 May 1878. He was working as a fisherman out of Grimsby when he married Elizabeth Ann Chalk there in 1903. In 1911 their children were George, Ellen and Emily. Thomas enrolled in the Royal Naval Reserve, Trawler section [RNR(T)] on 19 September 1914. After a few months service as an Engineman on the 161-ton Grimsby-registered trawler *Peterborough*, he joined *Laurel Crown*. His body was recovered from the sea after the mine explosion and is buried in Lyness Royal Naval Cemetery, in Grave B.99. Thomas died aged 38.

John Coull, Temporary Skipper RNR 1873WSA.[281]
John Coull was born in Port Gordon, Banffshire on 10 November 1873. He was a fisherman, and passed his Certificate of Competency as a Skipper on 3 May 1911. He enrolled in the RNR in Aberdeen on 18 August 1915 with the rank of Temporary Skipper and appointed in command of *Laurel Crown* the same day. John died aged 42. In the 1920s his widow received three Naval Prize Money awards totalling £101 5s.

Charles Durrant, Deck Hand RNR 8421DA.[282]
Charles Durrant was born in Lowestoft on 29 January 1899. In 1911 his family were living in Torry, Aberdeen and his father was Master of the steamship *Memsie*. Charles subtracted two years from his date of birth when he enrolled in the RNR in Aberdeen on 27 August 1915. Two days later he arrived in Orkney and reported to the Auxiliary Patrol Depot Ship HMS *Zaria* at Longhope, then joined *Laurel Crown*. Charles was the youngest crew member when she was sunk, aged only 17.

Robert Mitchell, Engineman RNR 1461ES.[283]
Robert Mitchell was born in Peterhead on 9 April 1890. Son of a fisherman, he was a marine engineer when he married dressmaker Mary Noble in Aberdeen in March 1914. He enrolled in the RNR in Aberdeen on 21 December 1914 and joined *Laurel Crown* on Boxing Day. Robert died aged 26.

Alfred Murphy, Deck Hand RNR 7018DA.[284]
Alfred Murphy was born in Manchester on 14 March 1884. In 1891 he was living in Stockton Heath, Cheshire as the adopted son of his uncle, a barge waterman. After he left school he worked as a general labourer. In 1908 he married Mary Elizabeth Wright, and in 1911 he was working as a bargeman out of lodgings in Birkenhead. He enrolled in the RNR in Grimsby on 19 May 1915 and joined *Laurel Crown* a week later. Alfred died aged 32.

Murdo Nicolson, Deck Hand RNR 7916DA.[285]
Murdo Nicolson was born at Calbost, Stornoway on 18 January 1872. He was working as a fisherman when he married Isabella McLeod in 1901. He enrolled in the RNR(T) on HMS *Zaria* on 22 July 1915 and served three months on the 76-ton Stornoway-registered drifter *Herring Fisher*. He joined *Laurel Crown* as a deck hand on 17 October. Murdo was probably the oldest crew member when she was sunk, aged 44.

George Petrie, Deck Hand RNR 11223DA.[286]
George Petrie was the only Orcadian on *Laurel Crown*. He was born at Wart, Burray on 8 August 1883, the oldest son of crofter George Petrie and Betsy Brown. He was working as a fisherman when he married Flora Taylor on 10 September 1914. They made their home at Wart and had a son, George Andrew. George enrolled in the RNR(T) at Kirkwall on 15 May 1916, reported to HMS *Zaria* at Longhope, and soon joined *Laurel Crown* as a deck hand. George died aged 32, after just five weeks service in the RNR. He is remembered on the family gravestone in Burray Cemetery.

Robert Slater, Second Hand RNR 4577DA.[287]
Robert Slater was born in Portknockie, Banff on 12 March 1886 and became a fisherman like his father. He enrolled in the RNR(T) on 6 March 1915 as a Second Hand and served on the 81-ton Banff registered drifter *Slains Castle*. He joined *Laurel Crown* in Scapa Flow on 25 March 1916. Robert died aged 30.

Clarence Percy Stephenson, Trimmer RNR 3322TS.[288]
Clarence Stephenson was born in Willerby, Yorkshire on 26 July 1893. After leaving school he worked as a boiler cleaner's labourer in Hull, where the family lived in Strickland Terrace. He enrolled in the RNR on 6 May 1915 and travelled north to Orkney to join *Laurel Crown* on 22 May. Clarence died aged 22.

---

[280] TNA BT377-7-130138.
[281] TNA BT377-7-126111; Navy Lists, Apr. and Sept. 1916, ID: 97149222.
[282] TNA BT377-7-54875.
[283] TNA BT377-7-130869.
[284] TNA BT377-7-53472.
[285] TNA BT377-7-54370.
[286] TNA BT377-7-57677.
[287] TNA BT377-7-51051.
[288] TNA BT377-7-113247.

Chapter 10

The Kitchener Memorial

by Neil Kermode

The Kitchener Memorial, Marwick Head, with the Brough of Birsay in the distance. (courtesy of Frankie Tait)

The Kitchener Memorial stands above the 85 metre high cliffs of the Marwick Head Reserve of the Royal Society for the Protection of Birds (RSPB), commanding stunning views across the Atlantic Ocean, of the Brough of Birsay to the north, and of Hoy to the south, with the stone stack of The Old Man of Hoy is clearly visible on a fine day. But how did this Memorial come about, why is it where it is, and what has changed since it was built? The story has several twists and turns, some of which arose soon after the idea was first floated, some of which have only recently come to light.

The building of the Memorial[289]

The memorial was first proposed by George W Scarth who was living in Twatt, Birsay.[290] The idea grew rapidly and a public meeting was held at the Old School in Twatt on 8 August 1916. This led to the formation of the Kitchener Memorial Trust, whose original members were Rev. C Meldrum, Rev. R Souter, Rev. J Ferguson,[291] GW Scarth (Secretary and Treasurer), PC Ballantyne, Quoylonga; Miss C Scarth, Twatt; Miss J Harvey, Wattle; Miss E Hunter, Gesetter; Miss J Comloquoy, Palace; J Fraser, Feaval; JG Stanger, Boardhouse; and John Spence, Hyan. A week later T Patterson, Loan, Miss H Harvey and Miss M Stanger joined the Trust. An appeal was launched and in the ensuing months a useful sum was built up.

The Trust approached others across the county and on 7 September a committee was formed to arrange the construction of a memorial. The Committee comprised WH Traill,[292] James Johnston (Convener of the County of Orkney), J Storer Clouston, WB Baikie (Provost of Kirkwall), PC Flett, William MacLennan, Andrew Wylie, Robert W Clouston (Provost of Stromness), R Slater, Rev. C Meldrum, JG Stanger and GW Scarth, with Mr WJ Heddle (Town Clerk of Kirkwall) as Hon. Secretary and Treasurer. Money was raised from the county and further afield, although no records survive of the individual donations made.

---

[289] The memorial at Marwick Head was but one of several initiatives around the country to mark the death of Lord Kitchener. The Lord Kitchener National Memorial Fund, headed by Queen Alexandra, raised £500,000 which was used to fund a bronze statue on the south side of Horse Guards Parade and an effigy in All Souls' Chapel in St.Paul's Cathedral, and the Lord Kitchener National Memorial Fund. The LKNMF awards scholarships (25 in 2015) to children of members of HM Armed Forces who are beginning their undergraduate studies. All those benefitting from these scholarships may join the Kitchener Scholars Association, still today a living memorial to the Field Marshal with over 600 members (see www.kitchenerscholars.org).

[290] George W Scarth (1881-1951) later went to McGill University, Montreal in 1920 and became a Professor of Botany.

[291] Meldrum, Souter and Ferguson were the Church of Scotland Minister of Birsay and the United Free Church Ministers of Birsay and Harray respectively.

[292] WH Traill of Woodwick, Evie accidentally shot himself in 1924 when climbing a fence with a loaded gun. He was replaced as Chairman by James Johnston.

Suggestions on the nature of the Memorial included a stained glass window in St.Magnus Cathedral in Kirkwall[293] and a massive stone tower or pyramid on the wild and rugged cliffs of Marwick Head, the closest point of land to where *Hampshire* sank. It was also suggested that the provision of a lighthouse would be useful to warn mariners, as there was then no light on the west coast of Orkney. Proposals were batted back and forth as to the merits of a lighthouse on Marwick Head or one on the Brough of Birsay, bearing in mind that the latter option would be the more logical location from the mariners' point of view.[294] However, momentum was lost and project lapsed for several years.

In early 1922 the wrecking of two trawlers on the Birsay shore with the loss of 10 lives provoked renewed debate in the *Orcadian* about whether the proposed memorial would be better built as a lighthouse than as 'a useless pile of stones'.[295] Eventually the Memorial Committee approached the Commissioners for Northern Lights to see if the two concepts could be combined, and offered the £700 raised for the Memorial towards the lighthouse. After an exchange of correspondence it was agreed the two schemes should not be amalgamated.[296]

Local architect JM Baikie was appointed to design and supervise the construction of the monument. By today's standards his specification and contract are delightfully simple, running to just four sides of paper each! The quarter-acre of land for the tower was purchased from Mrs. Taylor of Steddaquoy on 6 October 1924 for the nominal sum of five shillings. The tender for the work was placed with William Liddle of Cornesquoy, Orphir, for the sum of £734, and work commenced shortly afterwards. Apart from the inscribed plaque, construction was completed by September 1925,[297] on schedule.

The memorial takes the form of a simple square hollow castellated tower structure with plane walls inside and a tapering outer face. It stands 48ft high; at the base the footprint is 23ft 6ins and the walls are 4ft 6ins thick. It is built of stone from a local cliff top quarry and the detailing on the walls (base course, corbels and copings) is from the Clestrain quarry at Scorradale in Orphir.[298] The tower is roofed with a concrete slab cast in-situ. Two drainage spouts shed water from the roof onto the cast concrete apron below.[299] Some people consider the design ugly, but most think it a fitting tribute, unpretentious and uncompromising.[300]

The construction seems to have progressed well. Although un-dated, Tom Kent's photographs show some interesting construction details that make the blood run cold in today's more risk-averse times:

The hand-built ladders and the 'bespoke' scaffolding are all indicative of another era, although the pride of these skilled masons comes through in the photographs, and the condition of the structure today is testament to their skill.[301]

Top: (OA L4327-2)   Centre: George Brass and John Johnston. (OA L4327-3)   Right: note the ladders! (OA L2754-2)

---

[293] *Orkney Herald* 1 Aug. 1916.
[294] The Brough stands further to seaward, and being lower is said to be less prone to fog.
[295] This debate was addressed in more detail in Spence, 2013, from which some of this chapter was derived.
[296] The Brough of Birsay lighthouse was built by James Anderson and became operational in October 1925.
[297] *Orcadian* 24 Sept. 1925.
[298] Re-opening this quarry was approved in 2013, to supply the stone to re-pave the main street of Stromness.
[299] The monument was thought to have been orientated towards the wreck site, with its teak door facing seawards, but in 1983 it was noticed that this orientation was in error by about 30°. A new marker stone now points to the wreck site.
[300] Marwick 1966, reprinted in Robertson 1991, 420.
[301] The absence of permanent stairs within the structure contrasts with older tower constructions which typically use a spiral staircase to form a central column. Whilst there is no sign that a staircase was ever intended to be built, the internal volume would lend itself to such a construction, and it is peculiar that such a large hollow foot-print was designed without a staircase. It has been suggested that this was originally planned, but never executed: alas the original design sketches have not survived to show the initial intention.

10 – The Kitchener Memorial

The Aberdonian granite plaque was sited on the landward side of the memorial to protect it from the weather. Its inscription reads:

> *This tower was raised by the people of Orkney in memory of Field Marshal Kitchener of Khartoum on that corner of his country, which he had served so faithfully, nearest to the place where he died on duty.*
>
> *He and his staff perished along with the officers and nearly all the men of HMS Hampshire on 5th June 1916.*

(OA TK1901).

It is not easy for us today to appreciate why the erection of such a memorial to one man was felt necessary by Orcadians. As was shown in Chapter 3 above Kitchener was clearly a huge national figure, but why they felt moved to undertake such a work when he had never even set foot on the islands is not readily apparent. A century later the scale of the endeavour is still striking, although the motivations for such a strong statement remain unclear. Did the initiative stem at least in part from the outrage discussed in Chapter 7 above? Was it to remember the tragedy as a whole or just one man? To 21st century eyes the inscription is almost negligent in its implied dismissal of the sacrifice made by the others who died alongside Kitchener that night. The passing reference to the 'officers and nearly all the men of HMS *Hampshire*' was one of the triggers to use the occasion of the centenary to seek to better remember these sacrifices in a more fitting manner.

The unveiling ceremony

The Memorial was due to be unveiled on 5 June 1926, the 10th anniversary of the tragedy. However Lord Horne, the Minister of War,[302] was otherwise engaged and the date was set for Friday 2 July 1926.

The ceremony itself was a huge event for Orkney. A local public holiday was declared. It was estimated that between 4,000 and 6,000 people attended, and the photographs and film of the time show large crowds enjoying the summer weather. There are even reports of some individuals succumbing to the heat on the day – an unusual risk in Orkney, and of course a complete contrast to the weather in June 1916.

Plans had been developed to deal with the large crowds anticipated. There were increasing numbers of motorised vehicles in the county by this time although they were still a novelty for most. Some charabancs would have been present along with private cars and lorries, but horse-drawn carriages and carts would have been the most common form of transport. There are stories of people cycling from far and wide to come to the event, some with children on the cross-bar. A boat-load came direct from Rackwick in Hoy.

It is interesting to see the traffic management plan for handling the crowds on the front page of the *Orcadian* of 1 July 1926, along with instructions to road users on the signals that police officers would give to traffic. The fact that such instructions needed to be printed is testament to how unusual the traffic control would have been. It is noteworthy that this is some eight years before the introduction of the driving test, and even 90 years later Orkney has no dual carriageways or permanent traffic lights, and only eight roundabouts. The subsequent edition of the *Orcadian* notes that Superintendent Wood's traffic plan worked well and there were no accidents.

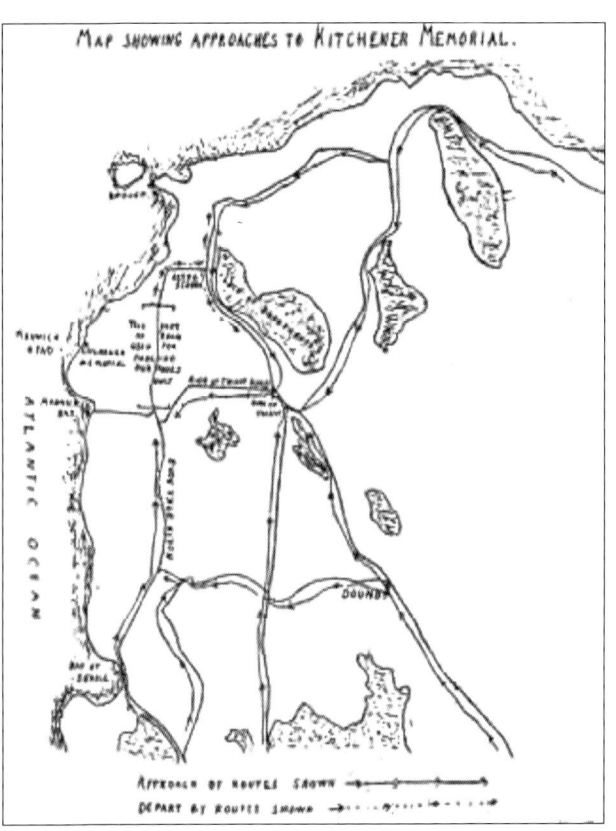

Traffic Management Plan for 2 July 1926. (*Orcadian* 1 July 1926)

Lord Horne had come to Orkney aboard the battleship HMS *Royal Sovereign* and arrived at the Memorial at noon. There he reviewed an armed guard of ex-servicemen mounted round the tower with arms reversed, organised by the Kirkwall Branch of the British Legion and in the charge of Sergt. Major J Rendall RGA.[303]

---

[302] General Lord Horne GCB KCMG of Stirkoke, Caithness had served with Kitchener and was a long-time friend. Admiral of the Fleet Earl Jellicoe sent his apologies for not attending the ceremony, but it was noted that no other senior government officials attended.

Within a temporary enclosure at each side of the tower were detachments of the Stromness Boys' Brigade, Kirkwall Town Band, Kirkwall Pipe Band, a choir, and what we would now call 'veterans', out of uniform but wearing their medals, under the command of Major Buchanan. Among the ex-officers on parade were Father Bruno Murphy,[304] Lieut. EW Clements RNR, Capt. G Barclay RGA, Capt. TR Mowat RGA, Lieut. JM Moar RGA, and Lieut. William Scott RGA. (OA L9818-3)

Ex-service men including
John Rendall, Jack Renshaw,
William "Jack" Crisp, G. Findlater,
J Kelday, D Peace, R Bichan,
D Wooldrage, J Muir, J Shearer,
J Corse, A MacKay, ? Marr.
(OA 4057-1)

Rev. Barclay of St.Magnus Cathedral led the prayers at the service. In his address before unveiling the Memorial, Lord Horne said:

And so this tower stands, and will stand, a landmark to those at sea, erected by a people who understand all that life at sea means – in memory of, and typical of, a great soldier – a mark of appreciation of the people of Orkney of a man who set his duty before him and did it.

At the time of the unveiling HMS *Royal Sovereign* and the destroyer HMS *Wessex* were at the wreck site. The former fired a 19-gun salute in recognition of Earl Kitchener's title. Officers and ratings from both ships attended the ceremony.

The opening itself was captured on film;[305] the Veterans removed their hats and the uniformed personnel present saluted.

The ceremony lasted about an hour, and afterwards the Kitchener Memorial Committee entertained a large number of guests to luncheon at the Stromness Hotel.[306]

Order of Service for the Unveiling Ceremony, 1 July 1926.
(*Orcadian* 8 July 1926)

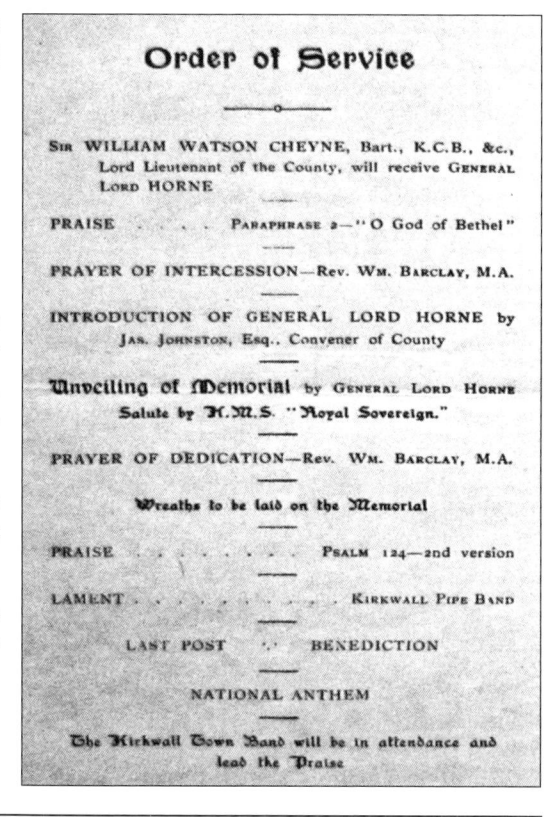

---

[303] Wylie 1996, 21-22. Major John MacKay was president of the branch (*Referee* 18 Apr. 1926).
[304] Father Bruno Murphy, Kirkwall's Roman Catholic priest, had served under Kitchener in Egypt.
[305] Scotland on Screen (https://scotlandonscreen.org.uk/browse-films/007-000-002-399-c);
British Pathe News (http://www.britishpathe.com/video/the-kitchener-memorial-cuts/query/Orkney).
[306] For details of the hosts, guests and speeches see *Orcadian* 8 July 1926.

Modern times

Little happened to the Memorial for 88 years after the unveiling other than the plaque suffering occasional damage, probably due to vandalism, and some changes to the doorway. This was originally closed with a teak door which had suffered during the intervening years and in the late 1950s it was removed. By this time the tower had become somewhat unsavoury with graffiti on the door and inner walls, and the site had been used as a toilet. A decision was taken to carefully fill the doorway with well-matched masonry. At the same time some remedial work was done to the door opening with the casting of a new lintel and also the blocking of the putlog holes in the walls which had been left for ventilation but were letting birds into the structure.

Over the years other minor works included some repair to the lettering on the plaque and the installation of interpretative boards at the entrance to the path from the car park by Mid Cumloquoy to the Memorial that were funded by the Kitchener Scholar's Association in 1989.[307] This coincided with the return of an illegally salvaged 3-pounder gun from HMS *Hampshire* which was mounted on a plinth nearby.[308]

In the 1970s the importance of the sea-cliffs to the resident bird population was becoming apparent and in 1976 the cliffs and a strip inshore (but excluding the land already sold for the memorial) were sold to the RSPB who established it as a bird reserve. Access to the tower is therefore over RSPB land, and the RSPB uses the landmark as a meeting point. But this sale was destined to have unforeseen consequences 40 years later.

On the afternoon of Sunday 6 July 1986, to mark the 70th anniversary of the deaths of the men who perished on HMS *Hampshire*, Rev. HWM Cant conducted an ecumenical service of remembrance at the memorial. Over 100 people attended the service, including the Field Marshal's great-nephew Lord Henry Kitchener and his sister Lady Kenya Tatton-Brown, Major General Tony Younger, a member of the Council of the Lord Kitchener National Memorial Fund, and twenty members of the Kitchener Scholars' Association.[309]

Restoration

The idea for the restoration in time for the 2016 centenary grew during 2011 when it was realised that there was an opportunity to use the inevitable focus on the events of a century ago to secure funding. Initial checks with likely bodies who might have had an interest in such a project showed that there were no competing schemes, and so an approach was jointly made to Orkney Islands Council (OIC) by the Orkney Heritage Society and the Birsay Heritage Trust to register interest. As the larger of these two bodies the Heritage Society took the lead on the restoration and new memorial project and formed a Project Team. This comprised Neil Kermode (Chairman), Andrew Hollinrake, David Murdoch, Spencer Rosie, Graham Brown, Lynn Campbell and initially Eleanor MacLeod and latterly Elizabeth Corsie and Alan Manzie. The group met approximately monthly through 2014 until the centenary. Each member of the team brought particular strengths, and their tireless efforts delivered the project on time and under budget.

Fundraising proved more challenging than originally anticipated. The Crown Estate's Coastal Communities Fund and the Heritage Lottery Fund both declined to assist, as did a number of other private charities. However the War Memorials Trust administered by Historic Scotland[310] was fully supportive, as were OIC at both Officer and Elected Member level. Both the Trust and the Council were able to offer useful grants and champion the funding call through their associated processes. In addition a number of generous donations were made by relatives of those lost, local businesses and individuals. An internet donation site was set up and appeals were made by direct mail and through widespread media coverage.[311]

A curious legal twist was discovered in 2013 when the idea of restoring the Memorial began to gain acceptance. To enable the work to proceed it became necessary for the OIC to lease the Memorial to the Orkney Heritage Society. At this point it was noticed that the tower had not been built at the originally intended location, but some distance inshore, i.e. not on the land bought for the purpose. Under Scots law landowners also own any structures built upon their land, so the Council realised they owned a tower-less section of the cliff top and had to break the news to the RSPB that they had inadvertently bought the Kitchener Memorial when they purchased the cliff edge in 1976! The OIC was thus unable to issue a lease since they did not own the piece of land upon which the tower stands. Fortunately for the project the local RSPB office was very pragmatic and keen to

---

[307] The source of this funding perhaps explains why these boards do not even include a passing reference to the sacrifice of the officers and crew of HMS *Hampshire*.
[308] This gun was refurbished for the Centenary by members of the Orkney branch of the Royal Naval Association.
[309] *Orcadian* 3 July 1986; OA RO5/255, RO7/315.
[310] Now Historic Environment Scotland.
[311] Including Scottish TV news, BBC Breakfast, BBC Radio 4 news, BBC Radio Orkney, *Financial Times*, *Sunday Times* and assorted magazines, periodicals and regional newspapers ranging from Orkney to Plymouth.

surrender their ownership of the Memorial, and following a fortuitous meeting of the RSPB Board in Orkney in May 2014 a bargain was stuck whereby OIC would swap with the RSPB the tower-less cliff edge it owned for the solum[312] of the Memorial. In doing so OIC took ownership of the tower and was then able to lease it to the Orkney Heritage Society, whilst the RSPB breathed a sigh of relief at having divested itself of the tower.

In early 2014 it was decided to re-open the doorway in order to inspect the roof before the restoration was begun. This proved prescient as the slab was subsequently found to be suffering from water ingress and had some cracks which, if left unchecked, would have resulted in the slab failing. Short portable beams were inserted under the slab in October 2015 to provide better support, and a fillet was cast on the roof to shed water from the walls and into the drainage spouts. It was also discovered that a hole had been beaten though the roof, probably to provide ventilation when the putlog holes were blocked. This feature has been retained, but regularised, as shown in the modern roof illustration opposite.

The new memorial wall

When the restoration of the Memorial was first suggested a number of schemes were put forward, including the installation of a staircase inside the structure to give public access to the roof-top and to place the names of the lost within the structure. Despite initial support, concerns were raised locally about this scheme and the staircase idea was dropped in favour of a low wall bearing the names of those lost. Discussions with relatives confirmed that this would be a suitable objective and they enthusiastically supported this approach. After examining numerous war memorials it was decided that this 21st century remembrance should be egalitarian in its approach. The inscriptions on the new wall therefore deliberately ignore rank and are a simple alphabetical listing of names. It was felt appropriate that the fourteen men of Kitchener's party should be listed separately from the 723 men lost of the ships' company. Together with the nine men lost from HM Drifter *Laurel Crown*, this results in there being 746 names inscribed on the new wall. It was also decided that the names should appear in capitals with all initials following the surname.[313]

A public consultation in March 2015 came out in favour of the wall just being on the seaward side and eventually the curved plan seen today was evolved by the Kirkwall architect Leslie Burgher, together with a clear marker pointing to the wreck site.

Samples of different granites and Caithness flags were obtained, and tests done on different fonts and surface preparation of the stone. The requirements for low maintenance and clarity of lettering when the stone is wet were studied, along with how to provide suitable means of leaving tributes at the site in future.

An unexpected phone call at Christmas 2013 led to an unusual contribution to the restoration. As a result of local publicity Regimental Training Major Mark Griffin of the local Army Reserve unit at Weyland Park Barracks in Kirkwall spotted the project. Warrant Officer Hazell got in touch and offered possible assistance because Kitchener had served in the Royal Engineers. During 2014 this initiative was developed into a full project and in late July 2015 a detachment of 12 military exchange personnel were mobilised to site with local support. The team comprised members of a bilateral US/UK forces exchange programme and those posted to Orkney to work came from the National Guard and the Air National Guard, both from South Dakota. They helped to rake out the mortar joints in the tower stonework, brought stone for the new memorial wall up to the site, and dug the foundation for this wall.

Tenders were issued for the works in May 2015. Casey Construction Ltd. of Kirkwall selected as the preferred tenderer and their craftsman John Hamilton from Harray commenced work in late June 2015. He recalled:

> *My first job was to take a couple of labourers and point the building, a mammoth task, but once I got into the pointing it soon started to take shape for the stone was in very good condition. The weather, now that was another story: there were days it battered down with rain and the winds had to be well over 100 miles per hour. The local farmers were not wrong when they warned me of the conditions I would have to work in. I finished the pointing in late November [when the scaffolding was taken down] and then took a break for the winter. It was mid March when I returned and we got the paths ready. The day we put the concrete in was promised to be fine but the Orkney skies opened again for two days solid. It was mid April before we could put up a shutter for the inside of the wall, then it was time for me to build the stone. The next part was the granite name plates to go on the inside. Paul Hewison, another stone mason, came and helped me put them on, and then the tops. The grass seed was in and Paul built the little information pillars with plenty time to*

---

[312] Solum: a Scottish legal term denoting the rights pertaining to the ground under a building, waterway etc.
[313] This decision gave rise to a small problem. It was found that there were 13 instances when the name and initials alone would be ambiguous, i.e. two men with the same surname and initials. On these instances the service numbers have been appended.

spare: we finished at 4 o'clock on 4 June 2016, one day before the ceremony. This job as my best and most satisfying job ever, I can always visit and remember all those kind words from all I spoke to each day, and of course the true meaning of the job, the people of HMS Hampshire. May all that visit enjoy it as much as I did.

Aerial view of the refurbishment. (Scott McIvor)

John Hamilton and Kevin Casey.

View of the Memorial with the new Commemorative Wall.
(copyright Colin Keldie K4 Graphics)

Detail of the names.
(copyright Colin Keldie K4 Graphics)

The unveiling ceremony on 5 June is described in Chapter 15 below.

The future

A further challenge has been to provide for the future protection of the site. Initially this responsibility rests with the Orkney Heritage Society. At the time of writing the project target of £150,000 has nearly been met, and further income, including the proceeds of this publication and on-site donations, will deal with any shortfall.

The Project Team found that the process of having the tower restored and the new wall constructed to better remember all those lost off Marwick Head in June 1916 set in train an unforgettable series of revelations and connections. They connected with an Oscar-winning playwright, with the Chief Commissioner of the Metropolitan Police, with residents of the town of Kitchener in Ontario, Canada, and most significantly, with scores of families who knew something of their loss, but often only had fragments of the picture. Some of these contacts are developed in the next chapter.

It is hoped that when visitors walk up to the beautiful cliff tops at Marwick Head and pause to read some of the names on the wall around the Memorial they will reflect on the terrible events of 1916. The rekindled ripples of interest in Lord Kitchener, HMS *Hampshire* and HM Drifter *Laurel Crown* will radiate from Orkney around the world and help these men to be remembered for years to come.

Chapter 11

The Men lost from HMS *Hampshire*

Following the sinking of HMS *Hampshire* the Admiralty sent a letter of regret dated 9 June 1916 to the next of kin of the deceased naval personnel; an example is illustrated on the right.[314] The names were listed in the national press on Monday 12 June.

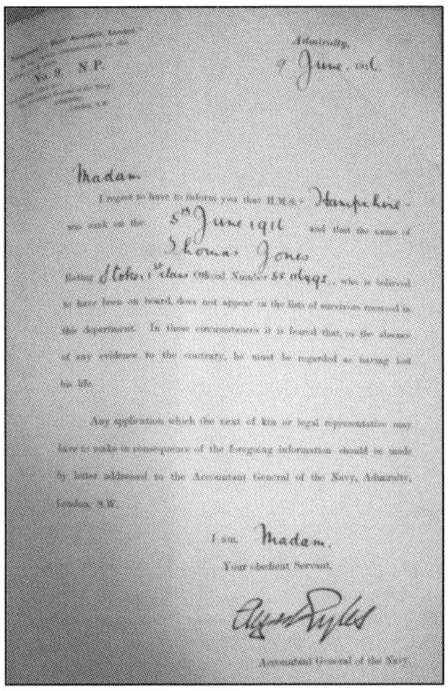

The bodies of the 166 men from *Hampshire* that were recovered are interred in the Lyness Naval Cemetery on Hoy, which had been opened in 1915. 122 lie in named graves, 44 in unnamed graves marked "Known unto God". One of the latter, and the Memorial to all those who "here lie buried", are shown below. The bodies of one of Kitchener's party, Robert Macpherson, and one from *Laurel Crown*, Thomas Baikie, are also interred at Lyness. The body of another of Kitchener's party, Oswald Fitzgerald, is buried in Eastbourne.

The names of all the ship's company of HMS *Hampshire* are engraved on one of the three Naval Memorials at Chatham, Portsmouth and Plymouth whose identical obelisks were designed by Sir Robert Lorimer and unveiled in 1924. The Chatham Memorial, sited above the Town Hall Gardens, overlooks the town. The Portsmouth Memorial, sited on Southsea Common, overlooks the Promenade and Spithead. The Plymouth Memorial, sited on the Hoe, overlooks the Sound.

Specimen letter (TNA ADM116/1526).

"Known unto God", Lyness.    Memorial, Lyness Naval Cemetery.   The Chatham Naval Memorial.

The Plymouth Naval Memorial.    The Portsmouth Naval Memorial.

---

[314] Like others killed in the Great War, their next of kin were later sent a memorial scroll and a bronze plaque ("death penny").

The three Naval Memorials bear the words "In honour of the Navy and to the abiding memory of these ranks and ratings of this port who laid down their lives in defence of the empire and have no other grave than the sea." Like the Lyness Cemetery, these Memorials are maintained fastidiously by the Commonwealth War Graves Commission.

The Roll of Honour

The Kitchener Memorial at Marwick Head, unveiled in 1926 (see Chapter 10 above), commemorates Field Marshall Kitchener "and his staff and the officers and nearly all the men of HMS *Hampshire*". The official number of men from *Hampshire* who lost their lives was just 643, but until recently there was uncertainty about the exact number. It was not until early in 2016, after meticulous research in consultation with the Commonwealth War Graves Commission, that a consensus emerged of the identities of the 737 men from *Hampshire* and 9 from *Laurel Crown*, thus enabling the 746 names to be listed in a single Roll of Honour and inscribed on the new wall at the Kitchener Memorial. The roll was used for the Orkney Heritage Society's Book of Remembrance (see Chapter 15 below), and copies may be seen at the Scapa Flow Visitor Centre and Museum, Lyness, Hoy, and at http://hmshampshire.org/. The Roll is now published for the first time as Appendix I below. Space has not permitted the inclusion of next-of-kin or other details.

The Officers and Men of HMS *Hampshire* lost on 5/6 June 1916

The average age of the 723 men who died was just over 25. 74 were under 18. The youngest was 16, the oldest 58. All of these individuals deserve a brief biography, as has been attempted for the members of Lord Kitchener's party, the crew of *Laurel Crown*, and the survivors in Chapters 3, 9 and 12 respectively; alas space and time prevent such treatment in this volume, although the naval careers of the survivors will have been typical of other crew members of *Hampshire* who lost their lives. However to give some context and depth to the Roll of Honour the authors have included the following notes and photographs that have come to their attention while preparing this volume. Of necessity the resulting entries below, which should be read in conjunction with Appendix I, are both selective and brief.

Philip **Alexander**, Chaplain, was the husband of Fannie who was a niece of the cricketer WG Grace (www.downendbromleyheath.org/home/the-history-of-the-war-memorial-downend/).

John **Bagley**, Stoker, is on the right in this photograph, with an unidentified friend (www.hmshampshire.co.uk).

Jack **Beechey**, Stoker, was born in Windsor, Berks but worked as a milkman in Wantage, Oxfordshire before joined the Navy in 1912. His niece treasures a pendant cross that Jack gave to his sister Doris during his last leave home.

Robert **Black**, Petty Officer Stoker: his great-niece Margaret Hartford says his widow Ethel, née Whatcott, lived until 1977. They had no children.

George **Bond**, Ship's Corporal, married Florence Greengrass in 1899 (http://www.standrewsgreatryburgh.org.uk/world-war-1-commemorations/those-who-served > George Harry Bond).

William **Bridges**, Private RMLI, wrote of Jutland in his last letter home to his parents. His great-niece, Alison Waudby-West, sent this photo of him taken in Bombay.

Harry **Browning**, Able Seaman, painted a picture of HMS *Hampshire* on an ivory nut, showing his artistic talent. His great-niece Anne Holland sent this photograph of him.

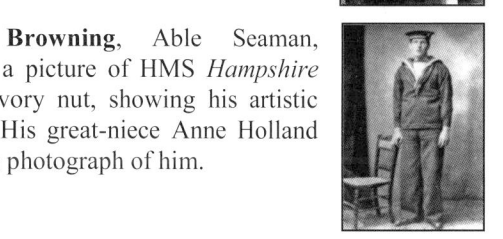

John **Buckenham**, Private, RMLI, had a half brother Arthur who a Royal Marine for 21 years (information from their great-nephew Len Buckenham, www.hmshampshire.co.uk).

Ralph **Buckingham**, Able Seaman, trained at HMS *Ganges* for torpedoes. His mother received his letter advising he had safely survived Jutland soon after his death, his great-great-nephew Lewis Buckingham said.

William **Cake**, Acting Petty Officer Stoker, joined the RN in 1896. He was a Cadet instructor at Osborne 1906-9. His widow Minnie received £43 gratuity and bounty, plus £2 18s monthly till her death in 1957.

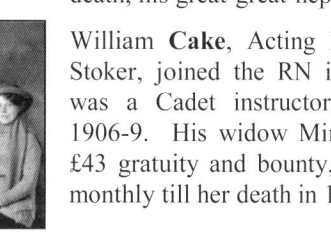

Stanley **Collier**, Able Seaman: his great-niece, Rosie Knights, has donated his remaining personal possessions to the Birsay Heritage Trust, including this photo.

Horatio **Cooke**, Petty Officer Plumber, joined the RN in 1901 and *Hampshire* about 1911. By his widow, Caroline Louise, he had 8 children including Mary who lived to 100 and campaigned to have the *Hampshire* wreck protected, writes her nephew Chris Hughes (*Derby Daily Telegraph*, 12 June 1916).

Arthur **Cossey**, Engineer-Commander, sent an account of the Battle of Jutland to his sister, Mrs VS Woods, of Mayfield, Retford (*Times* 13 June 1916; www.westsussexpast.gov.uk). He tried to flood some of *Hampshire*'s after tanks before she sank, and then ordered "abandon ship" (TNA ADM 116/2324A).

Manuel **Dasent**, Commander, was grandson of Admiral of the Fleet Sir Henry John Codrington, KCB (www.westsussexpast.gov.uk). His body was recovered by *Flying Kestrel* (ADM116/2324A).

John **Downes**, the Captain's Writer, was on Wesson's raft; he got ashore but died soon after from exposure (www.hmshampshire.co.uk).

Wilfred **Ellershaw**, Brigadier-General: in 2014 his grandson Philip scattered his mother's ashes in the sea near the *Hampshire* wreck, so that she would rest close to her father (*Living Orkney*, Aug. 2015, 12).

Walter **Ewing**, Able Seaman, had two brothers in the Army when he joined the RN in January 1914. A biography of him appears at https://mitchamwarmemorial.wordpress.com/2016/06/05/walter-ewing-lost-with-the-hampshire/

Edmund **Fellowes**, Midshipman, wrote 14 letters to his parents while on *Hampshire*, including an account of Jutland. He evidently collected ratings' cap tallies, 2 of which are held by the Imperial War Museum (IWM Ms.10969, INS7623, INS42827).

Frank **Glover**, Stoker 1st Class: his photograph appears at www.hmshampshire.co.uk.

Langton **Harris**, Boy 1st Class, was a friend of his namesake Sam **Harris**, Leading Seaman. Valerie and John Walter have some of his letters and the service sheet for the Memorial Service at St.Paul's Cathedral held 14 June 1916 (www.hmshampshire.co.uk).

Thomas **Hill**, Sergeant RMLI, had been dismissed from the RN for theft in 1897. He re-enlisted in 1903 using the name of his brother Reginald. The third Hill brother was notified that Reginald had died on 5 June, but must have been taken aback to find later that it was in fact Thomas who had died.

Thomas **Harwood**, Stoker 1st Class, joined the RN in 1902 and joined *Hampshire* just 12 days before she was sunk. His grandchildren David Townsend and Madeline Malthouse provided this photograph.

Vincent **Heneage**, Boy 1st Class, was a gardener before joining the Navy aged 15.

George **Hunter**, Warrant Engineer Officer RNR: his grandson Sandy Jamieson says he was from Carmyllie, Angus, an engineer, and moved to Paisley in 1910. He left behind his wife Janie and daughter Louie.

William **Innoles**, Private RMLI, was courting Florence Gilbert in 1916. After his death Florence married William's brother Harry; their son William was unable to attend the 2016 centennial events at the age of 85 due to ill health.

Herbert **Jennings**, Gunner, led the singing before slipping to the bottom of Wesson's raft (advice by his grandson, Eric Cook, www.hmshampshire.co.uk, quoting from Sunday Express 8 July 1934).

William **Lee**, Petty Officer Stoker: Patricia Bridgland, granddaughter, wrote lovingly on behalf of the family who never knew him, may he rest in peace.

Humphrey **Matthews**, Lieutenant, was Gunnery Officer. He was heard to shout "Make Way for Lord Kitchener" before *Hampshire* sank (Phillips 1930, 30). His body was washed ashore at Thurso, his life saving collar partially inflated and his wrist watch stopped at two minutes past eight (*Times* 13 June 1915).

George **Mayhew**, Private: 4 photographs and his Memorial plaque are held by the Imperial War Museum (IMW EPH2755).

Hugh **McNally**, Temporary Surgeon, graduated from Queen's University, Belfast in 1915. He had held a command in the Belfast Regiment of the Irish National Volunteers (www.westsussexpast.gov.uk).

Alexander **McPherson**, Stoker 1st Class, joined with his friend Stoker 1st Class John **Gordon**. Both perished on *Hampshire*. Alexander's niece, Florence Allan, has presented his Death Penny to the Birsay Heritage Trust.

William **Moreton**, Boy 1st Class, was one of 15 children. His niece Violet Chapman inherited his medals (www.hmshampshire.co.uk)

Peter **Mulvey**, Stoker, pictured with his family on his last trip home in this photograph sent by his grandson Christopher Lynch.

John **Novice**, Leading Seaman: his great-niece Trudy Risk advised that 28 years later her father John Novice, also in the RN, was at the D-Day landings.

Charles **Nye**, Stoker, had been a baker before enlisting in the RN for 12 years on 4 April 1913. His photograph was sent by his nephew Gordon Harris.

Mark **Nugent**, Assistant Paymaster RNR, was on Wesson's raft, but died at sea.

Harry **Payne**, Leading Seaman, died during his second period of service on *Hampshire*. Ian and Shirley Harman sent this photograph of their great uncle.

William and Albert **Pettett**, both Stokers RNR, were brothers who had consecutive service numbers, suggesting they had signed up on the same day.

Frank **Potter**, Boy 1st Class: a picture of him presented by Mrs Heather Phillips née Potter, of Camberley, Surrey, hangs in the Stromness Museum.

Gilbert **Sandom**, Private RMLI: photograph appears with some of his shipmates at www.submerged.co.uk. His nephew Gilbert Sandom, himself a former Royal Marine, visited Orkney in 2011.

Reginald **Sexton**, Signal Boy aged 17, the smallest member of *Hampshire*'s crew, sang "Tipperary" to the others on Bennett's raft before he died from exhaustion (TNA ADM116/2324A).

Walter **Sharp**, Chief Cook: his great-niece Rebecca Williams has a photograph (www.submerged.co.uk).

William **Sidebotham**, Lance Corporal, served 13 years in the RMLI. A letter he wrote to his parents describing *Hampshire*'s chasing of the German cruiser SMS *Emden* was published in his local paper on 17 June 1916 (www.hmshampshire.co.uk).

Edwin **Smith**, Able Seaman, worked down a coal mine before joining the RN. The many letters he wrote home to his family have been presented to the Birsay Heritage Trust by his niece Liz Granby.

George **Stallard**, Carpenter, was on Wesson's raft but died at sea.

Edward **Tipping**, Stoker 1st Class: his niece Jane Storey (1935-2013) set up www.hmshampshire.co.uk in memory of her uncle and his shipmates, who have no grave except the sea.

Charles **Tuck**, Ordinary Seaman, had volunteered at the age of 14. His brother was killed at Gallipoli. Their Australian niece, Audrey Peet, sent this memorial card to www.hmshampshire.co.uk.

Charles **Tucker**, Midshipman, wrote a letter describing his experiences during the Battle of Jutland (*Orkney Herald* 14 June 1916).

Humphrey **Vernon**, Sub-Lieutenant, had two brothers in the Army. Their father was chairman of the Great Northern Railway Company of Ireland (www.westsussexpast.gov.uk).

Frederick **Waight**, Petty Officer Stoker: his daughter, Freda, was born four months after *Hampshire* went down, reported his grandson Colin Nibbs.

Edwin **Walden**, Able Seaman, was the Captain's orderly (www.hmshampshire.co.uk).

Archibald **Watts**, Ordinary Seaman, known as "Mac": his nephew Charlie still has his ditty box. Mac's younger brother Herbert was lost in the sinking of HMS *Royal Oak* in Scapa Flow, 14 October 1939.

William **Williams**, Able Seaman RNVR, aged 29, had been a tin worker and a volunteer gunner in the First Glamorgan Royal Garrison Artillery. His lived with his wife in Morriston near Swansea. His grandson, Philip Dunn, has his "death penny". His great-nephew, Guy Jones, is trying to get William's name added to his local war memorial.

William **Wood**, Stoker: Bill Holden has posted his photograph and medals at www.submerged.co.uk.

Chapter 12

The Survivors

by Brian Budge

Twelve men survived from HMS *Hampshire*.[315] Their experiences during and immediately after the sinking have been described in Chapter 5 above.

Each survivor was interviewed on behalf of Captain Walker at about noon on 6 June.[316] The next day they were taken by car to Stromness and then by tug to the depot ship HMS *Blake* in Scapa Flow, arriving at 1500, for more clothing and medical attention. All were suffering more or less from shock and the results of exposure, and the majority from other disabilities as well.[317] A formal Court of Enquiry was then convened in the Captain's cabin and each was interviewed under oath.[318] They were transferred to HMHS *Soudan* on 8 June, and a day later the tender *Magic II* took them to Leith, whence they travelled by train to Haslar Hospital in Gosport.[319]

Below are brief accounts of their lives and careers before and after the sinking of HMS *Hampshire*.[320]

Warrant Mechanician William Bennet RN

Details of the birth and early service career of William Bennett are unknown as his service records have not been found.[321]

William was promoted to Acting Warrant Mechanician on 1 January 1915, and was on HMS *Arethusa* when she was torpedoed on 11 February 1916.

After HMS *Hampshire* he served on the battleship HMS *Glory* which from August 1916 till September 1919 was the Flagship of the squadron based at Archangel to protect supplies that arrived there for the White Russian Army.[322] In June 1926 he was serving as a Warrant Mechanician on the light cruiser HMS *Constance* and living in Rochester, Kent.[323] He was evidently promoted to Lieutenant before he retired from the Navy, for in 1939 he was listed as Lieut. (Engineer) W.E. Bennett Retd., serving at HMS *Eaglet*, the Royal Naval Reserve shore training establishment in Liverpool that became the Flagship of C-in-C Western Approaches during World War II. It is not known when William died.

---

[315] Power claimed there were three more survivors whom he identified as a private soldier, GHC. Revell, and an engineer and a man on deck, one being a Mr Green and the other a Mr Gulliver; he claimed the latter was living near Banbury in Oxfordshire in 1923 but died two years later (*Referee* 22 Nov. 1925, 10 Jan., 18 & 25 Feb., 6 June, 1 July 1926). The Admiralty determined that no one by the name of Revell or Gulliver was on board *Hampshire* in 1916, and though there were three ratings lost with the name of Green, their next-of-kin did not report the letters they received from the Admiralty dated 9 June 1916 having been inappropriate (TNA ADM116/1526).

[316] TNA ADM116/2323; http://www.hmshampshire.co.uk.

[317] Sims suffered from burns of the face sustained from flames from the initial explosion; Bennett, Buerdsell and Wesson suffered from contused and lacerated wounds and abrasions of feet and knees sustained while climbing over sharp rocks; lacerated wounds on Wesson's right hand were sceptic; Simpson had lacerated and abraded wounds of feet caused by other men treading on his bare feet on the raft; Cashman, Phillips and Rogerson had first degree frost bite in the lower extremities that were greatly improved under treatment; the others had no external injuries or frost bite but Sweeney, the oldest, suffered most seriously from shock, while Bowman, Farnden and Read suffered the least from shock (Journal of Medical Officer, HMS *Blake*, copied TNA ADM116/2324A).

[318] TNA ADM116/2323. Each survivor answered between 14 and 32 questions.

[319] TNA ADM226/2324A; *Orkney Herald* 21 June 1916; Phillips 1930, 48. Buerdsell was discharged from Haslar on 13 June, Wesson on 14 June, Bowman, Cashman, Farnden, Phillips, Read, Rogerson and Sweeney on 15 June, Sims on 19 June, and Simpson sometime after 27 June (TNA ADM116/1526). Instead of going to Haslar Bennett apparently went to another hospital ship before going to Chatham Hospital (TNA ADM116/2324A).

[320] The main source for these biographical details (apart from Bennett's) have been the individuals' service records, using Births, Deaths and Marriage registers, census records and the 1939 Register for more background when reasonable matches have been found. Ship details are taken from Colledge 2006, Dittmar 1972 and Jane's 2001. More complete versions of these biographies may be found at http://hmshampshire.org. It has proved difficult to recover details of the lives of some of the survivors after they left the Navy.

[321] Most of his details have been derived from the Navy Lists for Apr. 1916 (ID: 97149222), Dec. 1920, 550 (ID: 97490302), Dec. 1939 (ID: 92723494). The first two spell William's surname as Bennet, but it is clear they refer to the same individual.

[322] While in Russia Bennett met Surgeon Pickup again.

[323] TNA ADM116/2324A.

Able Seaman John Robert Bowman RN, J15315 (Po)

John Bowman, known as Jack, was born 31 March 1896 at Stalham, Norfolk, the son of an agricultural labourer. After leaving school he was a carpenter apprentice. He joined the Royal Navy as a Boy Class II on 19 January 1912.[324] He was 5ft 8ins tall, with brown hair, grey eyes, fresh complexion and had two small scars on his right ankle. After basic training at HMS *Ganges* at Shotley he was promoted to Boy Class I on 28 July, and two weeks later joined the Home Fleet battleship HMS *Commonwealth*. From November she served in the Mediterranean in the First Balkan War. On her return he joined HMS *Hampshire* on 3 January 1913. He signed on for 12 years on his 18th birthday as an Ordinary Seaman and was promoted to Able Seaman on 3 May 1915.

After *Hampshire* Jack was assigned to the destroyer depot ship HMS *Sandhurst* in Scapa Flow before joining the new destroyer HMS *Rapid*. He then spent 3 months in Portsmouth, followed by 15 months on the new sloop HMS *Ceanothus*, based in Malta.[325] The war over, he returned to Portsmouth before joining the sloop HMS *Foxglove* in January 1920. He was ashore at Portsmouth from February 1921 to May 1926, half of this time at the gunnery school there. He signed on to extend his naval service before serving 15 months on the light cruiser HMS *Calcutta* which sustained serious damage in Bermuda when she was dashed against a jetty by a hurricane in October 1926. He served on the light cruiser HMS *Despatch* during 1927-8. In February 1929 he joined the light cruiser HMS *Dauntless* while she was under repair after running aground off Halifax, Nova Scotia, and in May received a Long Service and Good Conduct Medal with a gratuity. He spent most of the next five years on HMS *Dauntless* and passed a rigger exam in 1933 before leaving the Navy with a pension on 1 April 1936.

Jack married Evelyn Rump in Norfolk in 1938; they had two children, alas both still-born. He was mobilized briefly during the Munich Crisis in 1938 and returned to Portsmouth on 5 September 1939 for war service. He joined the passenger ship *Ranpura* during her conversion to an Armed Merchant Cruiser and served on her until the end of 1941. He spent the rest of World War II based at Portsmouth. His final release from the Navy in September 1945 was from HMS *Daedalus*, the Fleet Air Arm base at Lee-on-Solent. Jack died of cancer in Norfolk in 1968, aged 72.

Jack's elder sister Alice ("Florrie") visited Orkney in 1930 and again in the 1970s, and corresponded with the family of Mina Sabiston née Phillips of Garson and then Skidge, Birsay for over 50 years.

Able Seaman Horace Llewellyn Buerdsell RN, J15527 (Po)

Horace Buerdsell was born at Bradford-on-Avon, Wiltshire on 3 March 1896. After leaving school he worked there briefly at a mattress and bedding factory. He joined the Royal Navy aged 15 as a Boy Class II on 22 January 1912.[326] He was 5ft 3½ins tall, with brown hair, brown eyes, a fresh complexion and had a scar at his right eye. He gave his occupation was "Wire Weaving".

He did his training in Portsmouth and on the school ship HMS *Impregnable* in Devonport. In February 1913 he became a Boy Class I and joined the cruiser HMS *Theseus*. On 5 May he joined the cruiser HMS *Vindictive* which in April 1918 played a heroic role in the Zeebrugge raid, where today her bow is preserved as a memorial.[327]

He was among a draft of sailors that the already obsolescent *Vindictive* carried out to join HMS *Hampshire* on the China station on 28 June 1913. He had grown to 5ft 6¼ins tall when he became an Ordinary Seaman on his 18th birthday and undertook to serve 12 years. Just two days before the sinking of *Hampshire* he was promoted to Able Seaman.

After *Hampshire* Horace was posted to HMS *Sandhurst* in Scapa Flow and later transferred to HMS *Rapid*, returning to Portsmouth in January 1919. After 10 weeks at the gunnery school HMS *Excellent* he joined the recently-built cruiser HMS *Caledon*. In August 1921 he attended the torpedo school, HMS *Vernon*. In January 1923 he joined the light cruiser HMS *Carlisle* and served 2½ years on the China station, including three months on the 625-ton river gunboat HMS *Cricket*. In October 1925 he returned home on the aging cruiser HMS *Weymouth*, reaching Portsmouth in time for some Christmas leave. He was discharged at Portsmouth on 2 March 1926.

---

[324] TNA ADM188/677/15315; ADM363/158/56: John Robert Bowman.
[325] Bowman's service records do not support Power's claim that he served on "Q" boats and latterly on the China Station.
[326] TNA ADM188/678/15527: Horace Llewellyn Buerdsell.
[327] Lake 2002.

Horace was unemployed during at least some of the 1930s. In 1939 he was working as a house and ship painter in Manchester and boarding in the household of John Lodge. He married Mona Chatterton, or Moslin, in Manchester in 1946. Horace died in Rochdale, Lancashire in 1977, aged 81.

Leading Seaman William Cashman RN, 228580 (Po)

William Cashman was born on 22 March 1888 in Aghada, Queenstown, Cork, the eldest son of Ellen Cashman. He had worked as a farm labourer, when he joined the Royal Navy as a Boy Class II at Portsmouth on 1 October 1903.[328] He gave his year of birth as 1886, for an age of 17. He did his basic training at Chatham, with a berth on the old armoured cruiser HMS *Northampton* and the steel corvette HMS *Cleopatra*. He was promoted to Boy Class I on 3 January 1904 and moved to Portsmouth later that month. When he signed on as an Ordinary Seaman to serve 12 years on his 18th birthday he was 5ft 8¾ins tall, with dark brown hair, brown eyes and a ruddy complexion.

His first sea-going service was 1904-07 on the armoured cruiser HMS *Good Hope* (which in November 1914 was lost with all hands at the Battle of Coronel). He was promoted to Able Seaman in August 1905. He served in 1908 on the Admiralty yacht HMS *Enchantress*, then for 1½ years on the battleship HMS *Swiftsure* in the Mediterranean. After a six month spell at Portsmouth gunnery school he re-joined *Enchantress* for another year. He then spent three years and started his Great War service on the armoured cruiser HMS *Minotaur* on the China station. He joined HMS *Hampshire* after she had joined the Grand Fleet in home waters, and was promoted to Leading Seaman in July 1915.

After *Hampshire* William returned to Portsmouth gunnery school. He signed on for another 12 years in September 1917, when his height was 5ft 10ins. He was promoted to Petty Officer on 1 November 1917 and to Acting Gunner on 6 February 1918. No record with details of William's post-war service has been located, but he is not included in the officer list in the December 1920 Navy List. He married and had two children: a son, also William, and daughter Lily, who resided at Hillside in Rostellan, Co.Cork and at Saleen respectively. After the war he probably retired after reverting to warrant officer rank. In 1926 he was living in Ballinacurra, Co.Cork. William died in Cobh, formerly known as Queenstown, in 1965, aged 71.

Stoker 1st Class William Charles Farnden RN, K18337 (Po)

Walter Farnden was born on 5 April 1892 at Barnham, Sussex, the first child of a nursery gardener. After leaving school he also worked as a gardener. On 18 March 1913 at Portsmouth he joined the Royal Navy as a Stoker Class II, to serve 12 years.[329] He was 5ft 11½ins tall, with light hair, grey eyes and a fresh complexion. After basic training at Portsmouth he spent two months on the elderly torpedo gunboat HMS *Dryad*, then a navigation school ship. After another six weeks at Portsmouth he boarded the elderly cruiser HMS *Europa* at Pembroke to travel to Colombo in Ceylon (now Sri Lanka) to join HMS *Hampshire* on 27 January 1914. On 18 March 1914 he was promoted to Stoker Class I.

After *Hampshire* Walter stayed ashore in Portsmouth until the end of 1916. He then served on mine clearance duties, first on the sloop HMS *Pansy*, later the minesweepers HMS *Sunflower* and HMS *Gentian*. He was promoted to Acting Leading Stoker on 1 February 1918. While sweeping in the Gulf of Finland on 15 July 1919 HMS *Gentian* was paired with HMS *Myrtle* when they exploded a mine. Both ships sank, each losing six engine-room sailors,[330] but Walter survived.

He returned to Chatham shore base and was confirmed as a Leading Stoker on 28 September. He transferred to the Royal Fleet Reserve in Portsmouth on 14 January 1920 and was called up to serve there as a Stoker Class I from April to June 1921. He married Emma Ansell in Brighton in 1936 and was living with her in Bognor Regis and working as a shunter with Southern Railway in 1939. The story of his *Hampshire* ordeal was published in 1938 in Part 15 of *The Great War, I Was There*. Walter died in Chichester in 1972, aged 80.

---

[328] TNA ADM188/404/228580: William Cashman.
[329] TNA ADM188/903/18337: Walter C Farnden. His brother Robert Cyril also survived WWI (TNA ADM188/937/35222).
[330] www.naval-history.net: Casualty Lists of the Royal Navy, compiled by Don Kindell from Admiralty Ledgers.

Shipwright William Charles Phillips RN, 343500 (Po)

William Phillips was born on 4 April 1886 at Pembroke Dock, where his father, Thomas, was a shipwright. He left school aged 14 and joined the Royal Navy as a Boy Shipwright at Pembroke Dock on 5 July 1900.[331] He was 5ft 4¼ins tall, with light hair, grey eyes and fair complexion, a mole under his armpit and a wart on his right hand. On his 18th birthday he undertook to serve 12 years in the Royal Navy and the next day travelled to Devonport for three months of basic naval training. On 4 October 1904 he moved to HMS *Indus*, the mechanics' training establishment and workshops at Devonport that was to be his home and workplace for a year. On 21 October 1905 he slung his hammock aboard the cruiser HMS *Sirius*, just returned from service on the China station to go into reserve at Devonport. He was promoted to Leading Shipwright when on 16 October 1906 he joined the cruiser HMS *Pelorus* on the Cape of Good Hope Station. He returned in April 1909 to Devonport, where worked on various postings until on 4 October 1910 he helped to commission the new cruiser HMS *Gloucester*, with alternating spells on the cruiser and ashore in Devonport and then Portsmouth, until travelling on HMS *Europa* to Ceylon to join HMS *Hampshire*. On 18 March 1916 he agreed to serve another 12 years in the Navy.

After convalescing in Wales from *Hampshire* William returned to Portsmouth where he remained until November 1917. He then took passage on the liner *Kenilworth Castle* to join the cruiser HMS *Minerva* patrolling off the East African coast. During five years based at HMS *Fisgard*, the Portsmouth training establishment for artificers and engineers, he also served on the cruiser HMS *Dido* July to October 1919 and the battleship HMS *Malaya* July to September 1923. He took his pension on 3 April 1926.

Shortly after *Hampshire* sank William wrote a detailed account of his time on the ship, and published an extended version in 1930.[332] In 1939 he was called up and reported at Portsmouth on 24 August, but was discharged six weeks later with high blood pressure. He died in Pembroke in 1946 aged 60.

Leading Stoker Alfred Ernest Read RN, K15762 (Po)

Alfred Read was born at Portsmouth on 23 October 1891. He worked as a painter and decorator and married Minnie Dibden in April 1911 before joining the Royal Navy as a Stoker Class II on 13 August 1912 to serve 12 years.[333] He was 5ft 8¼ins tall, with black hair, hazel eyes and fresh complexion. He had varicose vein scars on both thighs and legs.

After completing his training at Portsmouth he served on the cruisers HMS *Minerva* and HMS *Dido*. He was promoted to Stoker Class I after a year's service before travelling on HMS *Europa* to Ceylon to join HMS *Hampshire*. He became an Acting Leading Stoker on 16 March 1916.

After *Hampshire* Alfred returned to Portsmouth and was confirmed in the rank of Leading Stoker on 26 October 1916. He returned to sea duty on 16 April 1917 when he joined the cruiser HMS *Attentive*. She was serving as part of the Dover Patrol, responsible for defence against a series of German destroyer raids intended to provide cover for U-boats passing through the English Channel. The most famous of these raids took place on the night of 20-21 April, when the flotilla leaders HMS *Swift* and HMS *Broke* sank two German destroyers in a fierce and confused fight that cost the lives of 22 Royal Naval personnel.[334]

The stress of the blocking operation actions, on top of the trauma of the *Hampshire* sinking, was apparently more than Alfred could bear. His service record shows that he returned to Portsmouth on 1 July and was invalided out of the Navy on 9 August with Neurasthenia – the official term for the mental break-down, then known as "shell shock" and today as Post Traumatic Stress Disorder.

Alfred returned to work in Portsmouth as a painter and decorator although he was unemployed in 1926. He had been employed for two years by Portsmouth Corporation before retiring in 1956. He died in December 1957, aged 66, survived by his widow, four daughters and three sons.

---

[331] TNA ADM188/519/459, ADM363/284/8: William Charles Phillips.
[332] Phillips 1930.
[333] TNA ADM188/898/15762: Alfred Ernest Read.
[334] Marder 2014.

Leading Seaman Charles Walter Rogerson RN, 236059 (Po)

Charles Rogerson was born on 10 April 1890 in Hertford. He had been working as a baker's boy when he joined the Royal Navy as a Boy Class II at Portsmouth on 19 March 1906.[335] He was 5ft 1½ins tall, with brown hair brown, grey eyes and a fresh complexion.

Charles did his basic training on the school ship HMS *Impregnable* at Devonport, as a Boy Class I from 24 November. He then served the first 5 months of 1907 on the armoured cruiser HMS *Euryalus*, a boys' training ship on the West Indies station, and briefly on the battleship HMS *Goliath* and cruiser HMS *Gladiator*. He joined the cruiser HMS *Juno* serving in the Mediterranean in July 1907. When he signed on as an Ordinary Seaman to serve 12 years on his 18th birthday his height was 5ft 3ins. He was promoted to Able Seaman in July 1909. During the next five years he served on the cruisers HMS *Edgar*, HMS *Hawke*, HMS *Argonaut* and HMS *Ariadne*, and on the survey ship HMS *Waterwitch*. He sailed on HMS *Europa* to Ceylon to join HMS *Hampshire*. He was promoted to Leading Seaman in November 1915.

After *Hampshire* Charles served on the armed merchant cruiser HMS *Arlanza* for just over a year. In July 1917 he joined the light cruiser HMS *Royalist*, serving with the Grand Fleet. He returned to Portsmouth in January 1918 and was invalided out of the Navy on 4 April 1918 with the diagnosis "Neurasthenia", his ordeal on *Hampshire* no doubt having contributed to his condition. Charles died on 5 December 1923 in Auckland, New Zealand, aged just 33. Two years later his widow Isabella Rogerson was living in Hamilton in New Zealand.[336]

Able Seaman Richard Simpson RNVR, Tyne Z5589

Richard Simpson, known as Dick, was born on 4 August 1898 at Tynemouth, Northumberland, the elder son of a fish porter. After leaving school he worked as a butcher. He enrolled into the Royal Naval Volunteer Reserve on 29 June 1915.[337] He was 5ft 6¾ins tall, with dark brown hair, grey eyes and fresh complexion. His age was only 16, but the enrolment form shows his birth year as 1896, so aged 18. He trained for three months at Crystal Palace, the depot of the Royal Naval Division. He was rated Able Seaman when he joined *Hampshire* on 5 October 1915.[338]

After *Hampshire* Dick stayed in Portsmouth until October 1916, spending nearly a month at the gunnery school. He was then on the books of HMS *President* on the Thames for duty as a gunner on DAMS (defensively-armed mercantile ships, better known as DEMS in World War II) duty. His service record shows his first merchant ship gunnery posting as 1 February 1917. Along with fellow RNR gunner Donald Macleay and all 10 of the crew, Dick died when submarine *UC 63* sank the 403-ton steamer *Thames* just off the mouth of the Humber on 14 August 1917.[339] The ship was on passage with a cargo of pig iron from Middlesbrough to Fécamp in France, but was listed as overdue and missing, so Dick's family had to endure a long period waiting for confirmation of his death. The youngest of the twelve *Hampshire* survivors, Dick is commemorated on the Chatham Naval Memorial, and the Commonwealth War Graves Commission correctly records his age as 19 (but only by ten days).

Dick's father Ralph and his younger brother Thomas both served in the Army during the Great War and survived. His mother, Christina, gave Mina Sabiston née Phillips a set of knives when she married in 1923 and attended the dedication of the Kitchener Memorial in 1926, staying with the family, who had moved from Garson to Skidge in Birsay. They corresponded for many years. Thomas's daughter Kathleen Stewart recently renewed contact with the Sabiston family.

Ralph, Thomas, Christina and Dick Simpson.
(courtesy of Alice Garson)

---

[335] TNA ADM 188/419/236059: Charles Walter Rogerson
[336] TNA ADM116/2324A.
[337] TNA ADM 337/74/164: Richard Simpson.
[338] TNA ADM116/2324B.
[339] http://uboat.net/wwi/ships_hit/7391.html; Simpson's life has also been researched by the Tynemouth World War One Commemoration Project (Storer 2014, 64-9).

12 – The Survivors

Stoker Frederick Lot Sims RN, SS113673 (Po)

Frederick Sims was brought up at Bowerchalke near Salisbury.[340] He joined the Royal Navy as a Stoker Second Class on 18 March 1913, when he claimed his place and date of birth as Bermondsey, London on 12 March 1895. This made him less than a week over the 18 year age requirement. In 1913 he was 5ft 4ins tall (relatively short for the arduous duties of a stoker), with dark brown hair, hazel eyes, a fresh complexion and a scar on the left side of his chin. He gave his occupation as "Domestic Groom", and agreed to serve five years at sea and another seven years in the Fleet Reserve.

Frederick spent six months training at Portsmouth before joining his first ship, the armoured cruiser HMS *Venus*, in Pembroke on 10 September. After less than a month there he served briefly on the ageing armoured cruiser HMS *Thetis* in the Fleet reserve before returning to Portsmouth for another six weeks training. On 16 December he sailed on HMS *Europa* to join HMS *Hampshire*. He was promoted to Stoker First Class on 18 March 1916.

Frederick was the most seriously wounded of the *Hampshire* survivors, and he left many versions of his experiences.[341] After his discharge from Haslar Hospital in Portsmouth[342] he remained at Portsmouth for nearly two years, being promoted to Acting Leading Stoker on 4 September 1917. On 15 April 1918 he joined the cruiser HMS *Latona*, on minelayer duties in the Mediterranean. On 9 August 1918 he re-joined HMS *Europa*, then the flagship, at Mudros on the Greek island of Lemnos. He was confirmed in the rank of Leading Stoker on 4 March 1919. He served on a drifter returning from Malta to Scotland. On 9 July he was back in Portsmouth, where he was demobilized on 31 December. He served in the Royal Fleet Reserve in April-June 1921.

Frederick's service record suggests the effect of the trauma he suffered during the sinking of *Hampshire*: throughout his naval career his "Character" was recorded as "Very Good" and his Ability rating was recorded as "Superior" until 1917, but it slipped to "Satisfactory" thereafter.

After his demobilisation Frederick worked on trams in London: in 1926 he was a conductor for M.E. Tramways. He married Lydia Thomas in Hendon, Middlesex in December 1919 and they had five children, four of whom were still living in the family home in Hendon in 1939. During World War II he served in the Home Guard. The couple moved to a bungalow in Hemel Hempstead in 1956, and after driving trolley buses for four years Frederick retired in 1960. Lydia died in 1974, leaving Frederick a widower for 21 years until he died in Dacorum, Hertfordshire in 1995, aged 82.

Petty Officer 1st Class Samuel Edward Sweeney RN, 155874 (Po)

Samuel Sweeney joined the Royal Navy as a Boy Class II at Portsmouth on 4 June 1890.[343] He gave his place of birth as Fahan, Donegal and its date as 15 January 1875, for an age of 15. He was probably then only 14 years old, although his family details have not been determined. Samuel did his basic training at Devonport while berthed on the school ships HMS *Impregnable* and HMS *Lion*. He was promoted to Boy Class I in May 1891. He spent six months on the battleship HMS *Superb*, the Clyde guard ship. As an Ordinary Seaman on the training ship HMS *Calypso* he signed on for 12 years on 15 January 1893. He was 5ft 2¾ins tall, with brown hair, brown eyes and a dark complexion.

---

[340] Many of *Hampshire*'s young crew were probably under age when they volunteered to join up.
[341] The records relating to Frederick Sims are the most prolific of all the survivors:
  1913-1921 Service record (TNA ADM188/1119/113673: Frederick Lot Sims);
  1916, June 6: Survivors' statement (from TNA ADM116/3621, transcribed www.hmshampshire.co.uk);
  1916, June 7: Court of Enquiry (under oath) (TNA ADM116/2323);
  1916, June 7: Extract from Medical Officer's Journal, HMS *Blake* (TNA ADM116/2324A);
  1916, June 27: Note of phone call from Haslar Hospital to Admiralty (TNA ADM116/1526);
  1916, June 29: Letter from Admiralty to Mr Harvey, Stockan (TNA ADM116/2323);
  1916, July: Letter from Mrs Fanny Sims, London, to Mrs Harvey (papers of late Mrs Hourie);
  1916, Aug. 31: Letter from Stoker Sims to Mrs Harvey (Mrs A Hourie);
  1917, Nov. 22: Letter from Stoker Sims, HMS *Terrible*, to Mrs Harvey (Mrs Hourie);
  1926, May: Alleged statement to F Power by Mr FL Sims (*Referee* 2 May 1926; *Orcadian* 27 May 1926);
  1926, June 1-July 24: 7 letters between Admiralty to Stoker Sims concerning his interview with the Admiralty at which he made clear that he had never made the statements attributed to him in the press (TNA ADM116/2324A);
  1960: Interview of Sims (London Country Buses Company Magazine, 1960; www.hmshampshire.co.uk);
  1984: Interview by Trevor Royle with Stoker Fred Sims (Royle 1985, pp. 370, 372, 373);
  1991: Interview with Fred Sims (*Hemel Hempstead Gazette*, date unknown).
[342] Haslar's records show that Sims was discharged after 10 days (TNA ADM116/1526) but he later claimed he was there for about six weeks (ADM116/2324A).
[343] TNA ADM188/226/155874: Samuel Edward Sweeney.

Samuel served six months at sea on the armoured cruiser HMS *Narcissus*. During nine months on HMS *Himalaya* he was promoted to Able Seaman, but also served 27 days imprisonment. After a year at Portsmouth he joined the corvette HMS *Cordelia* in November 1895. Samuel deserted in March 1898 but was recovered in July 1899. After 90 days hard labour on HMS *Duke of Wellington* he spent 3 years on the cruiser HMS *Gladiator* and was promoted Leading Seaman. While serving on the tender HMS *Firequeen* at Portsmouth he was promoted Petty Officer Class 2 in February 1904. He served another 9 months on HMS *Gladiator*, then 15 months on the cruiser HMS *Venus* during which he was promoted to Petty Officer Class 1 and signed on for another 12 years; his height then was 5ft 5½ins. After 4 years ashore at Portsmouth he joined the battleship HMS *Hindustan* in October 1909 to serve 1½ years. In March 1911 he started an 18-month spell at HMS *Fisgard*. A year on board the battleship HMS *Britannia* was followed by another spell ashore at Portsmouth. In December 1913 he sailed on HMS *Europa* to join HMS *Hampshire*.

After *Hampshire* Samuel returned to Portsmouth, where was promoted to Acting Chief Petty Officer in June 1917. He returned to Orkney, joining HMS *Implacable* in April 1918 when she became the depot ship for the Northern Patrol. Samuel returned to Portsmouth less than two weeks after the Armistice was signed. He was invalided out of the Navy with a pension on 13 January 1919 because of an old injury to his right hand.

The Royal Navy was Samuel's family for nearly 30 years, that included good times and bad. He was the oldest survivor and suffered from shock more severely than the others. He committed suicide on the steamship *Teelin Head* in Belfast harbour in October 1926, aged 50, reputedly after murdering his wife.[344]

Petty Officer Wilfred Wesson RN, 201136 (Po)

Wilfred Wesson was born on 8 May 1883 in Hampstead, London. After working briefly as a labourer he joined the Royal Navy as a Boy Class II at Portsmouth on 8 September 1898.[345] He was 5ft 2ins tall, with light brown hair, grey eyes and a fresh complexion.

He did his basic naval training on the school ships HMS *Impregnable* at Devonport and HMS *Agincourt* at Portland, as a Boy Class I from 15 June 1899. When he signed on aged 18 in 1901 as an Ordinary Seaman to serve 12 years he had a tattoo of a "bird in flight, chasing a fly" on his right arm. So it was apt that he joined the destroyer HMS *Lapwing*, where he was promoted to Able Seaman on 7 November 1901. He served 1904-07 on the armoured cruiser HMS *Drake*.

Wilfred married Winifred Rathke in Portsmouth in early 1911 and their daughter, Winifred, was born later that year. After promotion to Leading Seaman in February 1912 he served a year on the battleship HMS *Hindustan*. He spent 1913 ashore at Portsmouth, except for two months on the navigation school ship HMS *Dryad*. When he signed on to serve another 12 years in May his height was 5ft 7½ins. On 16 December 1913 he boarded HMS *Europa* to travel to Ceylon and join HMS *Hampshire*. He was promoted to Petty Officer on 1 April 1915.

After *Hampshire* Wilfred returned to Portsmouth and stayed ashore until after the war. In October 1919 he joined the light cruiser HMS *Comus* and sailed for service in the East Indies. Promoted to Chief Petty Officer in April 1921, he joined the light cruiser HMS *Caroline*[346] in November, returning to the UK in February 1922. He was transferred to the Royal Fleet Reserve in May 1923 and paid his naval pension. He lived in Portsmouth for the rest of his life. In 1926 he was employed in a naval Institute, probably the Trafalgar Institute where he was working as a booking clerk in 1939. His wife died just before World War II started, and he then lived with his daughter Winifred. Winifred's husband was away in 1939, possibly serving in the Navy. Wilfred died in early 1946, aged 63.

Thus of the 12 survivors, one was killed later in the War, two died in the 1920s, two, possibly three in the 1940s, one in the 1950s, two in the 1960s, and two in the 1970s; the last to die was Frederick Sims, in 1995.

---

[344] OA TA/401.
[345] TNA ADM188/349/201136: Wilfred Wesson.
[346] HMS *Caroline*, built in 1914 and the last survivor of the Battle of Jutland, opened to the public in Belfast on 1 June 2016.

Chapter 13

Diving the Wreck

by Emily Turton and Ben Wade

Introduction

The wreck of HMS *Hampshire* lies in the Atlantic Ocean in Latitude 59°07'.024N, Longitude 3°23'.740W. This is 1½ miles off Marwick Head on the west coast of the Orkney Mainland. She lies completely upside down in approximately 65 metres of water, with the least depth over the upturned hull of approximately 55 metres. The seabed is largely flat and made up of coarse sand and stones. The underwater visibility is often about 25 metres, excellent for British waters.

Quite rightly, the Admiralty has always considered HMS *Hampshire* to be a war grave, and as such requests to salvage her have always been denied. However, it wasn't until early this century that she was awarded legal protection: on 30 September 2002, under the Protection of Military Remains Act of 1986, she was designated as a Protected Military Wreck and further diving on her was banned.[347] No diving can take place without permission from the Ministry of Defence (MOD) and this permission is only rarely given.

Her exposed location, depth and latterly the ban on diving, all contribute to the relatively small amount of diving that has ever taken place on HMS *Hampshire* in the 100 years since she sank. The divers still alive today who have had the privilege of diving her are few and far between.

Deep diving techniques have developed hugely in the last 20 years and there is now a global community of technical divers who dive beyond 60 metres recreationally. Technological advances and the availability of helium have made diving beyond 55 metres more accessible. However, the majority of recreational divers do not dive beyond 40 metres so given her depth and the tidal conditions, a dive on *Hampshire* would still be considered a demanding dive today.

Diving Expeditions

Over the years several diving expeditions on the wreck of the *Hampshire* have been reported. The information on the majority of these is scarce and to appreciate the possible scope of these expeditions and the likely veracity of the reports some understanding of the diving techniques of the time is required.

The 1920s and 1930s

All diving operations in the first half of the 20th century would have been conducted using "standard diving dress," similar to that shown on the right. This equipment was heavy, bulky and restricted movement. The diver wore a heavy, rubberised canvas suit, lead-soled shoes weighing approximately 34lbs and a helmet made of copper or brass. They also had to carry an additional 50lbs of lead weights on their chest and back. The standard dress diver could not swim, but had to walk on the seabed. Their air supply came from the surface via an umbilical hose which they had to drag behind them, and two people on the surface had to pump air to the diver for the entire duration of the dive.

This technique would have severely restricted the potential of the reported early diving expeditions to the *Hampshire*. The technique was used in Scapa Flow in the 1920's by Earnest Cox in the salvage of the German High Seas Fleet, but for the *Hampshire* the depth was greater and the dive more exposed, and therefore more weather dependent. The diver and dive vessel would have to contend with much stronger currents as well as the Atlantic swell making diving conditions more difficult. The risk of decompression sickness (the "bends") by

---

[347] Several other ships were given this protection at the same time and these include HMS *A7*, HMS *Bulwark*, HMS *Dasher*, HMS *Exmouth*, HMS *Formidable*, HMS *H5*, HMS *Natal*, HMS *Royal Oak**, HMS *Vanguard**, and *UB 81*. In keeping with our rich naval history, four of these wrecks, identified with an asterisk, lie in or close to Orkney waters.

diving to 65 metres would be great due to the lack of knowledge of decompression theory, and the lack of reliable decompression tables for this depth at that time.

In 2001 a lady claimed that her grandfather worked as a diver in the Royal Navy and was involved in an official dive on the *Hampshire* in 1916 to recover bodies.[348] However, there is no evidence that Kitchener's family were consulted on such an initiative, and in response to a Parliamentary question on 18 November 1918 the First Lord of the Admiralty stated that it "had not been possible either to examine or salve the vessel [nor] would it be possible to conduct such operations ... 30 fathoms down".[349]

The first published claim that *Hampshire* had been dived was made by the journalist Frank Power in 1926.[350] He claimed to have instigated a diving survey of the wreck, and found it lay in 37 fathoms (68 metres) in position 59° 07' 30"N, 03° 23' 00"W, "flattened out [with] considerable silting of sand over parts of the vessel [and] evidence of an internal explosion." Although Power's location and depth of the wreck are plausible, all of this information could, of course, have been ascertained without diving the wreck. His description of the wreck and seabed, however, is clearly inaccurate. Quite apart from the difficulties in diving to that depth with the equipment available at that time there is no substantive evidence to suggest that either of these alleged dives ever took place.

The Zaharoff Expedition of 1933

The second published account appeared in the Associated Press on 26 April 1933, stating that £15,000 (over £750,000 in today's money) had been recovered of an alleged £2 million of gold bars on board.[351] It was reported that this expedition was backed by the international arms dealer and industrialist Sir Basil Zaharoff (1849-1936), reputed to be one of the richest men in the world during his lifetime.

The salvage attempt was said to have been wrought with difficulties and incidents. Several divers are reported to have been injured, and two died, apparently in a mud slide inside the wreck. It is relevant to note that the *Hampshire* lies on a heavy sand and rock bottom, making an accumulation of mud inside the wreck highly unlikely. The diving technique is not described, but the use of oxyacetylene to cut underwater is mentioned, which if accurate would infer oxyhydrogen cutting equipment was used, an incredibly new technology for the depth at that time.

This story reappeared in the press repeatedly over the years, each time with greater embellishments, akin to a treasure hunting story found in a *Boys Own* annual. Each account describes retrieval of differing amounts of gold treasure, from nothing to a value of £15,000. The same three divers' names crop up in each account; a Mr Whitefield, a Mr Costello and a Mr Charles Courtney, who was a locksmith apparently specially trained as a diver so that he could go and unlock the ship's safe housed deep within a wreck at 65 metres![352]

A dive to this depth at this point in time is feasible, and as such could have taken place using the techniques described above. However wreck penetration using surface supplied air is challenging and sometimes impossible even today, so it is highly unlikely that the wreck penetration as described in these accounts would have occurred. Some accounts state that Mr Whitefield, or Weisfelt as he sometimes appears, died in the mud slide, others tell of his account being made from a hospital bed after the incident. The accounts are full of inconsistencies and the description of the diving is at times fanciful. It seems very likely, therefore, that these accounts are the work of fiction.

Post War developments

For nearly 50 years the wreck lay undisturbed. In 1948 the Naval Intelligence Department noted on an internal file that they had no security reservations concerning the wreck, and the Admiralty stated they were "not aware of any previous salvage operations."[353] In 1951 the Admiralty stated "the vessel is Admiralty property and we are not prepared to entertain proposals for salvage operations".[354] Two years later the Admiralty stated the vessel would not be sold as it was "now regarded as a war grave."[355]

---

[348] www.hmshampshire.co.uk > Hampshire Gold.
[349] Hansard; c.f. Boyle 1985, 389.
[350] *Orcadian* 4 Mar. 1926; *Referee* 21 Feb, 4 July 1926.
[351] Harris 1990, 116-124.
[352] See, for example, the posthumous account in the *Orcadian* 6 Apr. 1939. Courtney's tale is described in more detail in his autobiographical book *Unlocking Adventure* in 1951.
[353] TNA ADM137/1992, responses to queries by Texas Technical College who were attempting a theoretical salvage study.
[354] TNA ADM137/1992, response to queries by Lloyd Knight who was planning a salvage operation.
[355] HO WS *Hampshire* note following request in 1957 by Mr W Johnston to buy the vessel.

The 1970s and 1980s

Commercial diving techniques and equipment developed rapidly within the oil and gas industry in the late 1970s and early 1980s, enabling divers to work at depth in safety for long periods of time. The big development was saturation diving – see inset.

The *Stena Workhorse* expedition of 1983

The wreck was visited in 1977, 1979 and 1983 by a consortium led by the Californian businessman John R Breckenridge that included the West German film company Agus Underwater Films and the charterer Wharton Williams of Aberdeen.[356] The company received permission for their dives in 1977 and 1979, but were denied permission to salvage any of the ship or her cargo in 1983.[357] Ostensibly the dives were for historical research.

In 1977 they dived from the Swedish vessel *Deep Diver* using a bathysphere, but it was reported that weather caused the project to be abandoned. Breckenridge described the wreck in 1977 as being

> *in surprisingly good state of preservation ... what little footage we obtained on that visit definitely showed plates bent <u>inwards</u> on the bows*

In 1983 the same consortium chartered the larger oilfield support vessel *Stena Workhorse*, formally *Stena Welder*, equipped with a 100-ton crane, and hired a team of six saturation divers, allegedly to investigate the cause of the sinking. Namely, did the blast originate internally or externally? Was this sabotage and a way to remove Kitchener, or did the ship indeed hit a mine? The crew were informed of the gold "10 safes loaded in Glasgow with 100,000 sovereigns in each".[358] During the survey of the ship the divers reported the stern section in the area of the Captain's quarters to be damaged "as if a grab had been there before us." The starboard propeller and shaft were already laying off to one side and they were subsequently recovered by the diving team.

Despite permission to salvage never being given to the expedition, the starboard propeller, several guns and other items of bronze and brass were recovered. It seems unlikely that the dive expedition's primary goal was that of salvage, due to the amount and type of items that were recovered. The starboard propeller was already separate from the wreck and required no blasting. In essence an easy lift. The fact that the port propeller has not been touched suggests the crew were possibly after "easy pickings" to supplement income rather than systematic and wholesale salvage. Breckenridge and Wharton Williams claimed "Nothing was removed from the hull, and the hull was not disturbed in any way".

The ship was over the wreck from 5 to 8 August, when an equipment breakdown is reported to have prevented further work. She returned to Peterhead, arriving on 9 August, where the dive team demobbed. The next day the artefacts salvaged from the wreck were landed and impouned in the Customs bonded warehouse by the Receiver of Wreck on behalf of the MOD, who had asked they be returned to the wreck.[359] Later the MOD donated the artefacts to the Orkney Islands Council, who now turn display most of them at the Scapa Flow Visitor Centre and Museum in Lyness, Hoy.[360]

> Decompression sickness or "the bends" is one of the major safety concerns for any diver. It is the process of gas bubbles forming in your body tissues. The air you breathe is made up of oxygen and nitrogen. At the surface the nitrogen levels in your body does not change. When you dive, the pressure of the water surrounding you makes your body absorb more nitrogen. The deeper and longer you dive, the more nitrogen you absorb. On the ascent to the surface your body releases this nitrogen as the water pressure reduces. This has to be done slowly and in a controlled manor to avoid bubbles forming and causing the bends. This is done by conducting a series of decompression stops, a process of stopping your ascent at calculated depths for calculated periods of time on the way to the surface. The deeper you dive the more decompression stops you need.
>
> This diving technique restricted commercial divers working at depth until it was discovered that the human body can only absorb a fixed amount of nitrogen before it is then said to be saturated. This lead to the development of saturation diving. It was found that once the body was saturated with nitrogen for a given depth the diver would not need to do any more decompression stops, regardless of how long they stayed at that depth. This time could range from hours to days and even to weeks! Commercially this meant that divers could now work at depth for extended periods of time. Saturation divers live on board the dive support vessel in a special habitat pressurized to the same depth that they need to work in effectively a giant recompression chamber. To conduct their working shifts, they are lowered to and raised from the seabed in a pressurized bell. At the end of the job the pressure in the habitat is slowly reduced to mimic the divers ascending from depth and completing their decompression stops.

---

[356] OA/RO7/315; Royle 1985, 385, 389; HO WS *Hampshire*. The film company approached the Naval Law Department of the Admiralty for positional information. In 1977 the Imperial War Museum acquired a small rusted plate (see Appendix III below) which presumably was recovered during the first of these filming expeditions, possibly by a remotely controlled grab rather than by a diver.
[357] UKHO H3403/59.
[358] Personal communication by Pete Glazier, salvage diver. In fact HMS *Hampshire* never visited Glasgow
[359] *Aberdeen Press and Journal* 9, 10 Aug. 1983; *Orcadian* 11, 18 Aug. 1983; *Lloyds List* 16 Aug. 1983; UKHO H3875/26.
[360] See Chapter 14 and Annex III below.

The diver's report quoted above is compatible with a drawing by Capt. G Nilsson, Master of *Stena Workhorse* dated 8 August 1983 shown below:[361]

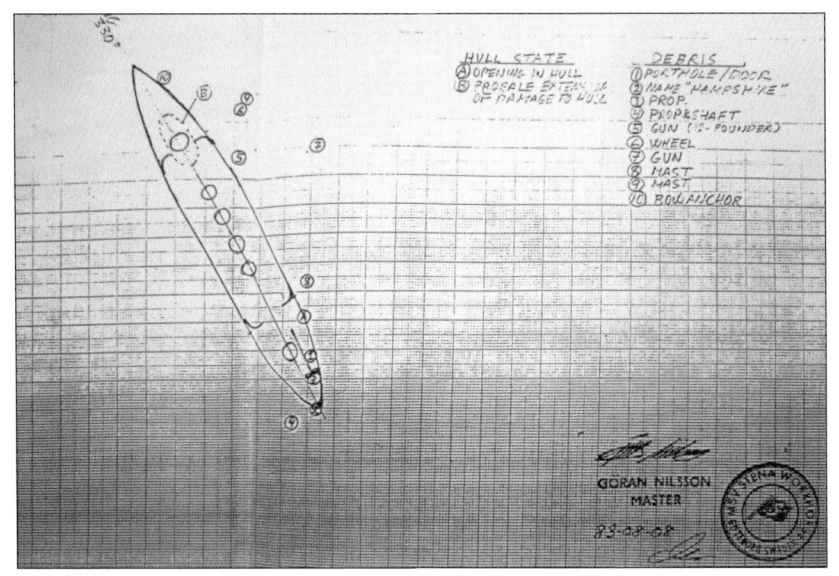

Plan of wreck of HMS *Hampshire*, 8 August 1983. (by courtesy of Stena Line Group)

While the reported primary function of this expedition was that of survey, the fact that the dive team were informed of the gold suggests an underlying secondary objective of treasure hunting. Prompted perhaps by the successful recovery two years earlier of 431 gold ingots from the wreck of HMS *Edinburgh*[362] at the much greater depth of 245m, it is almost certain that this expedition was hunting for the ship's alleged strong room, motivated by the possibility that it still contained gold.

The starboard propellor and shaft of HMS *Hampshire* now on exhibition at Lyness. (copyright Marjo Tynkkynen)

Recreational diving, c.1990-2002

After 1983 the wreck was apparently not dived again until technical advances made recreational diving to this depth possible. Scapa Flow as a wreck diving destination was pioneered in the early 1980s with the main attraction being the remaining wrecks of the German High Seas Fleet that were scuttled there in 1919. In fact one or two of those older pioneers are still operating today! By the early 1990s, Orkney's dive charter industry, based in Stromness, was thriving. Diving to 65 metres also became more accessible and more frequent amongst recreational divers. As a consequence, the *Hampshire* became a more popular destination for the more adventurous recreational diver. This is due in part to the availability of both technical diver training and more advanced diving techniques. As with all adventure sports, such developments allowed people to push boundaries. The numbers of divers visiting the wreck increased dramatically from this point until her protection in 2002. Initially a dive on the *Hampshire* could be added to a normal Scapa Flow diving week, given the right weather window. As the popularity of the wreck increased some groups booked entire charter weeks just to dive the *Hampshire,* such was her appeal.

The first recreational divers visiting the *Hampshire* would have been breathing air and using standard SCUBA (self-contained underwater breathing apparatus) diving equipment pioneered in the early days by the likes of Jacques Cousteau. The advances in deeper diving both commercially and recreationally see the addition of

---

[361] UKHO HH268/450/01. There is no provenance with this drawing.
[362] HMS *Edinburgh*, a 10,635 ton heavy cruiser, sistership of HMS *Belfast* now moored in the Pool of London, was built in 1936 and torpedoed in 1942 while escorting a return convoy from Murmansk and carrying 461 gold ingots weighing 4.57 tonnes and worth over £40 million as part payment for war supplies carried to Russia. The salvage was undertaken by Jessop Marine and Wharton Marine on behalf of the UK government.

helium to the breathing gas to allow safe dives beyond 60 metres. The 1990s saw the introduction of these "mixed gas" diving techniques recreationally. Technological advancements allowed the manufacture of better and more reliable equipment and the development of dive computers which calculated decompression for the diver, and displayed it on a wrist-mountable device, which allowed deeper and more complicated dives. We also see more technical dive equipment configurations with divers carrying multiple cylinders to extend their time underwater. By the late 1990s Closed Circuit Rebreathers were available on the recreational diving market. These electronically controlled machines allow for gas to be recirculated and therefore re-breathed, which hugely extends the gas supply. Deeper diving became safer. Had the *Hampshire* wreck not been protected she would today be visited on a regular basis by a large number of divers.

Modern surveys of the wreck

To mark the 2106 Centenary of the sinking of HMS *Hampshire* the MOD authorised two expeditions to ascertain the condition of the wreck.

2016 ROV Survey Expedition

The first of these expeditions was a remote survey using an ROV (remotely operated vehicle) and multibeam echosounder (MBES) technology. The project was led by Sandra Henry of the University of the Highlands and Islands Archaeology Institute.[363] The expedition ran from 6 to 12 May. Some of the initial findings were presented at lectures in Birsay and Kirkwall for the *Hampshire* centenary commemoration. Detailed findings are still being developed at the time of going to press.

Modern technology enables such remote survey images to highlight great detail over a wide area. The illustrations below show MBES and Single Side Scan Sonar images of the wreck and debris field. Note the extensive damage forward (top) and the debris including masts lying to east (right):

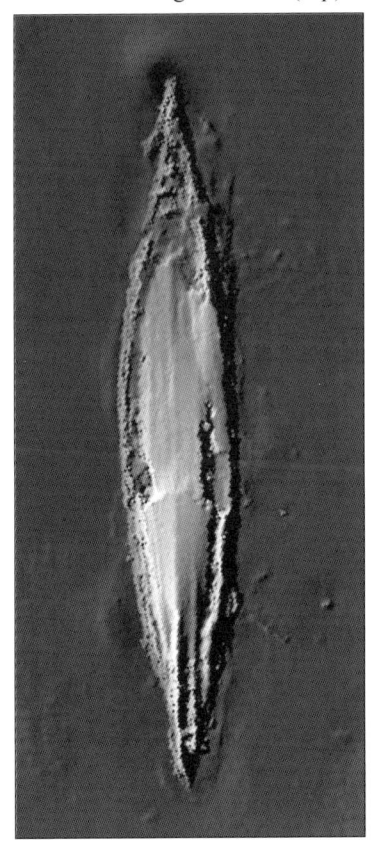

MBES image from SeaBat T50-P
by Teledyne Marine.
(copyright UHI Archaeology Institute)

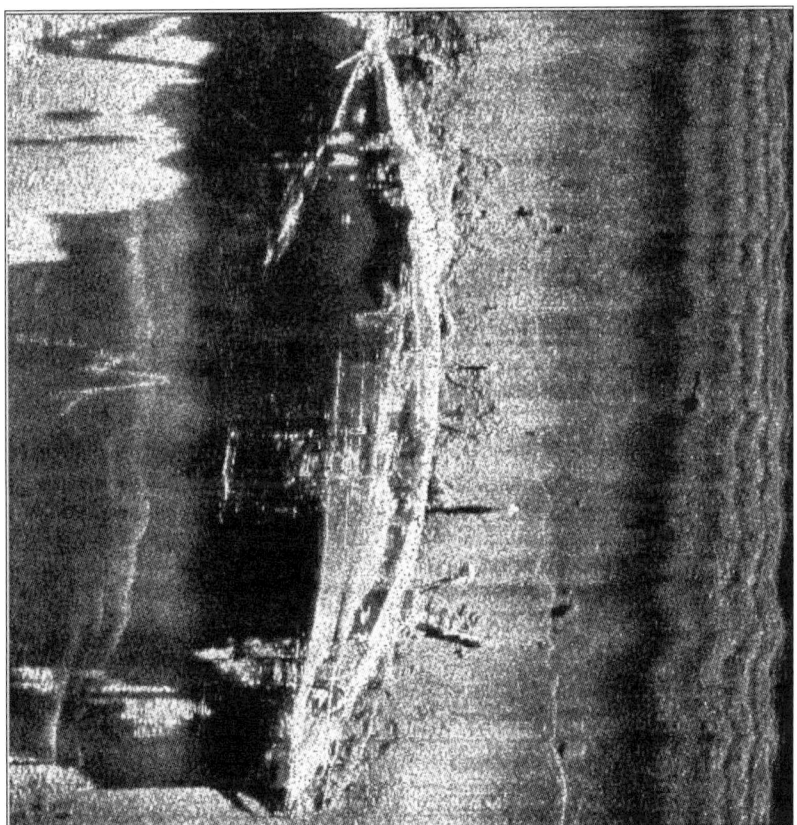

Side scan sonar image of *Hampshire*
(courtesy of Kevin Heath)

2016 Diving Expedition

In 2014 we sat down with our friends and diving colleagues Paul Haynes and Rod Macdonald to present an idea – a centenary diving expedition to HMS *Hampshire* to survey the ship in her 100th year underwater, using

---

[363] UHI were assisted by Seatronics, Teledyne Reson, Roving Eye Enterprises of Orphir, SULA Diving, and Trisom Marine Ltd. of Sanday.

modern techniques not in existence at the time of her closure in 2002. An application was made to the MOD and the expedition was licensed early in 2016 and also flagged by the Explorers Club.[364] A team of expert divers, diving from our Stromness based dive vessel *Huskyan* was assembled to conduct a photographic and 3D photogrammetry diver survey of the ship to coincide with the centenary of her sinking. The two-week expedition took place from 28 May to 10 June 2016.

The dive teams incorporated expertise from many fields of technical diving and the project was put together by four expedition organizers: Rod Macdonald, shipwreck author and license holder; Paul Haynes, leading diving educator; Ben Wade, leading diving professional and local wreck expert; and Emily Turton, professional skipper and local wreck expert. The other team members were chosen from a pool of international technical divers to include professional underwater photographers and experts in shipwreck photogrammetry.

Team Members, left to right: Ross Dowrie, Paul Toomer, Russ Evans, Gary Petrie, Kevin Heath, Immi Wallin, Emily Turton, Ben Wade, Paul Haynes, Brian Burnett, Rod Macdonald, Marjo Tynkkynen, Greg Booth, Kari Hyttinen, Chris Rowland, Mic Watson. Chris Woodhouse is missing from the photo. (copyright Marjo Tynkkynen)

Hampshire the shipwreck is exquisite. As a dive destination alone, she rivals any we have dived in the world. Diving *Hampshire* the war grave, however, was a huge privilege and an experience which will stay with each team member forever.

Eye-witness accounts describe the *Hampshire* sinking bow first but still upright. She would have hit the seabed before her stern slipped below the waves. It appears that she has only capsized once her bow has hit the seabed and now lies completely upside down with a large debris field to the south and east of the wreck. Contrary to previous accounts her bows are actually intact. Evidence of the mine damage lies further aft. The port anchor lies on the seabed still in its hawse.

The bow: upside down but intact.
(copyright Marjo Tynkkynen)

Just aft of the bow is an area of damage caused initially by the mine and then from her hitting the seabed and subsequently capsizing. Sticking prominently into the air and protruding out of this damaged area are the three forward anchor capstan drive shafts and wheels akin to three lollypop sticks.

Forward anchor capstan drive shafts.
(copyright Marjo Tynkkynen)

---

[364] In recognition of the historical importance of the loss of HMS *Hampshire* the prestigious Explorers Club awarded the expedition Explorers Club flag No 192. All major explorations since early 1900s have carried with them an Explorers Club flag, including expeditions to the Poles, Everest and the Moon. Flag No 192 was carried on 22 previous expeditions to Polar Regions, the Himalayas and has crossed the Atlantic twice by hot air balloon.

13 – Diving the Wreck

The keel is bent over to the starboard side. Armour plating has burst its seams on the port side, pushed out by the forward 7.5 inch gun hitting the seabed first as she capsized and this area is full of debris and wreckage. Notwithstanding the 1983 removal of artefacts, and contrary to rumour and supposition, the team agreed that the wreck does not appear to have been salvaged and there is no surviving underwater evidence to suggest that any cutting, grab salvage or blast salvage has taken place. Munitions litter the entire site from bow to stern. Cordite is scattered all over, some loose and some still in brass storage boxes with a concentration in areas close to magazines, when compard with the ship's plans. Large stacks of 6 and 7.5-inch shells are visible from outside the wreck, some in the forward damaged section and others where parts of the hull have deteriorated to an extent that openings have formed.

Shells for the forward 7.5 inch gun.
(copyright Marjo Tynkkynen)

Torpedo warheads lie at the bow alongside one of her forward torpedo tubes. These non ferrous warheads are clearly visible amongst the wreckage and have lifting eyes at the nose.

Torpedo warheads and debris in the bow.
(copyright Marjo Tynkkynen)

As to be expected with a ship of this age, parts of the wreck are decaying. This is clearly visible along the length of her armoured belt. Ships of this era were built with heavy armoured steel concentrated around the waterline to protect from direct shell fire and torpedo strikes. The weight of the amour has caused it to collapse towards the seabed, leaving a large longitudinal fissure along the top edge of the hull on both sides of the ship. This gap provides a glimpse into the engine rooms and four of the boiler rooms, where her very large four-cylinder steam engines, Yarrow boilers and Scotch boilers can be clearly seen.

Evidence of decay is also clearly visible at the stern but this may have been exacerbated by the huge impact the stern would have experienced when it finally hit the seabed. This impact might explain how the starboard propeller and shaft came to be broken and lying clear of the wreck, as described by the 1983 salvage team.

The remains of her stern seem to be mainly supported by the aft 7.5-inch gun and barbette and the port propeller its shaft.

The port propeller.
(copyright Marjo Tynkkynen)

The propeller is one of the best things we have seen underwater. As we descended down the rope to the wreck on the first dive of the expedition the visibility was incredible. At 35 metres and with a further 30 metres yet to descend the propeller was clearly visible below us and will remain "the image" of the expedition.

While the bulk of the very stern of the ship has collapsed, a section of plating containing nearly her complete name remains proud of the seabed.

The ships name at the stern.
(copyright Marjo Tynkkynen)

Exploring the debris field was as interesting and valuable as examining the main body of the wreck. We assume this debris has been deposited in the process of her capsizing. Items lie nestled amongst the seabed and time spent in even a small area turned up find after find, akin to beach combing. Solid brass portholes lie the entire length of the ship from stern to bow, having fallen away from the main body of the wreck as thinner hull plating has decayed.

Porthole on the seabed.
(copyright Marjo Tynkkynen)

HMS *Hampshire* had six twin barrelled Mk.VII 6-inch casemate guns. The lower barrels were removed as they proved to be too close to the water line, very wet and therefore relatively useless in any weather. They were subsequently mounted on the deck forward and aft of midships, two starboard and two port. One of these lies under the wreck but the remaining three have been deposited in the debris field with the farthest lying 30 metres away from the wreck. Two of these guns are rammed barrel-first into the seabed and have been nicknamed as tree guns by previous divers. The third rests horizontally on the seabed. Accounts of these guns were made by the 1983 saturation divers and by many recreational divers in the late 1990s.

Some of the most poignant sights were of the more mundane or day to day items, such as white porcelain wash hand basins, toilets, bathroom tiles and crockery, items that would have been used by each and every man aboard and hold the secrets and stories of those lost souls. A closer examination of the debris field reveals navigation lamps, inspection lamps, voice pipes and even a telegraph. One artefact spoke "*Hampshire*" to us above anything else: a solid brass plate with a rose surrounded by leaves – the county emblem of Hampshire. This is probably the front of a gun tampion but could also be from the ship's crest.

The wreck of HMS *Hampshire* has now been surveyed more thoroughly than ever before. The complete findings of the diver survey will be published in due course and should continue to help unravel some of the mystery surrounding the wreck.

Interestingly, the challenges of her exposed location with often temperamental surface weather conditions, the depth of the wreck and the strong tidal flow all contribute to fantastic underwater visibility which, in turn, contribute to the magical underwater experience that is a dive on *Hampshire*.

Amongst the divers who have had the opportunity to dive *Hampshire*, accounts of the wreck and her artefacts differ. However, one opinion amongst those privileged few appears to be constant: *Hampshire* is an incredible dive and would rank as one of the best wreck diving experiences in the world.

Chapter 14

The Artefacts Recovered

by Jude Callister

Many artefacts have been recovered from HMS *Hampshire*, some in the days immediately following the sinking, some many years later that were taken from the wreck by salvors.

The largest collection of *Hampshire* artefacts now belong to Orkney Islands Council. Most of the items in the collection were illegally salvaged from the wreck in 1983 and returned to Orkney in 1986.

Much of this collection is on display at the Scapa Flow Visitor Centre and Museum at Lyness in Hoy, which is centered around the former 1940s fuel oil pumping station at Lyness Naval Base and tells the story of Scapa Flow in the two World Wars. As you approach the museum the port propeller from *Hampshire* and a length of its drive shaft are on display in the forecourt. They weigh 43 tons. The propeller is 4.25 metres in diameter and made of manganese bronze. The collection also includes two of *Hampshire*'s eighteen 3-pounder deck guns,[365] a number of brass portholes, some with some of the steel plating still attached where they were torn from the ship's side, rims from escape hatches, and many smaller items.[366]

Scapa Flow Visitor Centre and Museum, Lyness. (OIC)

One of the few personal items is a fragment of a sailor's 'ditty' or 'diddy' box. In the days when sailors kept all their possessions in a kit bag, a small plain wooden box, 12x8x6ins, was used to store personal keepsakes such as letters and photographs and had the owner's name inscribed on a small brass plaque on the front. The box in the OIC's *Hampshire* collection belonged to Stoker Joseph Newman. It is unclear whether it was recovered illegally in 1980 or it came from the ditty box that is said to have contained a bundle of personal letters and old newspapers when it was found by an Aberdonian while fishing off Caithness in late June 1916.[367]

A recently acquired item is a vernacular metal dog collar inscribed "Lieut. Brock R.N. H.M.S. Hampshire". Its provenance is unknown, and there was no Lieut. Brock on the ship in June 1916, but it may have belonged to a ship's dog that was named after Staff Officer Vice Admiral Brock, or perhaps the dog was black and white and named after Brock the badger.

The other large collection of *Hampshire* artefacts, mostly remnants of her boats, is held by the Imperial War Museum. Most of this collection was donated by the Admiralty soon after she sank,[368] but one item is apparently from an illegal recovery in 1977.

The comprehensive inventory in Appendix III below includes several reports of flotsam from the wreck, but the whereabouts of most of these artefacts is not known today.

---

[365] A third 3-pounder gun is on display at Mid Cumloquoy in Birsay at the entrance of the footpath leading to the Kitchener Memorial.
[366] In 2016 six items from the collection were donated to the National Museum of the Royal Navy in Portsmouth.
[367] McCormick 1959, 204. No record of this ditty box has been found in the Admiralty or Police files held at TNA; nor in the many references therein to Detective-Inspector Vance is there any hint that he would have been involved in such a find.
[368] The provenance of the large sawn sections of the pinnace in the collection (pictured on p.24 above) was confirmed during the preparation of this volume by the discovery of relevant correspondence in TNA ADM116/2323. It is unclear whether the pinnace propeller and shaft at Lyness are from the same pinnace as the wooden hull sections at Duxford (one of which shows it to have had an engine).

Chapter 15

The Centenary Commemorations, 2016

by Neil Kermode and Keith Johnson

Commemorations of World War I and the Battle of Jutland

The centenary of the loss of HMS *Hampshire* was commemorated in Orkney by a number of organisations and in a variety of ways. The events overlapped with Orkney's hosting of the national commemoration of the centenary of the Battle of Jutland on behalf of the UK government's Department of Culture, Media and Sport. The associated events included a service in St.Magnus Cathedral on the morning of 31 May 2016 attended by over 400 guests and in the afternoon a further 300 attended a ceremony at the Lyness Royal Naval Cemetery in Hoy. Such were the number of guests that attendance had to be by invitation only.[369]

Other commemorative events not specific to HMS *Hampshire* included the "Poppies: Weeping Window", a cascade of some 4,500 handmade ceramic poppies originally seen pouring from a high window to the ground below at the Tower of London in the autumn of 2014 where 888,246 poppies were displayed, one to honour every death in the British and Colonial forces of the Great War. The display at St.Magnus Cathedral, from 22 April to 12 June 2016, was the first venue in Scotland for this 14-18 NOW presentation by artist Paul Cummings and designer Tom Piper.

The Weeping Window (courtesy *The Orcadian*).

The Orkney Museum at Tankerness House, Kirkwall mounted an exhibition entitled "The Battle of Jutland, Scapa Flow and the War at Sea" from 30 April until 30 September 2016. A number of concerts, films, public talks, guided walks, ship visits, dinners, dances and local radio broadcasts were also arranged.

Commemorations of the loss of HMS Hampshire

The initiatives of the Orkney Heritage Society, to refurbish the Kitchener Memorial and to build a low arc-shaped wall bearing the names of those who lost their lives from HMS *Hampshire* and HM Drifter *Laurel Crown* off Marwick Head in June 1916, have been described in Chapter 10 above. The two expeditions to survey the wreck of HMS *Hampshire* in May 2016 have been summarised in Chapter 13 above. This remainder of this Chapter addresses other initiatives in Orkney that related in whole or part to the *Hampshire* centenary.[370]

The Orkney Natural History Society Museum, Stromness

The Museum's annual summer exhibition for 2016 was "The Loss of HMS *Hampshire* and the Death of Lord Kitchener". The Society retained Tom Muir to mount the exhibition. The exhibition was open from 1 April to the end of October.

The HMS *Hampshire* Centenary Wood

746 young hawthorn, hazel and rowan trees were planted by the Woodland Trust Scotland and helped by members of the public, to create the HMS *Hampshire* Centenary Wood on 2 April 2016 on Orkney Islands Council (OIC) land in Kirkwall between Reid Crescent and the new Grammar School.

Councillor Stephen Hagan, Keith Welbon (Royal Naval Association), Jenny Taylor (Orkney Woodland Project) and Ruth Hyde (Woodland Trust) planting the Centenary Wood. (courtesy *The Orcadian*)

---

[369] The centenary was also commemorated at various locations outwith Orkney which space and time preclude inclusion in this volume.

[370] Further details of these and other events can be found at www.kitchenerhampshire.wordpress.com and associated social media sites.

A Fitful Sea

On the evenings of 3 and 4 June, at the Birsay Community Hall, the Birsay Drama Group and Friends presented "A Fitful Sea", a foy (pageant) comprising a programme remembering the *Hampshire* in narrative, poetry, music and song. The foy was commissioned by the Birsay Drama Group and the cast of twelve was directed by Issy Grieve. The words and poems were written by Pam Besant and the two songs written and sung by Sarah-Jane Gibbon, accompanied by her sister Emma Grieve. Two fiddle tunes were performed, one written by the late John J Fraser, father of the 12 year-old eye-witness John in 1916, the other by Kristan Harvey, a Birsay lass who won the BBC Radio Scotland Young Musician of the Year in 2011. Their last performance was preceded by four wartime tunes played by the Kirkwall Town Band and two songs by David and Sally McNeish, and followed by excerpts from "Oh! What a Lovely War" by the St.Magnus Players. Three further performances of the foy were performed at other events later in the year.

"Remembering the *Hampshire*" Exhibition

The Birsay Heritage Trust mounted an exhibition of artefacts, correspondence, pictures and other memorabilia entitled "Remembering The *Hampshire*" in the Board Room of the Birsay Community Hall, 3 through 6 June 2016. The exhibits had been loaned or presented by the OIC Museums Service, by individual Orcadians, and by relatives of *Hampshire* crew members. Over half of the 500 visitors recorded their names in the Visitors' Book, most of whom remarked on the quality of the exhibits.[371] Meanwhile on the 4th and 5th the Birsay Drama Group provided cream teas in the hall.

"Remembering The *Hampshire*" Exhibition.   (copyright Colin Keldie K4 Graphics)

Model of HMS *Hampshire*

The Birsay Heritage Trust commissioned Paul Tyer, of Peedie Models in Tankerness, to build a 900 mm model of HMS *Hampshire* from plans of her sister ship, HMS *Antrim*, (no plans of *Hampshire* having survived) that were provided by the Royal Maritime Museum, Greenwich. The model formed the centrepiece of the Trust's Exhibition.

Model of HMS *Hampshire*.
(courtesy Peedie Models)

---

[371] It is hoped that the model, many of the exhibition's other exhibits, and the Book of Remembrance (see below) will eventually form the basis of a permanent exhibition in the parish.

Royal Visit

HRH The Princess Royal and Vice Admiral Sir Tim Laurence returned to Orkney for a series of events on Sunday 5 June. They attended St.Magnus Cathedral, Kirkwall for Morning Service conducted by Rev. Fraser McNaughton. Princess Anne read the first reading, Acts 27:29 to 28:2, and The Lady Emma Fellowes, great-niece of Lord Kitchener read the second reading, recollections of Mina Phillips née Sabiston caring for some of the survivors of HMS *Hampshire*.

(courtesy Craig Taylor)

Rev. Fraser McNaughton, Lord-Lieutenant Bill Spence, The Princess Royal and Vice Admiral Sir Tim Laurence inspecting the poppies outside St.Magnus cathedral.

After the service the royal couple were shown around the Orkney Museum by Tom Muir, OIC Exhibitions Officer.

Tom Muir and The Princess Royal, with Jim Foubister (Vice Convener), Admiral Laurence and Bill Spence in the background.

(courtesy Orkney Photographic)

The Princess Royal and Admiral Laurence then visited the Birsay Community Hall and were received by the Vice Lord-Lieutenant, Keith Johnson. Over the preceding months the many community groups in Birsay had formed, with the help of OIC and Alan Manzie, a working group to organize a "*Hampshire* Week-end". Representatives of these organisations were presented to Her Royal Highness.

The Princess Royal, Keith Johnson, Margaret Irvine, Valerie Johnston, Alan Manzie, Anne Mathison and Rev. David McNeish.[372]   (courtesy Orkney Photographic)

This was followed by a tour of the *Hampshire* exhibition organised by Birsay Heritage Trust in the Board Room of the hall. Moving into the main hall, members of the Orkney Heritage Society Memorial Project Team along with the construction team were presented to the royal couple who then spent an hour meeting a hundred relatives who had travelled to Orkney from all over UK, and farther afield, to attend the commemoration events.[373] This was followed by a choir from Dounby Community School who sang "Let there be Peace" and a short prayer by Rev. David McNeish. After a brief introduction by Spencer Rosie, chairman of Orkney Heritage Society, Her Royal Highness was invited to unveil the "Book of Remembrance" which had been commissioned by Orkney Heritage Society and contained the names of 746 men who lost their lives on HMS *Hampshire* and HMD *Laurel Crown* off Marwick Head, and to sign the Visitors' Book.

Excerpt from the "Book of Remembrance".

---

[372] Margaret Irvine is Secretary, Birsay Drama Group; Valerie Johnston is Chair, Birsay Community Association; Alan Manzie is Birsay Community Development Coordinator; Anne Mathison is Secretary, Birsay Heritage Trust.

[373] These relatives were connected with twenty crew members from HMS *Hampshire*: Messrs. E Allen, C Bailey, W Bridges, H Browning, W Cake, F Collecott, S Collier, H Cooke, W Gibbs, T Harwood, V Heneage, T Hiscock, G Hunter, A McPherson, H Payne, G Sandom, J Shanks, R Thomson, F Waight and W Welsby, with six members of Lord Kitchener's party (Messrs. Brown, Donaldson, Ellershaw, Kitchener, McLoughlin, Robertson), with one of the rescuers (R Holloway), and with representatives of the Metropolitan Police and the Kitchener Scholars Association.

Princess Anne addressing relatives of those lost on HMS *Hampshire*, with Spencer Rosie (right),
with David McNeish and the Dounby School choir on the stage.   (courtesy Orkney Photographic)

Sheila Merriman, Alice Garson, and Ivy Ballantyne (centre), daughters of Mina Sabiston, with Ivy's son Ronnie behind her.
Mina's recollections of the night of 5/6 June 1916 were read at Morning Service in St.Magnus Cathedral by The Lady Emma
Kitchener, wife of Julian Fellowes (right). Ronnie is grandson of one of the original Kitchener Memorial Trustees.
Ivy was the only person to attend the ceremonies of both 1926 and 2016: at the age of five months,
she was carried up to the Kitchener Memorial by the mother of the survivor Richard Simpson.

After the royal couple departed for a private visit to the Kitchener Memorial, Orkney teas were served by the Hall Committee to the *Hampshire* relatives and local residents before the ceremony at Marwick Head.

The Centenary Commemoration and the Unveiling of the Commemorative Wall
The commemoration was held at 8pm on Marwick Head on a fine summer evening and attended by over 600 people. The event represented the culmination of a year of planning by many individuals who had worked tirelessly in the background to not only make the evening work, but also plan for last-minute variations in case of bad weather. In fact the weather turned out to be perfect: a cloudless sky, a gentle breeze and a smooth sea.

The logistics of 2016 echoed the arrangements for the traffic flow for the ceremony in 1926. Following the wet winter of 2015 the ground conditions were a major concern. Not knowing if the fields would be able to bear traffic it was decided early on that a shuttle service would be laid on to avoid cars near the tower. OIC hired coaches that ran from Kirkwall, Stromness and the Birsay Community Hall, and an internet ticketing facility that was set up to gauge demand took some 500 bookings. The ceremony was streamed live to an audience of about 50 people in the Birsay Community Hall hosted by Duncan Tullock, and to the internet.[374]

OIC staff led by Karen Greaves acted as site marshalls. The Stromness Royal British Legion Pipe Band welcomed attendees at the bottom of the hill before they made the 700 metre walk up the hill. Accompanying the climb,

---
[374] The internet web site was watched by over 5,000 people within a fortnight of the event.

the recorded voices of Dounby schoolchildren recited the names of the 746 men who gave their lives in 1916. Their names, together with those of the 12 survivors, were included in the Order of Service that were distributed.

Members of the Armed Services provided an Honour Guard flanking the Memorial, together with the colours of the Royal Naval Association and the Royal British Legion. Offshore, in the evening sun, the site of the wreck of HMS *Hampshire* was marked by the Type 45 destroyer HMS *Duncan*, and the site of the wreck of HM Drifter *Laurel Crown* by the Northern Lighthouse Board tender *Pharos*.

Rev. David McNeish, Minister of Birsay, Harray and Sandwick conducted the service, and Eileen Linklater, Andrew Hollinrake and Issy Grieve read verses of "Let there be Stones", a commemorative poem he had written for the occasion. The Rt. Rev. Dr Bob Gillies, Bishop of Aberdeen, Jamie Lowe, Sea Cadet Corps, and Jack Norquoy read short reflections and prayers. Music during the service was provided by members of the Stromness Royal British Legion Pipe Band, the Kirkwall Salvation Army Brass Band and the Kirkwall Town Band. Denise Stout directed a choir constituted specially for the event.

(l-r) Jack Norquoy, David McNeish, Jamie Lowe, Bob Gillies, David Dawson, Eileen Linklater and Issy Grieve. (courtesy *The Orcadian*)

Let there be stones, by Rev. David McMeish

Let there be a tower of stones.
A monument to a man and more.
A refuge from the inhospitable sea.
Hewn from rock,
Raised by the people of Orkney.

Let there be a tower of stones.
At the nearest point of land.
The highest point of survey.
A beacon of solidity.
A fixture for generations to come.

Let there be a tower of stones.

Let there be a wall of stones.
Gathered in an arc
The curve of horizons
And protective arms
The shelter stones of harbour
And safe passage.

Let there be a wall of stones.
Built on solid foundations
Strengthened against the battering wind.
And fashioned by hands who know how to neighbour rocks.
This is no hasty undertaking.

Let there be a wall of stones.
To better remember.
And on this wall.
Let every name be etched.
Every name recalled,
Every life valued and mourned
In grief and gratitude.

Let there be a wall of stones.
Let there be living stones.
People cut and crafted in different places.
Forged in different fires
Pressed in different circumstances.
Gathered in reflection.

Let there be a wall of stones.

Let there be living stones.
Succeeding generations
Of survivors, of relatives,
Of locals.
For voices that were silenced
May the stones themselves cry out.
Recalling details and dramas long since played out.
Petitioning the wind for forgiveness.

Let there be living stones.
Men and women who stand
Against all injustice
Against all hatred and tyranny.
Against every act of oppression
Whose lives are prayers for peace,
Vital poems of compassion
And monuments of mercy.

Let there be living stones

15 – The Centenary Commemorations 2016

Andrew Hollinrake reading from "Let there be stones". Denise Stout is on the right.

The Commemorative Wall was dedicated by Rev. David Dawson, Minister of St.Olaf's Episcopalian Church, Kirkwall, and unveiled by Bill Spence, Lord-Lieutenant of Orkney, flanked by his cadets Able Cadet Sam Henderson and Lance Bombardier Hudson Thomas-Johnson, by Admiral Sir Jock Slater on behalf of The Royal Navy, by Lieutenant Colonel Foulkes on behalf of The Army Reserve, by Keith Welbon on behalf of The Royal Naval Association (Orkney Branch), by Eddy Ross on behalf of The Royal British Legion, and by Neil Kermode and Andrew Hollinrake of the Orkney Heritage Society on behalf of the relatives of survivors and those who perished, and by James Gaudie (grandson of the 12 year old eyewitness in 1916), Steven Heddle (Convener of the OIC) and Jack Norquoy (a Scottish Youth MSP from Birsay) on behalf of the past, present and future people of Orkney. Wreaths were simultaneously cast into the sea from HMS *Duncan* and NLV *Pharos*.

At 8.45pm precisely, one hundred years after the moment HMS *Hampshire* struck the mine, HMS *Duncan* fired the first of two rounds to mark a two minute silence.

HMS *Duncan* firing gun salute over the wreck of HMS *Hampshire*. (courtesy *The Orcadian*)

The service deliberately finished with the final round to mark the start of the terrible fight for life that so few were to win. A lone piper struck up and walked playing from the hill. The guard were marched off quietly. The choir, bands and participants left the site, providing time and space for relatives and others to place tributes and wreaths against the newly unveiled wall.

In due course the crowd dispersed, the ships turned south, and the Memorial and wall were left alone on the cliff top overlooking the site of the tragedy, with just the tributes marking the day's events. But lodged in the minds of all those involved was the memory of a beautiful, thoughtful and haunting service, a service with a single purpose: Remembrance.

Conclusions

Although the objectives of this commemorative volume did not include the seeking of new interpretations of the events surrounding the loss of HMS *Hampshire* and HM Drifter *Laurel Crown*, the deaths of Lord Kitchener and so many others, or the consequential associated developments, so many fresh findings have emerged that it seems appropriate to bring them together. The objective of so doing is not to refute or apportion blame, but to help to correct some of the myths and mysteries that for too long have clouded the understanding of this disaster.

(1) With the last of the hitherto secret files held by the National Archives now open for public scrutiny, this volume is the first comprehensive account of the events to have been written without the caveat that relevant data was still being withheld under the Official Secrets Act. None of the previously published accounts of the disaster can be considered reliable.

(2) It transpires that Donald McCormick, hitherto regarded as authoritative, was, like Frank Power, a hoaxer.

(3) HMS *Hampshire* was sunk in an unseasonably cold NNW'ly gale by a moored mine laid by the German submarine *U 75*. Her loss was largely due to an extraordinary combination of ill-luck and coincidence.

(4) The mining of waters off Marwick Head was part of Germany's strategy that led to the Battle of Jutland.

(5) The "secret" of Kitchener's intended mission was compromised in London, in Russia, and even in the German press, although the German authorities were not aware of its timing or route.

(6) The criticisms by the Germans and others of Admiral Jellicoe's decision to route HMS *Hampshire* west of Orkney are unwarranted, and in particular the claims by several historians that he had ignored warnings of *U 75* having been sighted west of Orkney in early June.

(7) It seems likely that Capt. Walker forgot about the Stromness lifeboat rather than refusing permission for her to be launched, but while she might have saved some lives it is unlikely she could have saved many.

(8) There were several other significant shortcomings in the naval and military rescue efforts, but even the most zealous and competent response would not have prevented the loss of most of the 737 lives from drowning or hypothermia within an hour or so of the sinking.

(9) There were only 12 survivors. Some reached safety through their own efforts, some with assistance by local farmers, and some with assistance by Marines and Territorials from Ness Battery, Stromness, some of whom were at the cliff-tops shortly after the two rafts arrived.

(10) Contemporary evidence clearly shows that no bodies came ashore in Birsay, that the authorities generally welcomed civilians searching for and rescuing survivors, and that there was no general order that they should keep away from the cliffs. But it does seem likely that traditions to the contrary arose from an officer having stopped some farmers in Sandwick from lowering a colleague down a cliff on a rope, and from another officer later having ordered local inhabitants to disperse rather than witness or impede the difficult and gruesome task of moving mutilated bodies from the cliff tops to waiting lorries.

(11) The perception of the authorities having been incompetent, arrogant, insensitive and patronising caused deep sense of outrage amongst Orcadians that persists today.

(12) Given the public popularity of Lord Kitchener in 1916 it was inevitable that his death would trigger numerous conspiracy theories. These theories were exploited by Power, and the attempts in the Admiralty's Narrative of 1926 to refute them were not convincing. To his credit McCormick ridiculed many of these theories, but it is now clear that he added others. There is no substantive evidence to support any of the alternate theories on the cause of the sinking of HMS *Hampshire* or on the fate of Lord Kitchener.

(13) Recent surveys have shown that parts of *Hampshire's* hull are now seriously deteriorating, as is to be expected with a wreck of this age, but contrary to earlier reports there is no evidence of salvage damage.

(14) Orcadians have welcomed the centenary of the loss of HMS *Hampshire* as an opportunity to better remember and honour all those who gave their lives off Marwick Head in June 1916.

Given the extent of the records now available and of the inconsistencies and omissions they contain, and the constraints of time and space associated with the preparation this volume, it is not pretended that the above conclusions are the last word on this saga. But they have been developed with diligence and the benefit of hindsight, and without intentional bias. The authors apologise for any errors in the text, and regret it has not been possible to include all the memorabilia of their many correspondents or who attended the centenary events.

It is hoped that this volume is a fitting tribute to those 746 brave men. May their souls rest in peace.

Appendix I

ROLL OF HONOUR

MEMBERS OF THE MISSION TO RUSSIA

BROWN, Driver, DAVID CLIFFE, Age 32. 43rd Brigade Royal Horse Artillery. Commemorated on the Hollybrook Memorial, Southampton, panel 1.

DONALDSON, Temporary Brigadier-General, Sir HAY FREDERICK, KCB. Age 59. *Chief Technical Adviser to the Ministry of Munitions.* Commemorated on the Hollybrook Memorial, Southampton..

ELLERSHAW, Brigadier-General, WILFRID, Royal Artillery. Age 44. *War Office Representative. From Cosham, Hampshire.* Commemorated on the Hollybrook Memorial, Southampton.

FITZGERALD, Lieutenant-Colonel, OSWALD ARTHUR GERALD, CMG, 18th King George's Own Lancers. Age 40. *Personal Military Secretary to Field Marshal Lord Kitchener. Son of the late Colonel Sir Charles Fitzgerald.* Buried in Eastbourne (Ocklynge) Cemetery, East Sussex, grave X1677

GURNEY, Mr JAMES WALTER. *Valet to Mr O'Beirne.*

KITCHENER, Field Marshal the Right Honourable Lord, HORATIO HERBERT, KG, KP, GCB, OM, GCSI, GCMG, GCIE. Age 65. *Secretary of State for War.* Commemorated on the Hollybrook Memorial, Southampton and the Kitchener Memorial, Marwick Head, Orkney.

MACPHERSON, Second Lieutenant, ROBERT DAVID. Age 19. 8th Battalion Cameron Highlanders. *Russian Language Interpreter.* Buried at Lyness Royal Naval Cemetery, grave F.5A.

McLOUGHLIN, Detective Sergeant, MATTHEW. Age 37. *Scotland Yard Special Branch, Kitchener's personal protection officer. Born Co.Tipperary.* Commemorated in the Metropolitan Police Book of Remembrance, London.

O'BEIRNE, Mr HUGH JAMES, CVO CB. Age 49. *Minister, British Foreign Office.* Commemorated in the Chapel of Balliol College, Oxford.

RIX, Mr LEONARD CHARLES. Age 31. *Shorthand Clerk to Mr O'Beirne.*

ROBERTSON, Temporary Lieutenant-Colonel, LESLIE STEPHEN. Age 52. *Deputy Director of Production at the Ministry of Munitions.* Commemorated on the Hollybrook Memorial, Southampton.

SHIELDS, Mr WILLIAM. Age 24. *Valet to Lieut.-Col. Fitzgerald.*

SURGUY, Mr HENRY. Age 35. *Valet to Lord Kitchener.* Commemorated on the Roll of Honour at Freemason's Hall, London.

WEST, Mr FRANCIS PETER. Age 30. Valet to Brigadier-General Donaldson.

HMS *HAMPSHIRE* – SHIP's COMPANY

ABURROW, Officer's Cook 1st Class, JOHN ALBERT, 366364(Po), RN. Age 26. Buried at Lyness Royal Naval Cemetery, grave F.51.

ADAMS, Stoker 1st Class, HAROLD, K 18655(Po), RN. Age 22. *From Stapenhill, Burton-on-Trent.* Commemorated on the Portsmouth Naval Memorial.

ADAMS, Able Seaman, WALTER FREDERICK, J 19641(Po), RN. Age 19. *From Branksome, Bournemouth.* Commemorated on the Portsmouth Naval Memorial.

ADAMS, Private, WALTER HORACE, 18508(Po), RMLI. Age 18. Buried at Lyness Royal Naval Cemetery, grave F.111 Special Memorial.

ALEXANDER, Chaplain, PHILIP GEORGE, RN. Age 33. *From Portland Place, Bath.* Commemorated on the Portsmouth Naval Memorial.

ALLEN, Leading Stoker, ERNEST ALFRED, K 12783(Po), RN. Age 25. *From Camberley, Surrey.* Commemorated on the Portsmouth Naval Memorial.

ALLEN, Boy 1st Class, FRED HENRY, J 36182(Ch), RN. Age 17. Buried at Lyness Royal Naval Cemetery, grave F.105.

ALLEN, Stoker 1st Class, WILLIAM BRINKLEY, K 28354(Po), RN. Age 27. *From Featherstone, Pontefract.* Commemorated on the Portsmouth Naval Memorial.

ALLUM, Able Seaman, GEORGE ADIN, J 5224(Po), RN. Age 24. *From Portsmouth.* Commemorated on the Portsmouth Naval Memorial.

AMEY, Stoker 1st Class, NELSON PERCIVAL, K 23664(Po), RN. Age 19. *From Oving, Chichester.* Commemorated on the Portsmouth Naval Memorial.

AMEY, Private, WILLIAM JOHN, 15312(Po), RMLI. Age 21. *From Kingston, Portsmouth.* Commemorated on the Portsmouth Naval Memorial.

AMOS, Ordinary Seaman, JOSEPH JAMES, J 34405(Ch), RN. Age 18. Buried at Lyness Royal Naval Cemetery, grave F.529.

AMY, Shipwright 1st Class, WILLIAM MONAMY, 342066(Po), RN. Age 42. *From Southsea, Portsmouth.* Commemorated on the Portsmouth Naval Memorial.

ATTWOOD, Able Seaman, CHARLES ERNEST, J 17801(Po), RN. Age 19. *From Maidenhead, Berkshire.* Commemorated on the Portsmouth Naval Memorial.

ATTWOOD, Cook's Mate, GEORGE, M 3075(Po), RN. Age 24. *From Twickenham, Middlesex.* Buried at Lyness Royal Naval Cemetery, grave F.110A Special Memorial.

AUSTIN, Leading Seaman, ALBERT EDWARD, J 5810(Po), RN. Age 23. Buried at Lyness Royal Naval Cemetery, grave F.92.

AYLING, Stoker 1st Class, CHARLES GEORGE JOSEPH, K 18369(Po), RN. Age 22. *From Chichester, Hampshire.* Commemorated on the Portsmouth Naval Memorial.

AYTON, Ordinary Seaman, GEORGE, J 38127(Po), RN. Age 18. *From Harlesden, London.* Commemorated on the Portsmouth Naval Memorial.

BAGLEY, Stoker, JOHN LUKE, S 5069(Ch), RNR. Age 21. *From Middlesborough.* Commemorated on the Portsmouth Naval Memorial.

BAILEY, Petty Officer, CHARLES, 220840(Po), RN. Age 29. Commemorated on the Portsmouth Naval Memorial.

BAILEY, Leading Seaman, GEORGE, 220838(Po), RN. Age 29. *From Southwick, Brighton.* Commemorated on the Portsmouth Naval Memorial.

BAILEY, Able Seaman, HENRY RICHARD, 222144(Po), RN. Age 30. *From Kingston-on-Thames.* Commemorated on the Portsmouth Naval Memorial.

BAILEY, Officer's Steward 3rd Class, JOHN CHARLES, L 6110(Dev), RN. Age 24. *From Everton, Liverpool.* Commemorated on the Plymouth Naval Memorial.

BAINES, Stoker 1st Class, SAMUEL, K 23163(Po), RN. Age 19. Buried at Lyness Royal Naval Cemetery, grave F.103A.

BAKER, Private, FREDERICK GEORGE, 18006(Po), RMLI. Age 19. Commemorated on the Portsmouth Naval Memorial.

BAKER, Able Seaman, PERCY, J 2584(Po), RN. Age 23. Commemorated on the Portsmouth Naval Memorial.

BALLARD, Blacksmith, ROBERT GEORGE, 346630(Po), RN. Age 33. Buried at Lyness Royal Naval Cemetery, grave F.52.

BANCROFT, Able Seaman, ISAAC, 216601(Po), RN. Age 29. Buried at Lyness Royal Naval Cemetery, grave F.38A.

BANWELL, Stoker, ERNEST JOHN, S 9050(Ch), RNR. Age 33. Commemorated on the Chatham Naval Memorial.

BARBEARY, Able Seaman, CHARLES HENRY, J 18428(Po), RN. Age 21. *From Ilfracombe, Devon.* Commemorated on the Portsmouth Naval Memorial.

BARGEN, Boy 1st Class, THOMAS EDWARD, J 38133(Po), RN. Age 16. *From Hoxton, London.* Commemorated on the Portsmouth Naval Memorial.

BARNARD, Painter 1st Class, JAMES EDWARD THOMAS, 341857(Po), RN. Age 38. *From Buckland, Portsmouth.* Buried at Lyness Royal Naval Cemetery, grave F.30.

BARNETT, Able Seaman, JOHN, J 18938(Po), RN. Age 19. *From Hammersmith, London.* Commemorated on the Portsmouth Naval Memorial.

BARROW, Engine Room Artificer 4th Class, NORMAN, M 1508(Po), RN. Age 22. Commemorated on the Portsmouth Naval Memorial.

BARTLETT, Canteen Manager, FRANK HUBERT, Admiralty Civilian(Dev), . Age 58. Commemorated on the Plymouth Naval Memorial.

BARTLETT, Mechanician, GEORGE, 284537(Po), RN. Age 38. Commemorated on the Portsmouth Naval Memorial.

BARTLETT, Able Seaman, GEORGE, Sussex 4/172, RNVR. Age 24. Buried at Lyness Royal Naval Cemetery, grave F.66.

BARTLETT, Shipwright 2nd Class, VICTOR GEORGE, M 6528(Po), RN. Age 25. *From North End, Portsmouth.* Commemorated on the Portsmouth Naval Memorial.

BATES, Sailmaker, ARTHUR, 166115(Po), RN. Age 39. Commemorated on the Portsmouth Naval Memorial.

BATES, Petty Officer, BERNARD EMILE, 222551(Po), RN. Age 29. *From Hampstead, London.* Commemorated on the Portsmouth Naval Memorial.

BATES, Acting Leading Stoker, GEORGE, K 2105(Po), RN. Age 26. Commemorated on the Portsmouth Naval Memorial.

BAULK, Ordinary Seaman, ARTHUR STANLEY, J 35732(Po), RN. Age 20. *From London.* Commemorated on the Portsmouth Naval Memorial.

BAYNES, Stoker 1st Class, GEORGE ALBERT, K 25448(Po), RN. Age 29. Commemorated on the Portsmouth Naval Memorial.

BEAN, Acting Leading Stoker, FREDERICK FRANK, K 6026(Po), RN. Age 24. *From Broadstairs, Kent.* Commemorated on the Portsmouth Naval Memorial.

BEAR, Leading Telegraphist, JOHN VICTOR, J 9897(Ch), RN. Age 22. *From Ramsgate, Kent.* Commemorated on the Chatham Naval Memorial.

BEARMAN, Chief Armourer, WALTER JOHN, 146489(Po), RN. Age 45. *From Woolston, Southampton. Awarded Long Service and Good Conduct Medal.* Commemorated on the Portsmouth Naval Memorial.

BECK, Petty Officer Stoker, GEORGE EDWARD, 307322(Po), RN. Age 31. *From South Tottenham, London.* Commemorated on the Portsmouth Naval Memorial.

BEECHEY, Stoker 1st Class, JOHN WILLIAM HARRY, K 16587(Po), RN. Age 21. *From Wantage, Berkshire.* Commemorated on the Portsmouth Naval Memorial.

BEESTON, Able Seaman, GEORGE STANLEY, J 14129(Po), RN. Age 20. Buried at Lyness Royal Naval Cemetery, grave F.99.

BELCHAMBER, Leading Stoker, EDWARD, 303849(Po), RN. Age 32. *From East Dulwich, London.* Commemorated on the Portsmouth Naval Memorial.

BELL, Stoker 1st Class, WILLIAM ARTHUR, SS 116494(Po), RN. Age 19. Commemorated on the Portsmouth Naval Memorial.

BENNETT, Able Seaman, LESTER STONE, Sussex 5/112, RNVR. Age 24. Buried at Lyness Royal Naval Cemetery, grave F.69.

BENNETT, Leading Seaman, WILLIAM HENRY, 220975(Po), RN. Age 30. Commemorated on the Portsmouth Naval Memorial.

BENTLEY, Stoker 1st Class, FREDERICK, K 24268(Po), RN. Age 35. Commemorated on the Portsmouth Naval Memorial.

BEVERLEY, Able Seaman, ROBERT, J 15794(Po), RN. Age 20. *From Holbeck, Leeds.* Commemorated on the Portsmouth Naval Memorial.

BEX, Boy 1st Class, WILLIAM LUKE, J 31809(Ch), RN. Age 17. *From Richmond, Surrey.* Commemorated on the Portsmouth Naval Memorial.

BILLINGHAM, Stoker 1st Class, BERTIE, SS 112506(Po), RN. Age 27. *From Birmingham.* Commemorated on the Portsmouth Naval Memorial.

BILLINS, Corporal, WILLIAM EDWARD, 15603(Po), RMLI. Age 24. *From Isleworth, Middlesex.* Commemorated on the Portsmouth Naval Memorial.

BIRTLES, Boy 1st Class, ROBERT, J 35535(Po), RN. Age 17. *From Bootle, Liverpool.* Commemorated on the Portsmouth Naval Memorial.

BISHOP, Able Seaman, GEORGE SAMUEL JOHN, J 1036(Po), RN. Age 24. Commemorated on the Portsmouth Naval Memorial.

BLACK, Petty Officer Stoker, ROBERT BROTHERTON, K 13405(Po), RN. Age 26. *From Sunderland.* Commemorated on the Portsmouth Naval Memorial.

BLACKSHAW, Boy 1st Class, GEORGE, J 37182(Dev), RN. Age 17. *From Rochdale, Lancashire.* Commemorated on the Plymouth Naval Memorial.

BLAKE, Stoker 1st Class, EDWARD ALLAN JOHNIE, K 18723(Po), RN. Age 21. *From Worthing, Sussex.* Commemorated on the Portsmouth Naval Memorial.

BLANDFORD, Leading Stoker, SIDNEY TOM, K 3760(Po), RN. Age 29. *From Hampshire.* Commemorated on the Portsmouth Naval Memorial.

BLOOR, Boy 1st Class, THOMAS, J 35047(Po), RN. Age 17. *From Leek, Staffordshire.* Commemorated on the Portsmouth Naval Memorial.

BOBBETT, Leading Seaman, JOHN JOSEPH, 183495(Po), RN. Age 37. *From Bridport, Dorset.* Commemorated on the Portsmouth Naval Memorial.

BOND, Ship's Corporal 1st Class, GEORGE HARRY, 190843(Po), RN. Age 34. *From Portsmouth.* Commemorated on the Portsmouth Naval Memorial.

BONNICK, Able Seaman, HENRY ALEXANDER WILLIAM, J 15306(Po), RN. Age 20. Commemorated on the Portsmouth Naval Memorial.

BORAMAN, Private, RICHARD JOHN, 16464(Po), RMLI. Age 21. Commemorated on the Portsmouth Naval Memorial.

BORNE, Leading Seaman, JAMES HERBERT, J 8120(Po), RN. Age 22. Commemorated on the Portsmouth Naval Memorial.

BOSWORTH, Officer's Steward 3rd Class, MATTHEW JAMES, L 6929(Dev), RN. Age 32. Commemorated on the Plymouth Naval Memorial.

BOWEN, Stoker 1st Class, GEORGE WILLIAM, K 7676(Po), RN. Age 26. Commemorated on the Portsmouth Naval Memorial.

BRAGG, Engine Room Artificer 3rd Class, JAMES ALBERT, M 4425(Po), RN. Age 26. *From Eastbourne, Sussex.* Commemorated on the Portsmouth Naval Memorial.

BRAIN, Boy 1st Class, WILLIAM HENRY, J 37295(Ch), RN. Age 16. Commemorated on the Chatham Naval Memorial.

BRIDGES, Private, WILLIAM FITZHERBERT, 12019(Po), RMLI. Age 32. *From Southsea, Portsmouth.* Buried at Lyness Royal Naval Cemetery, grave F.27.

BRINDLEY, Stoker 1st Class, JOSEPH, K 11585(Po), RN. Age 25. *From Brierley Hill, Staffordshire.* Buried at Lyness Royal Naval Cemetery, grave F.112.

BRISCOE, Signal Boy, JOHN, J 32605(Po), RN. Age 17. *From St.Leonards-on-Sea, Sussex.* Commemorated on the Portsmouth Naval Memorial.

BROAD, Stoker 1st Class, WILLIAM HUGH, K 16856(Po), RN. Age 21. Commemorated on the Portsmouth Naval Memorial.

BROCKWAY, Boy Telegraphist, ALFRED GEORGE CHARLES, J 32560(Po), RN. Age 17. *From Buckland, Portsmouth.* Commemorated on the Portsmouth Naval Memorial.

BROWN, Stoker 1st Class, ROBERT, K 24050(Po), RN. Age 22. Commemorated on the Portsmouth Naval Memorial.

BROWN, Stoker, WILLIAM, S 4956(Po), RNR. Age 23. *From Whiteabbey, Co.Antrim.* Commemorated on the Portsmouth Naval Memorial.

BROWNING, Able Seaman, HARRY, J 15337(Po), RN. Age 20. *From Newhaven, Sussex.* Buried at Lyness Royal Naval Cemetery, grave F.91.

BUCKENHAM, Private, JOHN THOMAS, 8756(Po), RMLI. Age 37. *From Kings Lynn, Norfolk.* Buried at Lyness Royal Naval Cemetery, grave F.40A.

BUCKINGHAM, Able Seaman, RALPH ANGUS, J 12609(Po), RN. Age 21. *From Hethersett, Norfolk.* Commemorated on the Portsmouth Naval Memorial.

BUNTING, Able Seaman, THOMAS, Bristol Z/4941, RNVR. Age 18. *From Codnor, Derby.* Buried at Lyness Royal Naval Cemetery, grave F.104.

BURDEN, Stoker 1st Class, ERNEST, K 18703(Po), RN. Age 21. *From Stockwith, Doncaster.* Commemorated on the Portsmouth Naval Memorial.

BURFOOT, Able Seaman, CHARLES NELSON NEWBURY, J 15405(Po), RN. Age 20. Commemorated on the Portsmouth Naval Memorial.

BURREN, Engine Room Artificer 3rd Class, GEORGE PERCY, M 137(Po), RN. Age 24. Commemorated on the Portsmouth Naval Memorial.

BURROWS, Boy 1st Class, ALFRED, J 38128(Po), RN. Age 17. *From* Commemorated on the Portsmouth Naval Memorial.

BURTON, Acting Leading Stoker, JAMES ROBERT, K 2447(Po), RN. Age 25. Commemorated on the Portsmouth Naval Memorial.

BURY, Leading Signalman, FREDERICK, 224023(Po), RN. Age 28. Buried at Lyness Royal Naval Cemetery, grave F.109A Special Memorial.

BUSBY, Able Seaman, WALTER SYDNEY, 226842(Po), RN. Age 28. *From Southsea, Portsmouth.* Commemorated on the Portsmouth Naval Memorial.

BUTLER, Stoker 1st Class, FREDERICK EDWARD, K 18641(Po), RN. Age 21. *From New Cross, London.* Commemorated on the Portsmouth Naval Memorial.

BUTLER, Private, GEORGE INKERMAN, 7968(Po), RMLI. Age 39. Commemorated on the Portsmouth Naval Memorial.

BUTLER, Clerk, RALPH TWISDEN, RN. Age 20. Buried at Lyness Royal Naval Cemetery, grave F.4.

BYNG, Mechanician, JAMES, 286748(Po), RN. Age 38. Commemorated on the Portsmouth Naval Memorial.

CADBY, Ship's Corporal 1st Class, WILLIAM GEORGE, 229398(Po), RN. Age 29. *From Maida Hill, London.* Commemorated on the Portsmouth Naval Memorial.

CADMAN, Stoker 1st Class, CHARLES, SS 113678(Po), RN. Age 21. *From Mansfield, Nottinghamshire.* Commemorated on the Portsmouth Naval Memorial.

CAKE, Petty Officer Stoker, WILLIAM, 283898(Po), RN. Age 38. *From East Cowes, Isle of Wight.* Buried at Lyness Royal Naval Cemetery, grave F.37A.

CAMERON, Petty Officer Stoker, WILLIAM JAMES, K 3219(Po), RN. Age 25. *From Lower Edmonton, London.* Commemorated on the Portsmouth Naval Memorial.

CANNON, Ordinary Seaman, JAMES ALFRED, J 27906(Po), RN. Age 17. *From Forest Hill, London.* Commemorated on the Portsmouth Naval Memorial.

CARD, Ordinary Seaman, WILLIAM GEORGE BARNARD, J 34484(Ch), RN. Age 18. *From East Ham, London.* Commemorated on the Chatham Naval Memorial.

CARTER, Ordinary Seaman, CYRIL CHARLES WILLIAM ARTHUR, J 38287(Ch), RN. Age 18. *From Barnes, London.* Commemorated on the Chatham Naval Memorial.

CARTER, Petty Officer, THOMAS EDWIN, 195915(Po), RN. Age 27. *From Gosport, Hampshire.* Commemorated on the Portsmouth Naval Memorial.

CARVIN, Seaman, CHARLES, D 2115(Po), RNR. Age 48. *From Balbriggan, Co.Dublin.* Buried at Lyness Royal Naval Cemetery, grave F.10.

CHAMBERS, Shipwright 2nd Class, ARTHUR HARRY, 345776(Po), RN. Age 33. *From Landport, Portsmouth.* Commemorated on the Portsmouth Naval Memorial.

I – Roll of Honour

CHAPLIN, Surgeon, HAROLD GARRETT, RN. Age 28. Buried at Lyness Royal Naval Cemetery, grave F.2A.

CHARLTON, Lieutenant, ADOLPH COLES, RNR. Age 25. *From Northgate, Hartlepool.* Commemorated on the Portsmouth Naval Memorial.

CHEATER, Able Seaman, HARRY JAMES, 200894(Po), RN. Age 33. Commemorated on the Portsmouth Naval Memorial.

CHESWORTH, Petty Officer, ALEXANDER, 205341(Po), RN. Age 33. *From Southsea, Portsmouth.* Commemorated on the Portsmouth Naval Memorial.

CHILD, Cooper, ALBERT ERNEST, 342343(Po), RN. Age 38. *From Portsmouth.* Commemorated on the Portsmouth Naval Memorial.

CHITTY, Petty Officer Stoker, ALBERT, K 3738(Po), RN. Age 26. *From Arundel, Sussex.* Commemorated on the Portsmouth Naval Memorial.

CLARK, Master-at-Arms, WILLIAM, 180547(Po), RN. Age 38. *From Holt, Wiltshire.* Commemorated on the Portsmouth Naval Memorial.

CLAY, Leading Stoker, FRANCIS, 307315(Po), RN. Age 30. *From Quinton, Birmingham.* Commemorated on the Portsmouth Naval Memorial.

CLAYTON, Petty Officer 1st Class, WILLIAM, 162921(Po), RN. Age 40. *From Eastbourne, Sussex.* Commemorated on the Portsmouth Naval Memorial.

CLEARY, Stoker 1st Class, FRANK WILLIAM, SS 113682(Po), RN. Age 22. Commemorated on the Portsmouth Naval Memorial.

COLBECK, Signal Boy, PERCY, J 37186(Dev), RN. Age 16. Commemorated on the Plymouth Naval Memorial.

COLE, Telegraphist, FRANCIS GEOFFREY, J 18968(Po), RN. Age 19. *From Horsham, Sussex.* Commemorated on the Portsmouth Naval Memorial.

COLLECOTT, Boy 1st Class, FREDERICK GEORGE, J 34591, RN. Age 17. Buried at Lyness Royal Naval Cemetery, grave F.97A.

COLLETT, Ordinary Seaman, JOHN WILLIAM, SS 6825(Po), RN. Age 19. *From Southsea, Portsmouth.* Commemorated on the Portsmouth Naval Memorial.

COLLIER, Able Seaman, STANLEY, 234001(Po), RN. Age 28. *From Tring, Hertfordshire.* Buried at Lyness Royal Naval Cemetery, grave F.33A.

COLLINS, Leading Seaman, SAMUEL, J 8327(Po), RN. Age 23. *From Aldeburgh, Suffolk.* Commemorated on the Portsmouth Naval Memorial.

COLLIS, Able Seaman, WILLIAM THOMAS, J 19117(Po), RN. Age 19. *From Fratton, Portsmouth.* Commemorated on the Portsmouth Naval Memorial.

COMPTON, Private, ALFRED WALTER, 14780(Po), RMLI. Age 29. *From Bognor, Sussex.* Commemorated on the Portsmouth Naval Memorial.

CONNOLLEY, Stoker, PATRICK, S 8784(Ch), RNR. Age 26. Commemorated on the Chatham Naval Memorial.

CONSTABLE, Ordinary Seaman, LEONARD ALBERT LONGMAN, J 29980(Po), RN. Age 18. *From Farnborough, Hampshire.* Commemorated on the Portsmouth Naval Memorial.

COOGAN, Stoker 1st Class, JOHN, K 24407(Po), RN. Age 19. *From Liverpool.* Commemorated on the Portsmouth Naval Memorial.

COOK, Mate, FREDERICK, RN. Age 28. *From Wellingborough, Northamptonshire.* Buried at Lyness Royal Naval Cemetery, grave F.2.

COOKE, Plumber, HORATIO NELSON, 344481(Po), RN. Age 37. *From East Liss, Hampshire.* Commemorated on the Portsmouth Naval Memorial.

COOMBS, Petty Officer, JOSEPH REGINALD, 229114(Po), RN. Age 48. Commemorated on the Portsmouth Naval Memorial.

COOPER, Boy 1st Class, GEORGE HENRY, J 37120(Ch), RN. Age 17. Commemorated on the Chatham Naval Memorial.

COOPER, Able Seaman, WILLIAM LEONARD MARTIN, 176448(Po), RN. Age 38. Commemorated on the Portsmouth Naval Memorial.

COPE, Able Seaman, HERBERT, 178066(Po), RN. Age 37. Commemorated on the Portsmouth Naval Memorial.

COSSEY, Engineer Commander, ARTHUR ERNEST, RN. Age 40. Buried at Lyness Royal Naval Cemetery, grave F.1A.

COULTHARD, Able Seaman, THOMAS, Tyneside Z/1070(Ch), RNVR. Age 22. Commemorated on the Chatham Naval Memorial.

COVEY, Leading Stoker, JESSE EDMUND, 308428(Po), RN. Age 29. Buried at Lyness Royal Naval Cemetery, grave F.33.

COWLEY, Stoker 1st Class, GEORGE WILLIAM, SS 112510(Po), RN. Age 28. *From Clay Cross, Chesterfield.* Commemorated on the Portsmouth Naval Memorial.

COX, Carpenter's Crew, HENRY, 304514(Po), RN. Age 38. Commemorated on the Portsmouth Naval Memorial.

COX, Chief Stoker, JAMES, 281752(Po), RN. Age 39. *From Shorwell, Isle of Wight.* Commemorated on the Portsmouth Naval Memorial.

COX, Leading Signalman, JOHN CHRISTOPHER, 231899(Ch), RN. Age 29. *From Glasnevin, Dublin.* Commemorated on the Chatham Naval Memorial.

COYLE, Stoker 1st Class, JOHN, K 27971(Po), RN. Age 26. *From Manchester.* Commemorated on the Portsmouth Naval Memorial.

CROMPTON, Private, EDWARD, 18514(Po), RMLI. Age 18. *From Liverpool.* Commemorated on the Portsmouth Naval Memorial.

CROSS, Private, ANDREW, 13168(Po), RMLI. Age 30. *From Manningham, Bradford.* Commemorated on the Portsmouth Naval Memorial.

CRUSE, Staff Paymaster, PERCY, RN. Age 37. Commemorated on the Portsmouth Naval Memorial.

CULLINGTON, Signalman, FREDERICK THEODORE, Mersey 7/237, RNVR. Age 20. *From Bootle, Lnacashire.* Commemorated on the Plymouth Naval Memorial.

CUMMING, Leading Signalman, DONALD, 230025(Po), RN. Age 29. *From Portree, Isle of Skye.* Commemorated on the Portsmouth Naval Memorial.

CUNNINGHAM, Boy 1st Class, HENRY, J 34315(Po), RN. Age 17. *From Hackney Wick, London.* Commemorated on the Chatham Naval Memorial.

CUNNINGHAM, Seaman, JAMES, A 8031(Po), RNR. Age 38. *From Newry, Co.Down. Served in the Royal Irish Fusiliers and was wounded in the South African War.* Commemorated on the Portsmouth Naval Memorial.

DABBS, Chief Petty Officer, HERBERT, 173852(Po), RN. Age 38. Buried at Lyness Royal Naval Cemetery, grave F.111A Special Memorial.

DAGWELL, Stoker 1st Class, FRANK, K 15426(Po), RN. Age 23. Commemorated on the Portsmouth Naval Memorial.

DALLAS, Private, WILLIAM ALBERT EDWARD, 16959(Po), RMLI. Age 22. *From Portsea, Portsmouth.* Commemorated on the Portsmouth Naval Memorial.

DANIELS, Private, EDWARD, 14431(Po), RMLI. Age 27. *From Fareham, Hampshire.* Commemorated on the Portsmouth Naval Memorial.

DARBY, Blacksmith, WILLIAM GEORGE, 346868(Po), RN. Age 31. Commemorated on the Portsmouth Naval Memorial.

DASENT, Commander, MANUEL, RN. Age 37. Buried at Lyness Royal Naval Cemetery, grave F.12A.

DAVEY, Seaman, ERNEST, J 14256(Po), RN. Age 21. *From Stratford, London.* Commemorated on the Portsmouth Naval Memorial.

DAVIS, Signal Boy, ARTHUR, J 39824(Dev), RN. Age 16. Buried at Lyness Royal Naval Cemetery, grave F.106A.

DAWSON, Ship's Steward, ALFRED WILLIAM ARTHUR, 342334(Po), RN. Age 32. Commemorated on the Portsmouth Naval Memorial.

DAWSON, Private, JOHN BURROW, 17920(Po), RMLI. Age 19. *From Kirkby Lonsdale, Westmorland.* Buried at Lyness Royal Naval Cemetery, grave F.32.

DE STE CROIX, Petty Officer, WALTER BERTRAM, J 2836(Po), RN. Age 23. *From Milton, Portsmouth.* Buried at Lyness Royal Naval Cemetery, grave F.69.

DEAN, Serjeant, FRANK POYSER, 11666(Po), RMLI. Age 31. Buried at Lyness Royal Naval Cemetery, grave F.8.

DENHAM, Engine Room Artificer 1st Class, HERBERT SMITH, 269018(Po), RN. Age 43. *From East Cowes, Isle of Wight. Served in South African War. Awarded China Medal (1900). Awarded Long Service and Good Conduct Medal.* Commemorated on the Portsmouth Naval Memorial.

DENNIS, Stoker 1st Class, HARRY, K 26497(Po), RN. Age 24. Commemorated on the Portsmouth Naval Memorial.

DEVESON, Ordinary Seaman, PERCY WILLIAM, J 33172(Po), RN. Age 18. Buried at Lyness Royal Naval Cemetery, grave F.94A.

DEVLIN, Stoker, JAMES, S 5057(Ch), RNR. Age 35. *From Cookestown, Co.Tyrone.* Commemorated on the Chatham Naval Memorial.

DIAMOND, Petty Officer, CHARLES HENRY, 186566(Po), RN. Age 36. *From Kingston, Portsmouth.* Commemorated on the Portsmouth Naval Memorial.

DIAPER, Petty Officer 1st Class, HENRY JAMES, 182315(Po), RN. Age 36. Commemorated on the Portsmouth Naval Memorial.

DOCHERTY, Stoker, ROBERT, S 5278(Po), RNR. Age 31. *From Kyles Brae, Coleraine, Co.Londonderry.* Commemorated on the Portsmouth Naval Memorial.

DODD, Stoker 1st Class, WILLIAM, K 24689(Po), RN. Age 24. Commemorated on the Portsmouth Naval Memorial.

DOHERTY, Stoker, MICHAEL, S 4795(Po), RNR. Age 33. *From Assistant Superintendant of Shibden Industrial School, Halifax, Yorkshire.* Commemorated on the Portsmouth Naval Memorial.

DOMINEY, Private, CHARLES JOHN, 16411(Po), RMLI. Age 25. *From Wareham, Dorset.* Commemorated on the Portsmouth Naval Memorial.

DONNELLY, Able Seaman, GEORGE NICHOLSON, J 15300(Po), RN. Age 20. *From Kirkcudbright.* Commemorated on the Portsmouth Naval Memorial.

DOOLEY, Private, SEPTIMUS, 15817(Ch), RMLI. Age 26. *From Withington, Manchester.* Commemorated on the Chatham Naval Memorial.

DOVE, Ordinary Seaman, GEORGE WILLIAM, J 33497(Ch), RN. Age 18. Commemorated on the Chatham Naval Memorial.

DOWLAND, Private, SIDNEY JOSEPH, 8384(Po), RMLI. Age 40. *From Horton Heath, Wimborne, Dorset.* Buried at Lyness Royal Naval Cemetery, grave F.51A.

DOWNES, 3rd Writer, JOHN, M 12230(Po), RN. Age 23. *From London.* Buried at Lyness Royal Naval Cemetery, grave F.114 Special Memorial.

DOWSON, Stoker 1st Class, JOSEPH, SS 116366(Po), RN. Age 21. *From Middlesborough.* Commemorated on the Portsmouth Naval Memorial.

DRUMMOND, Stoker 1st Class, FREDERICK GEORGE, SS 116370(Po), RN. Age 20. *From Liverpool.* Commemorated on the Portsmouth Naval Memorial.

DUFF, Stoker, PETER, S 6916(Po), RNR. Age 22. Commemorated on the Portsmouth Naval Memorial.

DUFFIN, Stoker 1st Class, ANDREW JOE, SS 116500(Po), RN. Age 20. *From St.Denys, Southampton.* Commemorated on the Portsmouth Naval Memorial.

DUNCAN, Petty Officer, ALEXANDER JAMES CHARLES, 200356(Po), RN. Age 33. Buried at Lyness Royal Naval Cemetery, grave F.96.

DUNN, Telegraphist, LESLIE GEORGE ARTHUR, J 19122(Po), RN. Age 19. Commemorated on the Portsmouth Naval Memorial.

DURRANT, Petty Officer Telegraphist, GEORGE WYNN, 205599(Ch), RN. Age 32. Buried at Lyness Royal Naval Cemetery, grave F.34A.

DYER, Petty Officer, GEORGE, 160876(Po), RN. Age 40. *From North End, Portsmouth.* Commemorated on the Portsmouth Naval Memorial.

EADES, Able Seaman, JAMES, 238050(Po), RN. Age 26. *From Lewes, Sussex.* Commemorated on the Portsmouth Naval Memorial.

EAST, Stoker 1st Class, ERNEST RICHARD, SS 113679(Po), RN. Age 23. *From Far Cotton, Northampton.* Commemorated on the Portsmouth Naval Memorial.

ECCLESTON, Stoker, NORMAN, S 3263(Po), RNR. Age 26. Commemorated on the Portsmouth Naval Memorial.

EDWARDS, Private, IVOR STANLEY REGINALD REX, 17984(Po), RMLI. Age 19. *From Fromefield, Frome, Somerset.* Commemorated on the Portsmouth Naval Memorial.

ELLISON, Serjeant, VICTOR, 13015(Po), RMLI. Age 31. *From Battersea, London.* Commemorated on the Portsmouth Naval Memorial.

ELMER, Chief Stoker, GEORGE JONATHAN, 277097(Po), RN. Age 41. (Served as GEORGE KENNETT.) *From Southsea, Portsmouth.* Commemorated on the Portsmouth Naval Memorial.

ELSON, Ship's Steward's Assistant, REGINALD MALCOLM, M 11016(Po), RN. Age 19. *From Beckenham, Kent.* Commemorated on the Portsmouth Naval Memorial.

EPPS, Petty Officer Stoker, JOHN FREDERICK, 282938(Po), RN. Age 39. *From Faversham, Kent.* Commemorated on the Portsmouth Naval Memorial.

EVANS, Boy 1st Class, GEORGE MAFEKING, J 44718(Po), RN. Age 16. *From Gillingham, Kent.* Commemorated on the Portsmouth Naval Memorial.

EVANS, Mechanician, JOSEPH, 306289(Po), RN. Age 34. *From Burton-on-Trent.* Commemorated on the Portsmouth Naval Memorial.

EVANS, Private, PERCY, 16455(Po), RMLI. Age 20. Buried at Lyness Royal Naval Cemetery, grave F.31.

EVANS, Able Seaman, ROBERT, Tyneside Z/779, RNVR. Age 20. *From Chirton, North Shields.* Commemorated on the Chatham Naval Memorial.

EVANS, Boy 1st Class, WILLIAM ARTHUR, J 38126(Po), RN. Age 16. Buried at Lyness Royal Naval Cemetery, grave F.100.

EVERETT, Ordinary Seaman, WALTER, J 41770(Po), RN. Age 24. *From Fakenham, Norfolk.* Commemorated on the Portsmouth Naval Memorial.

EWING, Able Seaman, WALTER, J 29000(Po), RN. Age 18. *From Wimbledon, London.* Commemorated on the Portsmouth Naval Memorial.

EYRE, Stoker 1st Class, JAMES, K 18648(Po), RN. Age 21. *From Wingfield, Chesterfiled.* Commemorated on the Portsmouth Naval Memorial.

FALLOWFIELD, Acting Leading Stoker, ROBERT, K 26242(Po), RN. Age 27. Commemorated on the Portsmouth Naval Memorial.

FARINDON, Able Seaman, ARTHUR, 232486(Po), RN. Age 27. Commemorated on the Portsmouth Naval Memorial.

FARTHING, Private, WALTER THEOPHILUS, 13316(Po), RMLI. Age 33. *From Southsea, Portsmouth.* Commemorated on the Portsmouth Naval Memorial.

FEAR, Private, EDMUND CLAYWORTH, 17949(Po), RMLI. Age 18. *From Brislington, Bristol.* Commemorated on the Portsmouth Naval Memorial.

FELLOWES, Midshipman, EDMUND ETHELBERHT, RNR. Age 19. Commemorated on the Portsmouth Naval Memorial.

FELLOWS, Stoker 1st Class, BENJAMIN, K 18279(Po), RN. Age 22. Buried at Lyness Royal Naval Cemetery, grave F.94.

FERRETT, Yeoman of Signals, SYDNEY JAMES FRANCIS, 218658(Po), RN. Age 29. *From Southsea, Portsmouth.* Commemorated on the Portsmouth Naval Memorial.

FERRETT, Private, THOMAS CHRISTOPHER JAMES, 17553(Po), RMLI. Age 20. *From Verwood, Dorset.* Commemorated on the Portsmouth Naval Memorial.

FERRIMAN, Able Seaman, GEORGE FREDERICK WILLIAM, SS 4055(Po), RN. Age 25. *From Bulwell, Nottingham.* Commemorated on the Portsmouth Naval Memorial.

FIELD, Stoker 1st Class, GEORGE, K 15760(Po), RN. Age 23. *From Castleford, Yorkshire.* Commemorated on the Portsmouth Naval Memorial.

FIELDING, Signal Boy, PERCY, J 34598(Po), RN. Age 17. *From Rochdale, Lancashire.* Commemorated on the Portsmouth Naval Memorial.

FINCKEN, Artificer Engineer, CUTHBERT ABRAHAM TAYLOR, RN. Age 35. *From Plymouth.* Commemorated on the Plymouth Naval Memorial.

FISKEN, Warrant Engineer, PETER, RNR. Age 49. Buried at Lyness Royal Naval Cemetery, grave F.121.

FITCH, Ordinary Telegraphist, JOHN WALTER NEWLAND, J 30922(Po), RN. Age 17. Buried at Lyness Royal Naval Cemetery, grave F.106.

FITZGERALD, Stoker 1st Class, JOHN HENRY, K 24489(Po), RN. Age 19. *From Shirley, Southampton.* Commemorated on the Portsmouth Naval Memorial.

FLACK, Stoker 1st Class, FREDERICK, K 7187(Po), RN. Age 24. Buried at Lyness Royal Naval Cemetery, grave F.109 Special Memorial.

FLANAGAN, Boy 1st Class, BERNARD, J 38129(Po), RN. Age 16. *From Barnes, London.* Commemorated on the Portsmouth Naval Memorial.

FLAVIN, Leading Seaman, MICHAEL, 194183(Po), RN. Age 34. *From Rostellan, Co.Cork.* Commemorated on the Portsmouth Naval Memorial.

FLEMING, Canteen Assistant, JOHN HENRY, Admiralty Civilian (Ch). Age 19. *From Grimsby, Lincolnshire.* Commemorated on the Chatham Naval Memorial.

FLEMING, Signaller, MARTIN THOMAS, J 14984(Dev), RN. Age 20. *From Hammersmith, London.* Commemorated on the Plymouth Naval Memorial.

FLEXMAN, Leading Stoker, ERNEST FREDERICK, 221359(Po), RN. Age 29. Buried at Lyness Royal Naval Cemetery, grave F.8A.

FONEY, Ordinary Seaman, FRANCIS JOHN, J 43933(Po), RN. Age 20. *From St.Brelade's, Jersey.* Commemorated on the Portsmouth Naval Memorial.

FORREST, Able Seaman, GEORGE HENRY, 182501(Po), RN. Age 37. *From Dudley, Worcestershire.* Commemorated on the Portsmouth Naval Memorial.

FORREST, Stoker 1st Class, JOHN, K 27693(Po), RN. Age 24. *From Tullyhogue, Dungannon, Co.Tyrone.* Commemorated on the Portsmouth Naval Memorial.

FOSTER, Boy 1st Class(Bugler), EDWARD, J 34525, RN. Age 17. Buried at Lyness Royal Naval Cemetery, grave F.7.

FOSTER, Stoker 1st Class, JOB, K 24403(Po), RN. Age 24. Commemorated on the Portsmouth Naval Memorial.

FOTHERGILL, Able Seaman, EDWIN, 186166(Po), RN. Age 37. Buried at Lyness Royal Naval Cemetery, grave F.35A.

FOWLER, Canteen Assistant, ALFRED THOMAS, Admiralty Civilian(Ch). Age 18. *From Dover, Kent.* Commemorated on the Chatham Naval Memorial.

FRASER, Engine Room Artificer 4th Class, CECIL SAMUEL, M 19887(Po), RN. Age 23. Buried at Lyness Royal Naval Cemetery, grave F.9A.

FREEMAN, Able Seaman, WILLIAM ARTHUR, J 7559(Po), RN. Age 22. *From Portfield, Chichester.* Commemorated on the Portsmouth Naval Memorial.

FREEMAN, Private, WILLIAM CHARLES, 16779(Po), RMLI. Age 21. Commemorated on the Portsmouth Naval Memorial.

GALE, Petty Officer Stoker, HERBERT ARTHUR, 312109(Po), RN. Age 27. Commemorated on the Portsmouth Naval Memorial.

GALE, Able Seaman, WILLIAM, 183196(Po), RN. Age 36. *From Bridport, Somerset.* Commemorated on the Portsmouth Naval Memorial.

GANDER, Leading Stoker, JAMES, 307215(Po), RN. Age 32. *From Brighton, Sussex.* Commemorated on the Portsmouth Naval Memorial.

GARDNER, Boy Telegraphist, WALTER FLETCHER, J 31837(Dev), RN. Age 17. *From Manchester.* Commemorated on the Plymouth Naval Memorial.

GARRETT, Boy 1st Class, SAMUEL, J 34712(Dev), RN. Age 17. Commemorated on the Plymouth Naval Memorial.

GARRETT, Cook's Mate, WILLIAM JOHN, M 11809(Po), RN. Age 21. *From Farnham, Surrey.* Commemorated on the Portsmouth Naval Memorial.

GARSDEN, Artificer Electrical 2nd Class, JOSHUA WILLIAM VAUSE, 347074(Po), RN. Age 33. Commemorated on the Portsmouth Naval Memorial.

GEARNS, Boy 1st Class, JOHN CHARLES, J 38264(Dev), RN. Age 17. *From Horwick, Bolton, Lancashire.* Commemorated on the Plymouth Naval Memorial.

GEORGE, Able Seaman, EDWARD CECIL, SS 4090(Po), RN. Age 24. *From St.Catherine's, Lincoln.* Commemorated on the Portsmouth Naval Memorial.

GERRARD, Stoker 1st Class, FREDERICK EUSTACE, K 18303(Po), RN. Age 21. *From Portland, Dorset.* Commemorated on the Portsmouth Naval Memorial.

GIBBS, Petty Officer Stoker, WILLIAM JOHN, 286738(Po), RN. Age 37. *From Fratton, Portsmouth.* Commemorated on the Portsmouth Naval Memorial.

GIBSON, Engine Room Artificer 4th Class, WILLIAM, M 11416(Po), RN. Age 22. *From Radcliffe, Manchester.* Commemorated on the Portsmouth Naval Memorial.

GILDERSLEEVE, Boy 1st Class, HENRY, J 38120(Po), RN. Age 16. Commemorated on the Portsmouth Naval Memorial.

GILES, Engine Room Artificer 2nd Class, HARRY, 271830(Po), RN. Age 34. Commemorated on the Portsmouth Naval Memorial.

GISBORN, Private, JAMES FREDERICK, 14928(Po), RMLI. Age 26. Commemorated on the Portsmouth Naval Memorial.

GLOVER, Stoker 1st Class, FRANK, K 15764(Po), RN. Age 22. *From Birmingham.* Commemorated on the Portsmouth Naval Memorial.

GLOVER, Petty Officer, GEORGE ALBERT, 177130(Ch), RN. Age 38. Commemorated on the Portsmouth Naval Memorial.

GOBLE, Private, ALBERT ERNEST, 17664(Po), RMLI. Age 19. *From Landport, Portsmouth.* Buried at Lyness Royal Naval Cemetery, grave F.50A.

GOMM, Able Seaman, CHARLES, J 16024(Po), RN. Age 20. *From Denham, Buckinghamshire.* Buried at Lyness Royal Naval Cemetery, grave F.90A.

GOODFELLOW, Cook's Mate, BERTIE, M 3655(Po), RN. Age 22. *From Salisbury, Wiltshire.* Commemorated on the Portsmouth Naval Memorial.

GORDON, Stoker 1st Class, JOHN EWEN GLENNIE, K 23704(Po), RN. Age 18. *From Peterculter, Aberdeenshire.* Commemorated on the Portsmouth Naval Memorial.

GRACE, Leading Stoker, WILLIAM ERNEST, 295753(Po), RN. Age 34. *From Middle Wallop, Hampshire.* Commemorated on the Portsmouth Naval Memorial.

GRANT, Petty Officer Stoker, SAMUEL ALLEN, 307787(Po), RN. Age 29. *From Hampstead, London.* Commemorated on the Portsmouth Naval Memorial.

GREEN, Stoker 1st Class, GEORGE, K 23626(Po), RN. Age 20. *From Henley-on-Thames, Oxfordshire.* Commemorated on the Portsmouth Naval Memorial.

GREEN, Able Seaman, JOHN JOSEPH, 237506(Po), RN. Age 25. *From Bristol.* Commemorated on the Portsmouth Naval Memorial.

GREEN, Stoker 1st Class, JOSEPH, K 909(Po), RN. Age 30. Commemorated on the Portsmouth Naval Memorial.

GREENAN, Stoker, JOHN, S 5256(Ch), RNR. Age 21. *From Thornaby-on-Tees.* Commemorated on the Chatham Naval Memorial.

GREENHILL, Lieutenant, BENJAMIN PELHAM KNOWLE, RNVR. Age 35. Buried at Lyness Royal Naval Cemetery, grave F.48A.

GREENWOOD, Boy 1st Class, BENJAMIN THOMAS, J 37290(Dev), RN. Age 16. *From Rochdale, Lancashire.* Commemorated on the Plymouth Naval Memorial.

GREY, Lieutenant, ERIC VERNER, RN. Age 28. Commemorated on the Portsmouth Naval Memorial.

GRINYER, Stoker 1st Class, CHARLES EDMUND, K 23703(Po), RN. Age 23. *From Brighton, Sussex.* Commemorated on the Portsmouth Naval Memorial.

GROOMBRIDGE, Petty Officer, VICTOR ALBERT, 221414(Po), RN. Age 29. *From Hastings, Sussex.* Commemorated on the Portsmouth Naval Memorial.

GROVES, Able Seaman, THOMAS PERCY, J 8803(Po), RN. Age 23. Commemorated on the Portsmouth Naval Memorial.

GROVES, Able Seaman, WILLIAM ERNEST, J 20434(Po), RN. Age 18. *From Battersea, London.* Buried at Lyness Royal Naval Cemetery, grave F.39.

HACKEN, Private, ROBERT FREDERICK, 16467(Po), RMLI. Age 21. *From Ash Vale, Aldershot, Hampshire.* Commemorated on the Portsmouth Naval Memorial.

HAGAN, Stoker 2nd Class, JOHN, K 33263(Po), RN. Age 23. *From Doncaster, Yorkshire.* Commemorated on the Portsmouth Naval Memorial.

HAGAN, Carpenter's Crew, JOHN SIDNEY HENRY, M 6071(Po), RN. Age 23. *From Portsmouth.* Commemorated on the Portsmouth Naval Memorial.

HAINES, Shipwright 2nd Class, ALBERT WILLIAM, M 6535(Po), RN. Age 35. Commemorated on the Portsmouth Naval Memorial.

HAINSWORTH, Able Seaman, HENRY, J 7315(Po), RN. Age 21. Commemorated on the Portsmouth Naval Memorial.

HAMLIN, Leading Stoker, CHARLES HAROLD, K 5952(Po), RN. Age 25. Commemorated on the Portsmouth Naval Memorial.

HANSELL, Stoker 1st Class, ALBERT, K 22810(Po), RN. Age 20. Commemorated on the Portsmouth Naval Memorial.

HARDEN, Stoker 1st Class, CHARLES, SS 116361(Po), RN. Age 22. *From Liverpool.* Commemorated on the Portsmouth Naval Memorial.

HARDING, Leading Seaman, JOHN, 226183(Po), RN. Age 29. Buried at Lyness Royal Naval Cemetery, grave F.25.

HARGREAVES, Stoker 1st Class, JOSEPH HAROLD, K 27211(Po), RN. Age 27. Buried at Lyness Royal Naval Cemetery, grave F.107.

HARMAN, Boy 1st Class, DAVID JOHN, J 37854(Ch), RN. Age 17. Buried at Lyness Royal Naval Cemetery, grave F.36A.

HARPER, Able Seaman, ALFRED HENRY, London Z/2503(Ch), RNVR. Age 23. *From Twickenham, Middlesex.* Commemorated on the Chatham Naval Memorial.

HARRIS, Boy 1st Class, LANGTON WILLIAM, J 37265(Ch), RN. Age 17. Commemorated on the Chatham Naval Memorial.

HARRIS, Leading Seaman, SAMUEL JOHN, 203699(Po), RN. Age 32. *From Finsbury Park, London.* Buried at Lyness Royal Naval Cemetery, grave F.89.

HARRISON, Chief Ship's Cook, EDWIN GEORGE, 346362(Po), RN. Age 30. *From Baldock, Hertfordshire.* Buried at Lyness Royal Naval Cemetery, grave F.31A.

HARRISON, Private, JOHN WILLIAM, 14950(Po), RMLI. Age 27. Buried at Lyness Royal Naval Cemetery, grave F.43.

HARRISON, Leading Seaman, THOMAS, 164512(Po), RN. Age 43. *From Loftus, Yorkshire.* Commemorated on the Portsmouth Naval Memorial.

HART, Engine Room Artificer 4th Class, CLIFFORD GEORGE COLIN, M 15562(Po), RN. Age 21. Commemorated on the Portsmouth Naval Memorial.

HART, Stoker 1st Class, GEORGE, K 24482(Po), RN. Age 19. Commemorated on the Portsmouth Naval Memorial.

HARVEY, Boy 1st Class, JOHN ROBERT, J 34520, RN. Age 17. Commemorated on the Chatham Naval Memorial.

HARWOOD, Stoker 1st Class, THOMAS JOSEPH, 204985(Po), RN. Age 32. Commemorated on the Portsmouth Naval Memorial.

HAWKINS, Stoker 1st Class, EDWARD, K 18738(Po), RN. Age 26. *From Reading, Berkshire.* Commemorated on the Portsmouth Naval Memorial.

HAWKINS, Petty Officer Stoker, JOHN CHARLES, 306008(Po), RN. Age 32. *From Weymouth, Dorset.* Commemorated on the Portsmouth Naval Memorial.

HAWKINS, Private, WALTER, 17668(Ch), RMLI. Age 21. *From Leicester.* Commemorated on the Chatham Naval Memorial.

HAYES, Stoker 1st Class, HAROLD JAMES, SS 116486(Po), RN. Age 21. *From Doncaster, Yorkshire.* Commemorated on the Portsmouth Naval Memorial.

HAYLER, Leading Stoker, JOHN, K 3139(Po), RN. Age 26. Buried at Lyness Royal Naval Cemetery, grave F.37.

HAZEL, Ordinary Seaman, SYDNEY, J 31460(Po), RN. Age 18. *From Alderbury, Salisbury, Hampshire.* Commemorated on the Portsmouth Naval Memorial.

HAZEON, Captain, R.M.L.I., CYRIL STAFFORD, RM. Age 32. *From Bedford Park, London.* Buried at Lyness Royal Naval Cemetery, grave F.5.

HEAD, Private, GEORGE HENRY, 16468(Po), RMLI. Age 21. *From Whitchurch Hill, Oxfordshire.* Commemorated on the Portsmouth Naval Memorial.

HEATH, Stoker 1st Class, MAURICE, K 18656(Po), RN. Age 22. *From Brompton, London.* Commemorated on the Portsmouth Naval Memorial.

HEDGES, Wireman 2nd Class, EDWARD THOMAS, M 16670(Po), RN. Age 19. *From Watford, Hertfordshire.* Commemorated on the Portsmouth Naval Memorial.

HEGGS, Ordinary Seaman, JOSEPH HERBERT, J 26697(Po), RN. Age 18. *From Coalville, Leicester.* Commemorated on the Portsmouth Naval Memorial.

HENEAGE, Boy 1st Class, VINCENT, J 33128(Po), RN. Age 17. *From Scunthorpe, Lincolnshire.* Commemorated on the Portsmouth Naval Memorial.

HENNESSAY, Boy 1st Class, JAMES EDWARD, J 30845(Po), RN. Age 17. Commemorated on the Portsmouth Naval Memorial.

HENRY, Private, THOMAS WAUGH, 17564(Po), RMLI. Age 19. Commemorated on the Portsmouth Naval Memorial.

HENWOOD, Leading Stoker, DAVID, K 1631(Po), RN. Age 25. *From Portsmouth.* Commemorated on the Portsmouth Naval Memorial.

HESELWOOD, Petty Officer Stoker, ROBERT, 298739(Po), RN. Age 32. *From Bury, Lancashire.* Commemorated on the Portsmouth Naval Memorial.

HEWITT, Ordinary Signalman, FRANK, J 19271(Po), RN. Age 19. *From Hull, Yorkshire.* Commemorated on the Portsmouth Naval Memorial.

HICK, Private, HAROLD, 17960(Po), RMLI. Age 19. *From York.* Commemorated on the Portsmouth Naval Memorial.

HIGGINS, Ordinary Signalman, FRANK ALLPORT, Bristol Z/3491(Dev), RN. Age 19. *From Stourport, Worcestershire.* Commemorated on the Plymouth Naval Memorial.

HILL, Stoker 1st Class, EDWARD THOMAS, K 18149(Po), RN. Age 22. *From Cosham, Hanpshire.* Commemorated on the Portsmouth Naval Memorial.

HILL, Ordinary Seaman, GEORGE HENRY, J 37504(Po), RN. Age 18. *From Landport, Hampshire.* Commemorated on the Portsmouth Naval Memorial.

HILL, Stoker 1st Class, JOHN JAMES, SS 116484(Po), RN. Age 20. *From Crooke, Wigan, Lancashire.* Commemorated on the Portsmouth Naval Memorial.

HILL, Stoker 2nd Class, ROBERT, K 29580(Po), RN. Age 21. Commemorated on the Portsmouth Naval Memorial.

HILL, Serjeant, THOMAS PAGE, 12219(Po), RMLI. Age 35. (Served as REGINALD JOHN HILL.) *From Southsea, Hampshire.* Buried at Lyness Royal Naval Cemetery, grave F.42.

HILLS, Boy 1st Class, HERBERT GEORGE, J 34555(Po), RN. Age 17. *From Romford, Essex.* Commemorated on the Chatham Naval Memorial.

HIRTZEL, Engineer Lieutenant-Commander, GEORGE HENRY, RN. Age 37. Commemorated on the Portsmouth Naval Memorial.

HISCOCK, Private, JOHN THOMAS, 16986(Po), RMLI. Age 25. *From Shirley, Southampton.* Commemorated on the Portsmouth Naval Memorial.

HOBBS, Ordinary Seaman, FRANK NORMAN, SS 6747(Po), RN. Age 18. *From Sunninghill, Berkshire.* Commemorated on the Portsmouth Naval Memorial.

HOBSON, Artificer Engineer, MATTHEW BROOKS, RN. Age 35. *From Crewe, Cheshire.* Commemorated on the Portsmouth Naval Memorial.

HOCKLESS, Petty Officer, LESLIE HECTOR, 191335(Po), RN. Age 34. Commemorated on the Portsmouth Naval Memorial.

HODGKINSON, Boy 1st Class, JOHN, J 38226(Dev), RN. Age 17. *From Manchester.* Commemorated on the Plymouth Naval Memorial.

HOLBROOK, Petty Officer, WILLIAM, 202479(Po), RN. Age 34. Commemorated on the Portsmouth Naval Memorial.

HOLDEN, Ordinary Signalman, JOHN, J 36105(Dev), RN. Age 18. Commemorated on the Plymouth Naval Memorial.

HOLL, Stoker 1st Class, GEORGE WASHINGTON, K 24404(Po), RN. Age 19. *From East Dulwich, London.* Commemorated on the Portsmouth Naval Memorial.

HOLLAMBY, Corporal, FREDERICK HARRY, 15918(Po), RMLI. Age 26. *From Sutton Scotney, Hampshire.* Commemorated on the Portsmouth Naval Memorial.

HOLLEY, Able Seaman, JAMES FREDERICK, J 19503(Dev), RN. Age 20. *From Tiverton, Devon.* Buried at Lyness Royal Naval Cemetery, grave F.110 Special Memorial.

HOLLIS, Private, SAMUEL, 12023(Ply), RMLI. Age 36. Commemorated on the Plymouth Naval Memorial.

HOLLOWAY, Private, FRANK, 16294(Po), RMLI. Age 21. *From Chapel, Southampton.* Commemorated on the Portsmouth Naval Memorial.

HOLTOM, Officer's Steward 2nd Class, HENRY ERNEST, L 5962(Dev), RN. Age 36. *From Ladywood, Birmingham.* Buried at Lyness Royal Naval Cemetery, grave F.43A.

HOOK, Private, FREDERICK CHARLES, 16398(Po), RMLI. Age 22. *From Edgeware, Middlesex.* Commemorated on the Portsmouth Naval Memorial.

HOOKER, Shipwright 2nd Class, BERTRAM HAROLD, M 6530(Po), RN. Age 29. *From Sheerness, Kent.* Commemorated on the Portsmouth Naval Memorial.

HOOKHAM, Leading Stoker, BERT, 308841(Po), RN. Age 30. *From Eastbourne, Sussex.* Commemorated on the Portsmouth Naval Memorial.

HOPE, Private, CHARLES, 17991(Po), RMLI. Age 19. Commemorated on the Portsmouth Naval Memorial.

HORROCKS, Able Seaman, ARTHUR WALKER, 187981(Po), RN. Age 36. *From Buckland, Portsmouth.* Commemorated on the Portsmouth Naval Memorial.

HOUGHTON, Able Seaman, GEORGE, 223670(Po), RN. Age 31. Commemorated on the Portsmouth Naval Memorial.

HOWDEN, Private, WILLIAM HENRY, 12434(Po), RMLI. Age 34. Commemorated on the Portsmouth Naval Memorial.

HOWE, Signal Boy, HERBERT WILFRED, J 33496(Ch), RN. Age 17. *From Scarborough, Yorkshire.* Commemorated on the Chatham Naval Memorial.

HUDSON, Private, SIDNEY ALBERT, 16466(Po), RMLI. Age 19. *From Whitchurch Hill, Reading, Berkshire.* Commemorated on the Portsmouth Naval Memorial.

HUGHES, Boy 1st Class, REGINALD LAWRENCE, J 34710(Po), RN. Age 17. *From Romford, Essex.* Commemorated on the Portsmouth Naval Memorial.

HUMPHREY, Chief Stoker, ALICK, 283262(Po), RN. Age 43. *From Mont a L'Abbe, Jersey.* Commemorated on the Portsmouth Naval Memorial.

HUNT, Private, FRANK, 14285(Po), RMLI. Age 24. *From Portsmouth.* Commemorated on the Portsmouth Naval Memorial.

HUNTER, Stoker 1st Class, EDWARD, K 18730(Po), RN. Age 21. *From Wallsend-on-Tyne.* Buried at Lyness Royal Naval Cemetery, grave F.95A.

HUNTER, Able Seaman, EDWARD FRY, Tyneside Z/5617, RNVR. Age 31. Commemorated on the Chatham Naval Memorial.

HUNTER, Able Seaman, FRANCIS ARTHUR, 215264(Po), RN. Age 30. Commemorated on the Portsmouth Naval Memorial.

HUNTER, Warrant Engineer, GEORGE MITCHELL, RNR. Age 37. Buried at Lyness Royal Naval Cemetery, grave F.13.

INNOLES, Private, WILLIAM FRANK, 16768(Po), RMLI. Age 22. *From Brislington, Bristol.* Buried at Lyness Royal Naval Cemetery, grave F.26.

IRESON, Boy 1st Class, WILLIAM, J 34404(Ch), RN. Age 17. *From East Ham, London.* Commemorated on the Chatham Naval Memorial.

ISHERWOOD, Boy 1st Class, FRED, J 37862(Dev), RN. Age 17. *From Blackburn, Lancashire.* Commemorated on the Plymouth Naval Memorial.

IVES, Private, JOHN, 17903(Po), RMLI. Age 19. *From Bolton, Lancashire.* Commemorated on the Portsmouth Naval Memorial.

JAMES, Boy 1st Class, GILBERT, J 34703(Po), RN. Age 17. *From Wednesbury, Lancashire.* Commemorated on the Portsmouth Naval Memorial.

JAMIESON, Stoker 1st Class, WILLIAM, K 26742(Po), RN. Age 25. *From Cowdenbeath, Fife.* Commemorated on the Portsmouth Naval Memorial.

JARVIS, Stoker 1st Class, BERTIE, K 28953, RN. Age 27. *From Itchen, Southampton.* Commemorated on the Portsmouth Naval Memorial.

JARVIS, Stoker 1st Class, JOHN EDWARD, K 14689(Po), RN. Age 22. *From Walsall, Staffordshire.* Buried at Lyness Royal Naval Cemetery, grave F.96A.

JEFFRIES, Boy 1st Class, HENRY, J 34485(Ch), RN. Age 17. *From Stratford, London.* Commemorated on the Chatham Naval Memorial.

JELLEY, Officer's Cook 1st Class, THOMAS WILLIAM, L 56(Po), RN. Age 26. Buried at Lyness Royal Naval Cemetery, grave F.113 Special Memorial.

JENNINGS, Able Seaman, GEORGE THOMAS MURRAY, J 22016(Po), RN. Age 18. Buried at Lyness Royal Naval Cemetery, grave F.113 Special Memorial.

JENNINGS, Gunner, HERBERT JAMES, RN. Age 45. Buried at Lyness Royal Naval Cemetery, grave F.3A.

JENOURE, Leading Signalman, ARTHUR STANHOPE, J 8717(Po), RN. Age 22. Commemorated on the Portsmouth Naval Memorial.

JEWITT, Cook's Mate, LEWIS, M 12470(Po), RN. Age 19. Commemorated on the Portsmouth Naval Memorial.

JOELS, Bugler, ERNEST JAMES, 17529(Po), RMLI. Age 16. *From Gosport, Hampshire.* Commemorated on the Portsmouth Naval Memorial.

JOHNSTON, Stoker 1st Class, JAMES, K 24401(Po), RN. Age 18. *From Liverpool.* Commemorated on the Portsmouth Naval Memorial.

JOHNSTON, Stoker, JOHN, S 8299(Po), RNR. Age 38. Buried at Lyness Royal Naval Cemetery, grave F.104A.

JOHNSTONE, Able Seaman, LEO HENRI, J 4673(Po), RN. Age 22. *From Farnham, Surrey.* Commemorated on the Portsmouth Naval Memorial.

JONES, Master-at-Arms, COLIN, 173923(Po), RN. Age 38. *From Gloucester.* Commemorated on the Portsmouth Naval Memorial.

JONES, Boy Telegraphist, EVAN, J 37101(Dev), RN. Age 17. *From Wrexham.* Commemorated on the Plymouth Naval Memorial.

JONES, Private, HARRY, 16210(Po), RMLI. Age 24. Commemorated on the Portsmouth Naval Memorial.

JONES, Stoker, JOHN, S 1494(Po), RNR. Age 31. *From Leith.* Commemorated on the Portsmouth Naval Memorial.

JONES, Able Seaman, JOHN ALBERT, 214791(Po), RN. Age 30. *From Northam, Southampton.* Commemorated on the Portsmouth Naval Memorial.

JONES, Stoker 1st Class, THOMAS, SS 116492(Po), RN. Age 21. Commemorated on the Portsmouth Naval Memorial.

JONES, Stoker 1st Class, WILLIAM GRATTON, SS 116364(Po), RN. Age 22. Commemorated on the Portsmouth Naval Memorial.

JORDAN, Private, ARTHUR HENRY, 16458(Po), RMLI. Age 21. *From Bedminster, Bristol.* Commemorated on the Portsmouth Naval Memorial.

KANAAR, Midshipman, JOHN ADRIAN GERARD, RN. Age 19. *From Chiswick, London.* Commemorated on the Portsmouth Naval Memorial.

KEBBLE, Leading Seaman, ARTHUR ALFRED, 223032(Po), RN. Age 29. Commemorated on the Portsmouth Naval Memorial.

KEEPING, Petty Officer, THOMAS LEONARD, 227023(Po), RN. Age 28. Buried at Lyness Royal Naval Cemetery, grave F.26A.

KENDALL, Stoker 1st Class, ARTHUR, SS 111760(Po), RN. Age 23. Commemorated on the Portsmouth Naval Memorial.

KENNEDY, Able Seaman, JOHN, 177117(Po), RN. Age 38. Commemorated on the Portsmouth Naval Memorial.

KENNY, Stoker, THOMAS, S 7200(Po), RNR. Age 27. *From Drogheda, Co.Meath.* Commemorated on the Portsmouth Naval Memorial.

KENWARD, Stoker 1st Class, HENRY CHARLES, K 16231(Po), RN. Age 21. *From Arundel, Sussex.* Commemorated on the Portsmouth Naval Memorial.

KIMBER, Signalman, WILLIAM JOHN, London Z/4346(Ch), RNVR. Age 18. Commemorated on the Chatham Naval Memorial.

KIRBY, Stoker 1st Class, JAMES HENRY, SS 111977(Po), RN. Age 22. Commemorated on the Portsmouth Naval Memorial.

KIRBY, Petty Officer Stoker, WILLIAM JOHN, 307320(Po), RN. Age 31. Commemorated on the Portsmouth Naval Memorial.

KIRKUP, Stoker 1st Class, FREDERICK, K 15761(Po), RN. Age 22. Commemorated on the Portsmouth Naval Memorial.

KNIGHT, Leading Stoker, GEORGE HENRY, 310704(Po), RN. Age 29. *From Brighton, Sussex.* Commemorated on the Portsmouth Naval Memorial.

KNIGHT, Private, HENRY, 14081(Po), RMLI. Age 25. *From East Southsea, Portsmouth.* Commemorated on the Portsmouth Naval Memorial.

KNIGHT, Able Seaman, JOHN GEORGE, J 15148(Po), RN. Age 20. Buried at Lyness Royal Naval Cemetery, grave F.49A.

KNOWLSON, Cook's Mate, JAMES WILFRED, M 11659(Po), RN. Age 21. *From Leeds.* Commemorated on the Portsmouth Naval Memorial.

LACEY, Leading Stoker, REGINALD, K 2491(Po), RN. Age 27. Buried at Lyness Royal Naval Cemetery, grave F.98A.

LACY, Engine Room Artificer 4th Class, ARTHUR, M 3067(Po), RN. Age 26. *From Carlisle, Cumberland.* Commemorated on the Portsmouth Naval Memorial.

LAITY, Petty Officer, JOSEPH HENRY, 188576(Dev), RN. Age 36. Commemorated on the Portsmouth Naval Memorial.

LAMB, Ordinary Telegraphist, JOSEPH HENRY, J 35192(Dev), RN. Age 17. *From Newbottle, Co.Durham.* Commemorated on the Plymouth and Portsmouth Naval Memorials.

LAMPARD, Leading Seaman, ALBERT EDWARD, 229487(Po), RN. Age 28. *From Fareham, Hampshire.* Commemorated on the Portsmouth Naval Memorial.

LAMPITT, Able Seaman, JOHN, 229522(Po), RN. Age 28. *From Hockley, Birmingham.* Commemorated on the Portsmouth Naval Memorial.

I – Roll of Honour

LARKING, Midshipman, ALFRED GEORGE, RNR. Age 20. *From Brighton, Sussex.* Commemorated on the Portsmouth Naval Memorial.

LARKINS, Petty Officer, HERBERT, 216344(Po), RN. Age 30. *From Lincoln.* Commemorated on the Portsmouth Naval Memorial.

LATTER, Leading Seaman, WILLIAM THOMAS, 234187(Ch), RN. Age 28. *From Bermondsey, London.* Commemorated on the Chatham Naval Memorial.

LATTIMORE, Able Seaman, GEORGE CHARLES, J 394(Po), RN. Age 24. *From Plaistow, London.* Commemorated on the Portsmouth Naval Memorial.

LAWLER, Ordinary Seaman, WILLIAM, SS 5202(Po), RN. Age 20. *From Dublin.* Commemorated on the Chatham Naval Memorial.

LAWLER, Boy 1st Class, WILLIAM GEORGE, J 38134(Po), RN. Age 16. *From Battersea, London.* Commemorated on the Portsmouth Naval Memorial.

LAWRENCE, Telegraphist, LEONARD JAMES, J 18010(Po), RN. Age 19. *From Mere, Wiltshire.* Commemorated on the Portsmouth Naval Memorial.

LEACH, Petty Officer, THOMAS WILLIAM, 170692(Po), RN. Age 39. *From Kilburn, London.* Commemorated on the Portsmouth Naval Memorial.

LEADER, Private, LEONARD JOHN, 11522(Po), RMLI. Age 28. *From Gosport, Hampshire.* Buried at Lyness Royal Naval Cemetery, grave F.29.

LEDGER, Able Seaman, ARTHUR ERNEST, J 8206(Po), RN. Age 22. *From Isleworth, Middlesex.* Commemorated on the Portsmouth Naval Memorial.

LEDWOOD, Able Seaman, JOHN WILLIAM, SS 4266(Po), RN. Age 21. *From Pitsmoor, Sheffield.* Commemorated on the Portsmouth Naval Memorial.

LEE, Petty Officer Stoker, WILLIAM HENRY ARTHUR, 310388(Po), RN. Age 32. Commemorated on the Portsmouth Naval Memorial.

LESLIE, Able Seaman, FRED PERKINS, 238951(Po), RN. Age 24. *From Wadsley Bridge, Sheffield.* Commemorated on the Portsmouth Naval Memorial.

LEWIS, Stoker 1st Class, JAMES GREGORY, SS 116340(Po), RN. Age 20. *From Eston, Yorkshire.* Commemorated on the Portsmouth Naval Memorial.

LEWIS, Stoker 1st Class, JOHN HENRY, K 17781(Po), RN. Age 21. *From Beaminster, Dorset.* Commemorated on the Portsmouth Naval Memorial.

LILLEY, Boatswain, ARTHUR LEONARD, RN. Age 32. Buried at Lyness Royal Naval Cemetery, grave F.13A.

LIND, Stoker 1st Class, CHARLES NOEL, K 18338(Po), RN. Age 24. *From Shoreham-by-Sea, Sussex.* Commemorated on the Portsmouth Naval Memorial.

LIPSCOMBE, Petty Officer Stoker, CHARLES WILLIAM, K 3409(Po), RN. Age 25. *From Earlsfield, London.* Commemorated on the Portsmouth Naval Memorial.

LITTLE, Private, REGINALD THOMAS, 17910(Po), RMLI. Age 19. *From East Pennard, Shepton Mallett, Somerset.* Commemorated on the Portsmouth Naval Memorial.

LITTLEWOOD, Able Seaman, HARIPH REGINALD, 215102(Po), RN. Age 30. *From London.* Commemorated on the Portsmouth Naval Memorial.

LOCKER, Stoker 1st Class, GEORGE WILLIAM, K 15765(Po), RN. Age 21. *From Small Heath, Birmingham.* Commemorated on the Portsmouth Naval Memorial.

LOVEGROVE, Cook's Mate, THOMAS GEORGE, M 12241(Po), RN. Age 22. *From Winchfield, Hampshire.* Commemorated on the Portsmouth Naval Memorial.

LOWE, Stoker 1st Class, JAMES, SS 111658(Po), RN. Age 22. *From Leicester.* Commemorated on the Portsmouth Naval Memorial.

LOWE, Petty Officer Stoker, THOMAS, 308946(Po), RN. Age 28. *From Beaulieu, Hampshire.* Commemorated on the Portsmouth Naval Memorial.

LOWE, Stoker 1st Class, WILFRED CHAMBERS, SS 112615(Po), RN. Age 25. *From St.Botolph's, London.* Commemorated on the Portsmouth Naval Memorial.

LOWERY, Stoker 1st Class, HARRY, SS 116355(Po), RN. Age 20. *From Pleasley, Mansfield, Nottinghamshire.* Commemorated on the Portsmouth Naval Memorial.

LYFIELD, Leading Seaman(Boatman,C.G.), ALBERT GEORGE, 202893(Po), RN. Age 32. *From Portsmouth.* Commemorated on the Portsmouth Naval Memorial.

LYNCH, Stoker, JOHN, S 6933(Po), RNR. Age 34. (Served as JOHN KELLY.) *From Dublin.* Commemorated on the Portsmouth Naval Memorial.

LYNN, Private, ALBERT EDWARD, 16177(Po), RMLI. Age 20. *From Fulham, London.* Commemorated on the Portsmouth Naval Memorial.

McADAM, Stoker 1st Class, WILLIAM, SS 116360(Po), RN. Age 19. Commemorated on the Portsmouth Naval Memorial.

McCOOL, Stoker 1st Class, DANIEL, K 23925(Po), RN. Age 19. *From Liverpool.* Commemorated on the Portsmouth Naval Memorial.

McDONNELL, Stoker, PATRICK, S 8468(Po), RNR. Age 25. Commemorated on the Portsmouth Naval Memorial.

McFARLANE, Able Seaman, ROBERT MCROBBIE, 156816(Po), RN. Age 41. Buried at Lyness Royal Naval Cemetery, grave F.24A.

McGARRIGLE, Stoker 1st Class, DANIEL, SS 116376(Po), RN. Age 20. Commemorated on the Portsmouth Naval Memorial.

McGARVIE, Able Seaman, WALTER CLYDE, Clyde Z/6039, RN. Age 22. Commemorated on the Portsmouth Naval Memorial.

McGOWAN, Ordinary Seaman, FRANCIS GEORGE, J 46405(Po), RN. Age 27. Buried at Lyness Royal Naval Cemetery, grave F.108A Special Memorial.

McGRATH, Stoker, HENRY, S 8397(Po), RNR. Age 30. *From Anderston, Glasgow.* Commemorated on the Portsmouth Naval Memorial.

MacGREGOR, Ordinary Seaman, JOHN DONALD, J 35776(Po), RN. Age 17. Commemorated on the Portsmouth Naval Memorial.

McINTYRE, Able Seaman, ARCHIBALD, Clyde Z/6896, RNVR. Age 27. *From Glasgow.* Commemorated on the Portsmouth Naval Memorial.

McLAUGHLIN, Leading Seaman, JOHN, 176819(Po), RN. Age 38. *From Belfast. Served in the Naval Brigade under Sir George White at the Seige of Ladysmith.* Commemorated on the Portsmouth Naval Memorial.

McLOUGHLIN, Stoker, ROBERT JOSEPH, S 6955(Po), RNR. Age 23. *From Newry, Co.Down.* Commemorated on the Portsmouth Naval Memorial.

McNALLY, Surgeon, HUGH FRANCIS, RN. M.B., B.A. Age 24. *From Portaferry, Co.Down.* Commemorated on the Portsmouth Naval Memorial.

McNEILL, Stoker, ROBERT, S 5534(Po), RNR. Age 24. *From Musselburgh, Edinburgh.* Commemorated on the Portsmouth Naval Memorial.

McPHERSON, Stoker 1st Class, ALEXANDER JOHN, K 23705(Po), RN. Age 18. *From Peterculter, Aberdeenshire.* Commemorated on the Portsmouth Naval Memorial.

MALLARD, Ordinary Seaman, JOHN ARTHUR, J 31961(Po), RN. Age 18. *From Hay Mills, Birmingham.* Commemorated on the Portsmouth Naval Memorial.

MALLET, Midshipman, CLEMENT STANLEY BERTRAM, RNR. Age 18. *From St.Helier, Jersey.* Commemorated on the Portsmouth Naval Memorial.

MALLETT, Private, HAROLD FREDERICK, 17662(Po), RMLI. Age 19. *From Kingston, Portsmouth.* Commemorated on the Portsmouth Naval Memorial.

MANSER, Leading Seaman, FREDERICK SPENCER JOHN, J 11753(Po), RN. Age 21. *From St.Leonard's-on-Sea, Sussex.* Commemorated on the Portsmouth Naval Memorial.

MARINER, Private, ERNEST, 16423(Po), RMLI. Age 20. Commemorated on the Portsmouth Naval Memorial.

MARNER, Leading Stoker, GEORGE ARTHUR, K 21178(Po), RN. Age 28. *From Langport, Portsmouth.* Commemorated on the Portsmouth Naval Memorial.

MARSHALL, Stoker 1st Class, ARTHUR, K 7872(Po), RN. Age 24. Commemorated on the Portsmouth Naval Memorial.

MARSHALL, Ordinary Seaman, FREDERICK GEORGE, SS 4483(Po), RN. Age 21. *From Batt's Corner, Farnham, Surrey.* Commemorated on the Portsmouth Naval Memorial.

MARSHALL, Private, GEORGE EDWARD, 14974(Po), RMLI. Age 26. Commemorated on the Portsmouth Naval Memorial.

MARTIN, Stoker 1st Class, CHARLES, 292765(Po), RN. Age 35. *From Goring-by-Sea, Sussex.* Commemorated on the Portsmouth Naval Memorial.

MARTIN, Ship's Cook, GEORGE FREDERICK, 347295(Po), RN. Age 29. *From Gosport, Hampshire.* Commemorated on the Portsmouth Naval Memorial.

MARTIN, Able Seaman, ROBERT PERCY, J 16477(Po), RN. Age 20. *From Millwall, London.* Buried at Lyness Royal Naval Cemetery, grave F.36.

MASKELL, Chief Engine Room Artificer 2nd Class, JOHN ERNEST, 268297(Po), RN. Age 49. Commemorated on the Portsmouth Naval Memorial.

MASTERS, Able Seaman, BENJAMIN WILLIAM, J 22941(Po), RN. Age 20. Commemorated on the Portsmouth Naval Memorial.

MATTHEWS, Lieutenant, HUMPHREY, RN. Age 28. *From Hampshire.* Buried at Lyness Royal Naval Cemetery, grave F.14.

MAXTED, Stoker 1st Class, HARRY, K 18376(Po), RN. Age 21. *From Broadstairs, Kent.* Buried at Lyness Royal Naval Cemetery, grave F.91A.

MAYHEW, Private, ERNEST GEORGE, 12637(Po), RMLI. Age 29. Commemorated on the Portsmouth Naval Memorial.

MEDHURST, Stoker 1st Class, CHARLES ALFRED, SS 112507(Po), RN. Age 25. *From East Dulwich, London.* Commemorated on the Portsmouth Naval Memorial.

MELHUISH, Private, WILLIAM JOHN, 16514(Po), RMLI. Age 21. *From Bingston, Yeovil, Somerset.* Commemorated on the Portsmouth Naval Memorial.

MERRITT, Assistant Steward, CHARLES HAROLD, M 3099(Po), RN. Age 24. *From North End, Portsmouth.* Buried at Lyness Royal Naval Cemetery, grave F.7A.

MERWOOD, Leading Stoker, REGINALD, 360692(Po), RN. Age 30. *From Ryde, Isle of Wight.* Commemorated on the Portsmouth Naval Memorial.

MEW, Private, JOSEPH, 16469(Po), RMLI. Age 20. *From Moortown, Ringwood.* Commemorated on the Portsmouth Naval Memorial.

MIDDLETON, Stoker, ROBERT CLARENCE, S 5341(Ch), RNR. Age 22. *From Sheringham, Norfolk.* Commemorated on the Chatham Naval Memorial.

MITCHNER, Able Seaman, HARRY, 235318(Po), RN. Age 26. *From Kenilworth, Warwickshire.* Commemorated on the Portsmouth Naval Memorial.

MOORE, Stoker 1st Class, GEORGE WILLIAM, K 17789(Po), RN. Age 21. *From Stamshaw, Portsmouth.* Commemorated on the Portsmouth Naval Memorial.

MOORE, Leading Stoker, RICHARD, K 924(Po), RN. Age 28. *From Greenheys, Manchester.* Commemorated on the Portsmouth Naval Memorial.

MORETON, Boy 1st Class, WILLIAM ALBERT, J 39321(Po), RN. Age 17. *From Bampton, Oxfordshire.* Commemorated on the Portsmouth Naval Memorial.

MORLEY, Leading Stoker, ARTHUR, 311491(Po), RN. Age 28. Commemorated on the Portsmouth Naval Memorial.

MORPHEW, Electrical Artificer 3rd Class, GEORGE ADAMES, M 5649(Po), RN. Age 25. Commemorated on the Portsmouth Naval Memorial.

MORRIS, Stoker 1st Class, EDWARD OSWALD, K 24475(Po), RN. Age 19. *From Wavertree, Liverpool.* Commemorated on the Portsmouth Naval Memorial.

MORRIS, Private, FRANK SIDNEY, 17908(Po), RMLI. Age 22. *From Worcester.* Commemorated on the Portsmouth Naval Memorial.

MORRIS, Private, FREDERICK ARTHUR, 16182(Po), RMLI. Age 21. *From Hulme, Manchester.* Commemorated on the Portsmouth Naval Memorial.

MORTIEAU, Signal Boatswain, ARTHUR JAMES, RN. Age 43. Commemorated on the Portsmouth Naval Memorial.

MORTON, Private, ARTHUR FREDERICK, 10418(Po), RMLI. Age 34. Commemorated on the Portsmouth Naval Memorial.

MORTON, Stoker 1st Class, CYRIL ELSTON ANDREW, SS 116358(Po), RN. Age 20. Commemorated on the Portsmouth Naval Memorial.

MOULD, Able Seaman, ALBERT CHARLES, 232938(Po), RN. Age 27. *From Plumstead, London.* Commemorated on the Portsmouth Naval Memorial.

MUDIE, Leading Seaman, DOUGLAS BLAKELY, 228592(Po), RN. Age 29. *From Edinburgh.* Commemorated on the Portsmouth Naval Memorial.

MULLEN, Able Seaman, DANIEL, Tyneside Z/5666(Ch), RNVR. Age 20. Commemorated on the Chatham Naval Memorial.

MULLENS, Petty Officer Stoker, FREDERICK CHARLES, 305455(Po), RN. Age 31. Commemorated on the Portsmouth Naval Memorial.

MULVEY, Stoker, PETER, S 6889(Po), RNR. Age 27. Buried at Lyness Royal Naval Cemetery, grave F.11.

MUNTON, Stoker 1st Class, ALBERT, K 14703(Po), RN. Age 22. *From Whaplode Dove, Lincolnshire.* Commemorated on the Portsmouth Naval Memorial.

MUSSON, Private, THOMAS, 11956(Po), RMLI. Age 32. *From Hinckley, Leicestershire.* Commemorated on the Portsmouth Naval Memorial.

NAYLOR, Sick Berth Attendant, ALBERT GODFREY SANDERSON, M 6821(Po), RN. Age 20. *From Northampton.* Commemorated on the Portsmouth Naval Memorial.

NEELD, Able Seaman, ALBERT WILLIAM, J 16495(Po), RN. Age 20. *From Sparkbrook, Birmingham.* Buried at Lyness Royal Naval Cemetery, grave F.40.

NEWBEGIN, Petty Officer Stoker, JAMES, K 816(Po), RN. Age 26. *From Newcastle-on-Tyne.* Commemorated on the Portsmouth Naval Memorial.

NEWMAN, Stoker 1st Class, JOSEPH, K 18736(Po), RN. Age 25. Commemorated on the Portsmouth Naval Memorial.

NINEHAM, Chief Petty Officer, WALTER EDWARD, 181548(Po), RN. Age 37. *From Lymington, Hampshire.* Buried at Lyness Royal Naval Cemetery, grave F.23A.

NOEL, Stoker 1st Class, HARRY, K 18283(Po), RN. Age 24. *From Portfield, Chichester, Sussex.* Commemorated on the Portsmouth Naval Memorial.

NORRINGTON, Leading Stoker, THOMAS ERNEST, K 18148(Po), RN. Age 22. Commemorated on the Portsmouth Naval Memorial.

NORRIS, Stoker 1st Class, ALLAN COLQUHOUN, SS 111654(Po), RN. Age 23. Commemorated on the Portsmouth Naval Memorial.

NORTH, Leading Stoker, ARTHUR, K 2(Po), RN. Age 26. Commemorated on the Portsmouth Naval Memorial.

NORTH, Able Seaman, GEORGE, J 11336(Po), RN. Age 21. Buried at Lyness Royal Naval Cemetery, grave F.101.

NORTHOVER, Armourer's Crew, SIDNEY JAMES, M 13493(Po), RN. Age 18. *From Tisbury, Wiltshire.* Commemorated on the Portsmouth Naval Memorial.

NOVICE, Leading Seaman, JOHN ARTHUR, 229759(Po), RN. Age 28. *From Isleworth, Middlesex.* Buried at Lyness Royal Naval Cemetery, grave F.10A.

NOWLAND, Stoker 1st Class, FRED, K 28357(Po), RN. Age 23. *From Holbeck, Leeds.* Commemorated on the Portsmouth Naval Memorial.

NUGENT, Assistant Paymaster, MARK LAVALLIN O'REILLY, RNR. Age 25. Commemorated on the Portsmouth Naval Memorial.

NYE, Stoker 1st Class, CHARLES WILLIAM, K 18645(Po), RN. Age 21. *From Brighton, Sussex.* Commemorated on the Portsmouth Naval Memorial.

O'CONNELL, Able Seaman, ALBERT ALFRED, J 16487(Po), RN. Age 20. *From Woolston, Hampshire.* Commemorated on the Portsmouth Naval Memorial.

OLIVER, Engine Room Artificer 3rd Class, FREDERICK CHARLES, M 3636(Po), RN. Age 26. Commemorated on the Portsmouth Naval Memorial.

OLIVER, Stoker, JOHN WRIGHT, S 8715(Ch), RNR. Age 18. Commemorated on the Chatham Naval Memorial.

ORMONDE, Petty Officer Stoker, WILLIAM ARTHUR, 362955(Po), RN. Age 30. Commemorated on the Portsmouth Naval Memorial.

OUBRIDGE, Leading Stoker, WILLIAM BERTRAM, K 3188(Po), RN. Age 29. Commemorated on the Portsmouth Naval Memorial.

OULTON, Boy 1st Class, WILLIAM HENRY, J 34458(Po), RN. Age 16. *From South Tottenham, London.* Commemorated on the Chatham Naval Memorial.

OWEN, Private, NORMAN, 18238(Po), RMLI. Age 18. *From New Silksworth, Sunderland.* Commemorated on the Portsmouth Naval Memorial.

PAGE, Able Seaman, JOHN HERBERT, 220900(Po), RN. Age 30. *From Wimborne, Dorset.* Commemorated on the Portsmouth Naval Memorial.

PAMPLIN, Stoker 1st Class, JOHN HENRY, K 24507(Po), RN. Age 22. (Served as John E. MAGGS.) Commemorated on the Portsmouth Naval Memorial.

PARKER, Stoker 1st Class, GEORGE HENRY, K 18274(Po), RN. Age 21. Commemorated on the Portsmouth Naval Memorial.

PARKER, Armourer's Crew, JAMES, M 13494(Po), RN. Age 25. Commemorated on the Portsmouth Naval Memorial.

PARKHURST, Ship's Steward's Assistant, ALEC JOHN, M 19458(Po), RN. Age 29. *From Westerham, Kent.* Commemorated on the Portsmouth Naval Memorial.

PARKS, Stoker, WILLIAM, S 4663(Ch), RNR. Age 25. Commemorated on the Chatham Naval Memorial.

PARSONS, Officer's Steward 3rd Class, HARRIE, L 5179(Dev), RN. Age 19. *From Huish, Yeovil, Somerset.* Commemorated on the Plymouth Naval Memorial.

PARSONS, Signalman, STANLEY CHARLES, J 18297(Po), RN. Age 19. *From Littlehampton, Sussex.*orated on the Portsmouth Naval Memorial.

PARSONS, Able Seaman, WILLIAM ROBERT, Sussex 5/101(Po), RNVR. Age 24. *From Hastings, Sussex.* Commemorated on the Portsmouth Naval Memorial.

PASHLEY, Officer's Steward 3rd Class, ALFRED EDWARD, L 5796(Dev), RN. Age 18. Commemorated on the Plymouth Naval Memorial.

PATON, Boy 1st Class, DAVID, J 35396(Dev), RN. Age 17. *From Levenshulme, Manchester.* Commemorated on the Plymouth Naval Memorial.

PATTENDEN, Leading Stoker, ALBERT, K 14510(Po), RN. Age 24. Commemorated on the Portsmouth Naval Memorial.

PAYNE, Ordinary Seaman, ARCHIE, J 23842(Po), RN. Age 18. *From Itchen, Southampton.* Commemorated on the Portsmouth Naval Memorial.

PAYNE, Leading Seaman, HARRY, J 1776(Po), RN. Age 25. *From Brighton, Sussex.* Commemorated on the Portsmouth Naval Memorial.

PAYNE, Stoker 1st Class, HARRY EDWARD, SS 116487(Po), RN. Age 20. Commemorated on the Portsmouth Naval Memorial.

PEARCE, Shipwright 1st Class, ARTHUR JAMES JOHN, 343042(Po), RN. Age 32. Commemorated on the Portsmouth Naval Memorial.

PELLETT, Ordinary Seaman, ERNEST ALFRED, J 34615(Dev), RN. Age 18. *From Walthamstow, London.* Commemorated on the Plymouth Naval Memorial.

PENGILLY, Sick Berth Steward, PERCY WILLIAM, 351081(Po), RN. Age 32. Commemorated on the Portsmouth Naval Memorial.

PERRY, Leading Stoker, DUKE, K 6007(Po), RN. Age 26. Commemorated on the Portsmouth Naval Memorial.

PERRY, Private, PERCY EDWIN, 9215(Po), RMLI. Age 36. *From Portsea, Portsmouth.* Commemorated on the Portsmouth Naval Memorial.

PESSELL, Ordinary Seaman, PERCY JOHN, J 35361(Ch), RN. Age 29. Commemorated on the Chatham Naval Memorial.

PETERS, Leading Stoker, WILLIAM ROBERT, K 6037(Po), RN. Age 25. Buried at Lyness Royal Naval Cemetery, grave F.50.

PETTETT, Stoker, ALBERT EDWARD, S 8320(Po), RNR. Age 20. *From Southwick, Sussex.* Commemorated on the Portsmouth Naval Memorial.

PETTETT, Stoker, WILLIAM JAMES, S 8321(Po), RNR. Age 21. *From Southwick, Sussex.* Commemorated on the Portsmouth Naval Memorial.

PHILLIPS, Leading Seaman, ARTHUR, J 7670(Po), RN. Age 23. Commemorated on the Portsmouth Naval Memorial.

PIPER, Private, FRANK SYDNEY, 16419(Po), RMLI. Age 20. Commemorated on the Portsmouth Naval Memorial.

POLLARD, Chief Stoker, JAMES, 289394(Po), RN. Age 41. *From Fratton, Portsmouth.* Commemorated on the Portsmouth Naval Memorial.

PONSFORD, Able Seaman, CLAUDE HENDERSON, 227479(Po), RN. Age 29. *From Penge, London.* Commemorated on the Portsmouth Naval Memorial.

PORTER, Leading Seaman, ALLAN JAMES, J 5819(Po), RN. Age 24. *From Brighton, Sussex.* Commemorated on the Portsmouth Naval Memorial.

POTTER, Boy 1st Class, FRANK, J 39711(Po), RN. Age 16. *From Wokingham, Berkshire.* Commemorated on the Portsmouth Naval Memorial.

POWELL, Stoker, JOHN, S 3612(Ch), RNR. Age 31. *From Stockton-on-Tees.* Commemorated on the Chatham Naval Memorial.

POWELL, Ordinary Seaman, WILLIAM GEORGE, J 28619(Po), RN. Age 16. Commemorated on the Portsmouth Naval Memorial.

PRAGNELL, Private, GORDON VICTOR, 15691(Po), RMLI. Age 26. *From Surbiton Hill, Surrey.* Commemorated on the Portsmouth Naval Memorial.

PRAGNELL, Ship's Corporal 1st Class, WILLIAM, M 6635(Po), RN. Age 28. Commemorated on the Portsmouth Naval Memorial.

PURNELL, Boy 1st Class, EDGAR, J 34472(Ch), RN. Age 17. *From Sleaford, Lincolnshire.* Commemorated on the Chatham Naval Memorial.

QUINTON, Able Seaman, WILLIAM EDWARD, J 1975(Po), RN. Age 24. *From Southampton.* Commemorated on the Portsmouth Naval Memorial.

RAGLESS, Able Seaman, PERCY JAMES, 234512(Po), RN. Age 26. Buried at Lyness Royal Naval Cemetery, grave F.102A.

RAMSEY, Able Seaman, PERCY RUFUS, SS 135(Po), RN. Age 32. Commemorated on the Portsmouth Naval Memorial.

RANDELL, Stoker 1st Class, GILBERT, K 18286(Po), RN. Age 23. *From Walworth, London.* Commemorated on the Portsmouth Naval Memorial.

RAWLINS, Able Seaman, WILLIAM EDWARD, J 15752(Po), RN. Age 20. Commemorated on the Portsmouth Naval Memorial.

REDFERN, Stoker 1st Class, THOMAS HENRY, SS 110756(Po), RN. Age 24. Commemorated on the Portsmouth Naval Memorial.

REED, Able Seaman, GEORGE EDWARD, J 18125(Po), RN. Age 19. *From Penge, London.* Commemorated on the Portsmouth Naval Memorial.

REED, Lance Corporal, WILLIAM, 14218(Po), RMLI. Age 24. *From Gosport, Hampshire.* Buried at Lyness Royal Naval Cemetery, grave F.112 Special Memorial.

REES, Able Seaman, WILLIAM HOPKIN, J 15244(Po), RN. Age 20. *From Barry, Glamorgan.* Commemorated on the Portsmouth Naval Memorial.

REEVE, Yeoman of Signals, GEORGE EDWARD, 232867(Po), RN. Age 28. *From Newhey, Rochdale, Lancashire.* Buried at 6Lyness Royal Naval Cemetery, grave F.63.

REYNOLDS, Stoker 1st Class, GEORGE, K 19786(Po), RN. Age 26. *From Bushbury, Wolverhampton.* Commemorated on the Portsmouth Naval Memorial.

REYNOLDS, Stoker 1st Class, PALMER, K 17622(Po), RN. Age 21. *From South Bermondsey, London.* Commemorated on the Portsmouth Naval Memorial.

REYNOLDS, Boy 1st Class, SIDNEY HENRY, J 37967(Po), RN. Age 16. *From Earlsfield, Lonidon.* Commemorated on the Portsmouth Naval Memorial.

RICHARDS, Private, ERNEST, 15451(Po), RMLI. Age 38. Commemorated on the Portsmouth Naval Memorial.

RIGBY, Boy 1st Class, JAMES EDWARD, J 37868(Dev), RN. Age 16. Commemorated on the Plymouth Naval Memorial.

RILEY, Private, ERNEST, 16370(Po), RMLI. Age 22. Buried at Lyness Royal Naval Cemetery, grave F.41A.

RIORDAN, Boy 1st Class, THOMAS JOSEPH, J 31927(Dev), RN. Age 17. *From Cork, Ireland.* Commemorated on the Plymouth Naval Memorial.

ROBERTS, Chief Armourer, PERCY BENTLEY, 344639(Po), RN. Age 32. *From Southsea, Hampshire.* Buried at Lyness Royal Naval Cemetery, grave F.6A.

ROBERTSON, Stoker 1st Class, JAMES WALLACE, K 18733(Po), RN. Age 22. Commemorated on the Portsmouth Naval Memorial.

ROBERTSON, Able Seaman, WILLIAM HARRY, 224692(Po), RN. Age 28. *From Portsmouth.* Commemorated on the Portsmouth Naval Memorial.

ROBEY, Leading Seaman, WILLIAM CHARLES, J 2231(Po), RN. Age 23. *From Southsea, Portsmouth.* Commemorated on the Portsmouth Naval Memorial.

ROBINSON, Stoker 1st Class, ARTHUR FRANK, K 19129(Po), RN. Age 24. *From Soho, London.* Commemorated on the Portsmouth Naval Memorial.

ROBINSON, Boy 1st Class, ERIC FRANCIS HENRY, J 34709(Po), RN. Age 17. *From Romford, Essex.* Commemorated on the Portsmouth Naval Memorial.

ROGERS, Petty Officer Stoker, EDWIN JOHN, 292603(Po), RN. Age 35. Commemorated on the Portsmouth Naval Memorial.

ROGERS, Able Seaman, WILLIAM, Wales Z/1348(Dev), RNVR. Age 21. *From Cwmbwrla, Swansea.* Commemorated on the Plymouth Naval Memorial.

ROGERS, Stoker 1st Class, WILLIAM EDWIN, K 24479(Po), RN. Age 19. *From Alton, Hampshire.* Buried at Lyness Royal Naval Cemetery, grave F.23.

ROSE, Private, REGINALD JOHN, 16401(Po), RMLI. Age 21. *From Basingstoke, Hampshire.* Buried at Lyness Royal Naval Cemetery, grave F.24.

ROSSITER, Seaman, THOMAS, A 3095(Dev), RNR. Age 25. *From Wexford, Ireland.* Commemorated on the Plymouth Naval Memorial.

ROWELL, Stoker 1st Class, WILLIAM GEORGE, K 18751(Po), RN. Age 21. *From Winchester, Hampshire.* Commemorated on the Portsmouth Naval Memorial.

ROWLEY, Chief Stoker, JOSEPH, 280555(Po), RN. Age 39. *From Southsea, Portsmouth.* Commemorated on the Portsmouth Naval Memorial.

RUSSELL, Officer's Cook 1st Class, FREDERICK, 361320(Po), RN. Age 28. *From Buckland, Portsmouth.* Commemorated on the Portsmouth Naval Memorial.

RYAN, Stoker, STEPHEN, S 6218(Po), RNR. Age 36. Commemorated on the Portsmouth Naval Memorial.

RYAN, Able Seaman, WILLIAM, J 13526(Po), RN. Age 21. *From Limehouse, London.* Commemorated on the Portsmouth Naval Memorial.

RYLES, Stoker 1st Class, MATTHEW, K 18278(Po), RN. Age 25. *From Gateshead-on-Tyne.* Commemorated on the Portsmouth Naval Memorial.

SALISBURY, Engine Room Artificer 4th Class, WILLIAM HUNTER, M 3780(Po), RN. Age 19. *From Anfield, Liverpool.* Buried at Lyness Royal Naval Cemetery, grave F.120.

SALOWAY, Signal Boy, WILLIAM LUKE, J 32006(Po), RN. Age 17. Commemorated on the Portsmouth Naval Memorial.

SANDOM, Private, GILBERT CHARLES, 15853(Po), RMLI. Age 22. Commemorated on the Portsmouth Naval Memorial.

SAUNDERS, Stoker 1st Class, ARTHUR, K 18153(Po), RN. Age 21. Commemorated on the Portsmouth Naval Memorial.

SAVILL, Captain, HERBERT JOHN, RN. Age 46. *From Bocking, Braintree, Essex.* Commemorated on the Portsmouth Naval Memorial.

SCHEURER, Stoker 1st Class, ARTHUR LOUIS, K 6806(Po), RN. Age 26. Commemorated on the Portsmouth Naval Memorial.

SCRIVEN, Petty Officer, THOMAS GEORGE, 232477(Po), RN. Age 26. *From Westham, Weymouth, Dorset.* Commemorated on the Portsmouth Naval Memorial.

SEE, Private, CHARLES WILLIAM, 16426(Po), RMLI. Age 21. Buried at Lyness Royal Naval Cemetery, grave F.122A.

SEMPLE, Able Seaman, ROBERT, Clyde Z/5111(Po), RNVR. Age 20. *From Flemington, Motherwell, Lanarkshire.* Commemorated on the Portsmouth Naval Memorial.

SEXTON, Signal Boy, REGINALD PHILIP AMOS, J 28570(Po), RN. Age 17. Buried at Lyness Royal Naval Cemetery, grave F.101A.

SEYMOUR, Able Seaman, HERBERT JOSEPH, J 15790(Po), RN. Age 19. *From Slough, Buckinghamshire.* Commemorated on the Portsmouth Naval Memorial.

SHAILL, Boy 1st Class, THOMAS EDWIN, J 32523(Po), RN. Age 17. Commemorated on the Portsmouth Naval Memorial.

SHANKS, Chief Engine Room Artificer 2nd Class, JOHN, 270194(Po), RN. Age 40. *From Edinburgh.* Commemorated on the Portsmouth Naval Memorial.

SHANKS, Stoker 1st Class, JOHN, K 27968(Po), RN. Age 22. Commemorated on the Portsmouth Naval Memorial.

SHARP, Chief Ship's Cook, WALTER HENRY, 343916(Po), RN. Age 34. Commemorated on the Portsmouth Naval Memorial.

SHARPLES, Sub-Lieutenant, THOMAS HENRY WILFRID, RN. Age 21. *From Constable, Burton, Yorkshire.* Buried at Lyness Royal Naval Cemetery, grave F.3.

SHAW, Corporal, JAMES PEARSON, 12228(Po), RMLI. Age 31. Buried at Lyness Royal Naval Cemetery, grave F.121A.

SHEARMAN, Stoker 1st Class, CHARLES NEWMAN, 289048(Po), RN. Age 38. Commemorated on the Portsmouth Naval Memorial.

SHEPHERD, Ordinary Seaman, FREDERICK ROBERT, J 49848(Po), RN. Age 19. *From York.* Commemorated on the Portsmouth Naval Memorial.

SHEPHERD, Ordinary Telegraphist, WILLIAM, J 39057(Ch), RN. Age 17. *From Stramshall, Uttoxeter, Staffordshire.* Commemorated on the Chatham Naval Memorial.

SHERWIN, Telegraphist, CYRIL ERNEST, J 25178(Po), RN. Age 18. Commemorated on the Portsmouth Naval Memorial.

SHIELDS, Able Seaman, WALTER, J 21616(Dev), RN. Age 20. *From Girvan, Ayrshire.* Commemorated on the Plymouth Naval Memorial.

SHORT, Boy 1st Class, WILLIAM HENRY, J 32325(Po), RN. Age 17. *From Taunton, Somerset.* Commemorated on the Portsmouth Naval Memorial.

SIDEBOTHAM, Lance-Corporal, WILLIAM, 13006(Po), RMLI. Age 31. *From Ryde, Isle of Wight.* Buried at Lyness Royal Naval Cemetery, grave F.102.

SILK, Officer's Steward 2nd Class, ERNEST GIBBS, L 1054(Dev), RN. Age 23. *From Devonport.* Commemorated on the Plymouth Naval Memorial.

SILLS, Stoker 1st Class, ERNEST EDWARD, K 16815(Po), RN. Age 22. *From Enfield Wash, Middlesex.*

SIRDIFIELD, Stoker 1st Class, JAMES THOMAS, K 18336(Po), RN. Age 22. *From Mansfield, Nottinghamshire.* Commemorated on the Portsmouth Naval Memorial.

SKINNER, Stoker 1st Class, WILLIAM, K 24484(Po), RN. Age 19. Commemorated on the Portsmouth Naval Memorial.

SKYNNER, Lieutenant, WILLIAM WALKER, RN. Age 27. Commemorated on the Portsmouth Naval Memorial.

SMEDLEY, Stoker 1st Class, JOSEPH HENRY, K 24163(Po), RN. Age 21. Commemorated on the Portsmouth Naval Memorial.

SMITH, Stoker 1st Class, ALBERT, K 18646(Po), RN. Age 22. Commemorated on the Portsmouth Naval Memorial.

SMITH, Stoker 1st Class, ALBERT, SS 114387(Po), RN. Age 20. *From New Wortley, Leeds, Yorkshire.* Commemorated on the Portsmouth Naval Memorial.

SMITH, Private, ALFRED, 15494(Po), RMLI. Age 24. Commemorated on the Portsmouth Naval Memorial.

SMITH, Mechanician, BENJAMIN, 297766(Po), RN. Age 31. *From Kingsdown, Box, Wiltshire.* Commemorated on the Portsmouth Naval Memorial.

Appendix II
Weather and Tides, early June 1916

by Keith Johnson

Synoptic conditions

The weather report from the Meteorological Office of the British Isles for June 1916 had as its headline: "Abnormally cold and dull". The summary goes on to say:

> the atmospheric conditions over the British Isles were of a most unstable and unseasonal character. The mean distribution of air pressure was of a distinctly northerly type so that winds from points in the northerly half of the compass prevailed nearly all through the month. The most striking feature of the month was the very unusual persistency of cool to cold days. It was noted by one observer that it was the coldest June in 40 years.

To illustrate the unsettled nature of weather at beginning of June 1916, the information below covers the synoptic weather charts from the UK Meteorological Office for period 4-6 June.

Sun 4 June: A slow moving area of low pressure 995mb off the west coast of Scotland with winds from South East force 5 (22 knots).[375] Temp.: 45°F. An area of high pressure (1020mb) west of Portugal.

Mon 5 June: A slow moving area of low pressure 985mb centred on the Firth of Forth with winds from North East force 6 (24 knots). Temp.: 46°F. An area of high pressure (1015mb) west of Portugal.

Tues 6 June: A slow moving area of low pressure 990mb to the East of Wick/Orkney with winds from North North East force 6 (24 knots). Temp.: 45°F.

A depression of 985mb is not particularly low and would not necessarily mean gale force winds unless there was an area of high pressure close-by, thus squeezing the isobars and giving rise to a steep pressure gradient and thereby strong winds. Weather records show that 64% of the Junes from 1891 to 2015 were free of gales.

The Meteorological Office forecasts for Orkney and Shetland for the following 24 hours were as follows:

Noon Sunday 4 June: Fresh or strong Southerly winds veering Westerly later, dull, rainy, improving later, rather cold.

Noon Monday 5 June: Strong or high North Easterly wind, decreasing later, dull, some rain, improving, cold.

This latter forecast may have had some bearing on the decision to route HMS *Hampshire* West of Orkney.

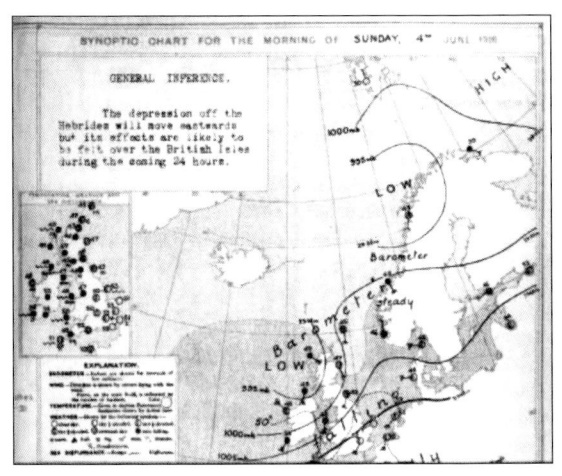

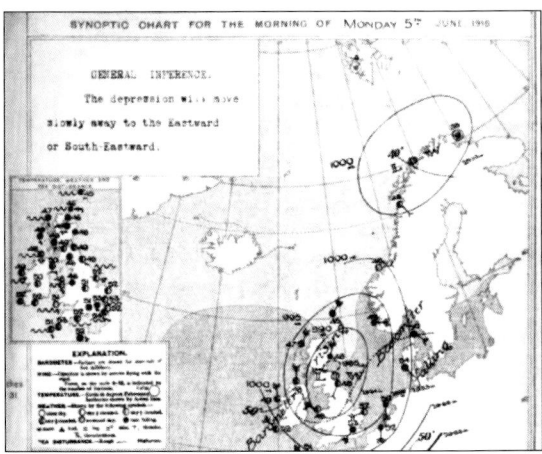

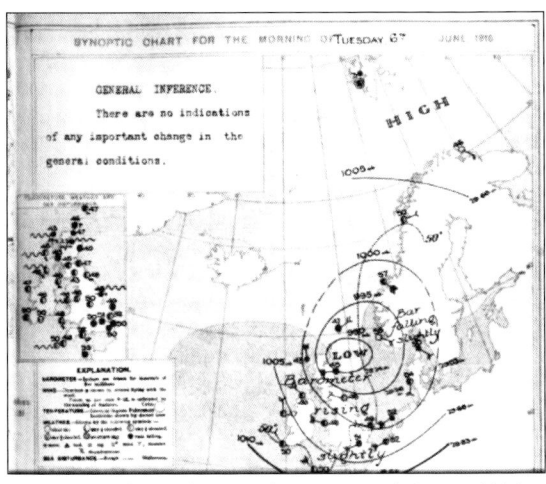

Met. Office Daily Weather Reports, 4-6 June 1916.

---

[375] The relationship between wind speed and wind force has been revised from time to time since Admiral Beaufort devised his scale in 1808, but the relationship in use in 1916 and shown below is very similar to that in use today:

Beaufort force		mph	knots
Fresh breeze	5	19-24	16-21
Strong breeze	6	25-31	22-27
High wind/Near Gale	7	32-38	28-33
Gale	8	39-46	34-40

II – Weather and Tides

Local Weather
The Meteorological Office forecasts tie with the weather observations taken by their accredited climate observer Magnus Spence at his "Normal Climatological Station" at Quoybellock in the centre of the parish of Deerness.[376] Relevant data is shown in the tables below and right:

24 hours from 0900	Mean Wind		Temperature			Rain
			Max.	Min.	Mean	
June 4	SE	19 knots	52°F	48°F	48°F	9mm
June 5	NNE	24 knots	46°F	44°F	44°F	23mm
June 6	N	19 knots	49°F	46°F	46°F	11mm

Wind at Deerness			
June GMT	Wind	mph	force
5 0400	NE	20	5
0800	NNE	24	6
1200	NNE	33	7
1300	N	32	7
1400	N	34	8
1500	N	34	8
1600	N	33	8
1700	NNW	35	8
1800	NNW	36	8
1900	NNW	39	8
2000	NW	40	8
2100	NW	34	8
2200	NW	33	7
2300	NW	34	7
2400	NW	32	7
6 0100	NW	23	6
0200	N	14	4
0300	NNE	16	5
0400	NNE	16	5
0800	N	21	5
1200	N	21	5
1600	N	18	5

The mean temperature in Deerness for June 1900-1920 was 50.4°F. On the day of the *Hampshire* sinking the mean temperature was 43.5°F [6.4°C], which is approximately 7°F lower than the average June temperature.

Wind speeds are generally higher over the sea than on land, so it appears that at the time of the sinking there was a North Westerly gale blowing, compounded by cold air temperatures and heavy rain. The wind chill at the time of sinking meant that the air temperature would have felt like about 32°F. With a sea temperature about 48°F it meant survival for those in the water would be very difficult.

Quoybellock station (TK1030).

HMS *Victor* recorded wind from NbyE force 5-6 with rough seas at 1800, just before she turned back. The tender *Flying Kestrel* reported a NW'ly wind force 7-8 with 15-20ft seas on her way north from Stromness. The steam yacht *Zaza* reported wind force 9 with waves over 25ft high when she left Kirkwall at 2125.[377]

Daylight
Sunset off Birsay on 5 June was at 2120, and twilight about 2230; the next morning off Sandwick twilight was about 0150 and sunrise 0311. The moon was new on 31 May and reached its first quarter on 8 June. On the overcast night of 5/6 June 1916 reports said it got dark at about 11pm and light again at about 3am.[378]

Tides
At Kirkwall High Water is 2.4m above Low Water at Springs and 1.1m at Neaps. The times of the tides were:[379]

	High Water		Low Water		High Water		Low Water	
Stromness	5/1200		5/1730		6/0000		6/0600	
Birsay	5/1212		5/1745		6/0015		6/0630	
Kirkwall	5/1316	2.2m	5/1856	1.0m	6/0115	2.5m	6/0748	0.8m

So if *Hampshire* sank at 2000 this was about 4¼ hours before HW Birsay, and if the rafts came ashore at 1am this was near enough at High Water.

Tidal Streams
Around Orkney the flood tide is generally an east-going stream, but off the West Mainland this stream divides to seaward of Bay of Skaill, running South along the coast towards Stromness and North along coast towards Birsay. This north-going stream begins at 4¼ to 4½ hours after HW Birsay and runs at a rate of up to 1 knot at spring tides. At 1¾ to 1½ hours before HW Birsay this flood stream weakens and its direction becomes irregular and subject to eddies, implying the southerly flow due to the ebb stream is weak.[380]

After *Hampshire* sank her rafts would have experienced the last 2 hours of the north-going flood, and thereafter a south-going ebb. But these tidal streams would have been weaker than the wind-induced current, which we now know would in theory flow 30° to the right of the down wind direction, i.e. in a SSE'ly direction if the wind was from the NW. In practice the rafts did drift in a SSE'ly direction, covering about 4 miles in about 4 hours.

---
[376] TNA ADM116/2324A. Magnus Spence, c1853-1919, a Birsay man and a Fellow of the Educational Institute of Scotland, was headmaster of Deerness School 1891-1919, and author of *Flora Orcadensis* (Eunson 2005, 130-7; Hewison 1998, 147).
[377] It was the report of *Zaza* that the Admiralty seems to have adopted in 1926. The weather actually experienced by *Hampshire* may have been less extreme, but alas the weather reports in the log books of the rescue vessels for 5th/2000 (when all were still in sheltered waters) and for 6th/0000 (when the weather off Marwick Head was moderating) don't give a clear picture.
[378] As in the main text, times given in 24 hour notation are GMT, those given "am" or "pm" are BST.
[379] These times are predictions by the UK Hydrographic Office; predictions for Kirkwall in *Peace's Almanac* differ by up to 5 minutes.
[380] These predictions are from the Admiralty's *North Coast of Scotland Pilot Book* (1975). The Admiralty *Tidal Stream Atlas for Orkney Islands* (NP209) is inconclusive about the tidal streams inshore close to the coast of Birsay. The *Clyde Cruising Club Tidal Atlas* for the Birsay area implies the Spring rates are less than 2.3 knots and Neap rates less than 1 knot.

unscrupulous blackguard I have yet encountered in journalism",[391] while Kitchener's brother publicly described him as "a mischievous rumourmonger".[392]

Power's populist campaign led directly to an Adjournment Debate in the House of Commons on 19 July 1926, and to the publication of the Admiralty's Narrative on 9 August. It climaxed with his sensational claim that he had found Kitchener's body buried in Norway and brought it back to Britain. However the widespread support for his vendetta collapsed when "Kitchener's Coffin" was opened by officials on 16 August and found to be empty.[393] Power claimed "there must have been a substitution" and denied he had hoaxed anyone. But it soon transpired that while in Orkney for the unveiling of the Marwick Head Memorial on 1 July 1926 Power had bought "Kitchener's Coffin"[394] and had it shipped to Newcastle where it arrived on 28 July. Meanwhile he was in Norway from 20 July till 4 August, during which time he hired an empty coffin, covered it with a Union Jack, and arranged for it to be filmed in a mock funeral in Stavanger. On his return to Newcastle he had "Kitchener's Coffin" shipped from Newcastle to Southampton on 7 August, and then six days later by rail from Southampton to London where he had its arrival filmed. The coffin was seized by police the following afternoon, a Saturday, and taken to Lambeth Mortuary; it was opened there on the morning of Monday 16th, in the presence of officials (but not Power, whom the police had excluded), and found to have never contained human remains.

On 17 August *The Daily Sketch* revealed that Frank Power was the assumed name Arthur Vectis Freeman, "a Hampshire man who had begun his career by studying for the Bar. Then he took up criminology and spent much time in investigations concerning big cases of crime."[395] In 1913 he was employed as a clerk by a firm of solicitors in the City of London, doing some journalism in his free time; for many years he made a living as the editor of technical journals; in 1916 he was managing a soldiers' rest house at Notting Hill Gate; in 1919 he was on the staff of the magazine *John Bull*.[396] In 1921 he became financially involved in a film "How Kitchener was Betrayed";[397] to help publicise this film Mr Singleton Gates told *The Daily Sketch* that it was he who had invented the story of Kitchener's body having been found in Norway, with the connivance of Freeman. In 1924, under his own name, Freeman published a small book criticising the management of the Great Eastern Railway.[398] In 1926 he was aged 44 and living with his wife in Shepherd's Bush, then Kensington.[399]

It appears that Freeman did not invent his assumed name but instead borrowed it from a Frank Power who had been correspondent for *The Times* during the siege of Khartoum (March 1884 to Jan. 1885) and whose *Letters from Khartoum, written during the Siege* was published in 1885.[400] McCormick claimed that after the death of Kitchener, Power "was obsessed by a passionate desire to solve what he regarded as almost a 'national crime' and probe the full story of *Hampshire*'s loss."[401] However in 1998 Melvin Harris[402] pointed out that Frank Le Poer Power, the war correspondent and British Consul at Khartoum, had been killed in September 1884![403]

What were the strengths and weaknesses of Freeman's stories? At one level he deserves considerable credit, for it is clear that without his publicising the issues several notable valuable contributions to the historiography might have gone unwritten: in 1925 Major John MacKay wrote an informative criticism of Jellicoe's routeing decision and the naval authorities' management of the rescue efforts,[404] albeit from a soldier's point of view; in mid-1926 survivor WC Phillips updated his detailed account of his time on HMS *Hampshire* that he had written 4 or 5 weeks after the accident, albeit this was not published until 1930; and in July 1926 the "Terrier" John Shearer recorded the "gruesome task" of Kirkwall RGA men recovering bodies.[405] More significantly, the Admiralty would not have published their Narrative of 1926, nor undertaken their extensive associated background enquiries,[406] albeit these would not be released to public view for at least 50 years (see below).

---

[391] Bridgeman 22 July 1926, TNA ADM116/324A; 24 July 1926 ADM116/3621.
[392] *Weekly Despatch* 22 Aug. 1926.
[393] See page 45 above.
[394] Contrary to Power's unsubstantiated claim that it had been made in England (*Referee* 13 June 1926), Kitchener's coffin was probably constructed by carpenters on HMS *Victorious*, the Scapa Flow depot ship, in June 1916 (*Orcadian* 19 Aug. 1926). It was so named because it was better built than others, in case Kitchener's body was recovered. The coffin was auctioned off in July 1925 and bought by Samuel Baikie of Bea Cottage, Stromness, who in turn had sold it to Power for £10 on 2 July 1926 (TNA ADM116/3621; *Daily News* 19 Aug. 1926, *Orcadian*, 19 Aug. 1926).
[395] *Orcadian* 19 Aug. 1926.
[396] McCormick 1959, 132; TNA MEPO2/2469.
[397] This film, based on information provided by Freeman, depicted the betrayal of Kitchener to a German woman by Rasputin. Private showings to members of Kitchener's family and a large number of Members of Parliament in November 1921 caused "great consternation", and despite it being banned by London County Council, Freeman made limited showings to the public in 1922 and February 1923 (TNA ADM116/3621; *Daily Sketch* 20 Aug. 1926).
[398] Freeman 1924.
[399] TNA MEPO2/2469.
[400] This book ran to three editions, the third of which at least was edited by Frank Power's brother Arnold.
[401] McCormick 1959, 132.
[402] Melvin Harris (1930-2009), the author, broadcaster and sceptic.
[403] http://www.casebook.org/dissertations/maybrick_diary/mb-mc.html.
[404] Three versions of MacKay's account survive: a lengthy typescript titled "H.M.S. *Hampshire*" evidently written in 1925 that was held in the *Orcadian*'s files (now held as OA D1/1204/45), a shorter article titled "What Might have been Done" (*Orcadian* 1 July 1926), and loose quotations of the former by Power (*Referee* 22 Nov., 13 Dec. 1925).
[405] Phillips 1930; *Orcadian* 1 July 1926.
[406] e.g. Tom Kent's statement ran to 4 pages, and c.80 graves of British WWI sailors in Norway were checked (TNA ADM 116/2324A).

Nor, in the absence of official denials until this Narrative was published, should he be criticised for his beliefs in the Admiralty's (erroneous) publication that HM Drifter *Laurel Crown* sank on 2 June, that no rescue vessels were despatched until 7am on 6 June, or that records were being withheld that would reveal serious incompetence of several service personnel in positions of responsibility.

But Freeman also exploited officialdom's secretive instincts, enhancing and publicising information that he garnered without critical examination, and shamelessly fabricating many details himself, including:
- his alleged 13th, 14th and 15th survivors;
- his claim that there was considerable delay in despatching the rescue vessels;
- his claim that there was an argument over launching the Stromness lifeboat;
- his claim that survivors were deliberately posted overseas;[407]
- his claim that Kitchener's Coffin was made in London before Kitchener's death;[408]
- his claim that the publication of the Admiralty Narrative added little to what was already known;[409]
- his embellishments of the tales that civilians were forbidden to assist in rescue efforts (see Chapter 6 above);
- many of the conspiracy theories addressed in Chapter 8 above, including the stories that *Hampshire* was attacked by a submarine in the Mediterranean, to which a spy had signalled; the unsuitability of *Hampshire* for the mission; her poor record and condition; negligent navigation; the shooting of two spies in Belfast in Feb. 1916 and the knowledge then that she would visit Russia; that any explosions subsequent to the first were attributable to a bomb on board; that Kitchener was seen boarding a boat; that he and two others survived for a day and two nights; that Fitzgerald had been the victim of foul play by spies; that his body was found in a boat; and that a body in Norway in khaki uniform with medal ribbons had been associated with *Hampshire*.

Several of his correspondents, including Phillips, Rogerson, Sims, Wesson and Kitchener's brother, felt he had manipulated their relationship,.[410]

Freeman was questioned by Scotland Yard on 17 August 1926 but not arrested. Kitchener's family,[411] the government, the Admiralty and the police were all anxious that the affair should be allowed to blow over as quickly as possible. The next day Freeman declared his intention "to go on with my investigations to find the body", but after his dénouement he was ridiculed in the national press – even by the editor of the *Sunday Referee*[412] – and he disappeared from public view.[413]

But if Freeman/Power fell from grace with his credibility shattered, many of his embellishments of the disaster took on a life of their own and were accepted as facts by successive generations both in Orkney and elsewhere. Some were further embellished by later conspiracy theorists.

The Admiralty Narrative White Paper of August 1926[414]
This account of the disaster, published most reluctantly by the Admiralty,[415] has been widely criticised, not least by McCormick, but the records now available at The National Archives show it to be a much more credible account than its sceptics have claimed.[416] The authorities were even confident enough to time its publication, and to include a denial that Kitchener's body was buried in Norway, at the very time Power was claiming he had found the body. Nevertheless the Narrative has several weaknesses, including:[417]
- the fallacy that Kitchener's visit to Russia was a secret, even if the Admiralty was not to blame (p4);
- the Admiralty's argument that *U 75* laid her mines in the wrong position (p12, footnote);
- the Admiralty's claim that moored mines laid of 7 metres below High Water should not have posed a threat to *Hampshire* (p12);
- the weakness (and irrelevance) of the Admiralty's disassociation with the pinnace and dinghy (pp10, 25-6);
- the dismissal of the possibility that the Stromness lifeboat could have rescued some survivors before the rafts foundered (p19);
- the overlooking of the failures to mobilise the Stromness Rocket Apparatus Brigade, to requisition some vehicles, and to enlist local guides (pp17, 19-20);

---

[407] *Orcadian* 7, 25 Feb. 1926. Curiously Power did not enlarge on his claim that Col. Slater, a Territorial, was posted to the Far East.
[408] *Referee* 13 June 1926.
[409] McCormick 1959, 141.
[410] TNA ADM 116/2324A; McCormick 1959, 203; *Weekly Despatch* 22 Aug. 1926.
[411] *Daily Mail* 17 Aug. 1926; *Weekly Despatch* 22 Aug. 1926.
[412] *Referee* 22 Aug. 1926.
[413] The Metropolitan Police kept a file on Power. In Dec. 1926 he told them he was earning his living as a typist and shorthand writer and not in good financial circumstances (TNA MEPO2/2469). He may have been the staff of *John Blunt's Monthly* on 15 October 1929 when the editor thereof resurrected several of his old claims in an article 'Who Murdered Kitchener?' (TNA ADM116/324A).
[414] An annotated typescript copy of a draft of the Admiralty Narrative of 1926 by Fleet Paymaster V Weekes, donated by Mr P Parkes to the Orkney Archive where it is held as OA D1/843, adds nothing of substance; nor do the drafts in TNA ADM116/2324A.
[415] Although Power claimed the Admiralty Narrative raised some "controversial matters" (*Referee* 15 Aug. 1926) he never developed these points. Coincidentally the Narrative was published while the alleged remains of Kitchener were en route between Newcastle and Southampton, so enabling Power to claim he was more preoccupied with the body than with the Narrative.
[416] In particular TNA ADM116/2324A has several draft copies which suggest the Admiralty had few substantive issues to keep concealed but were naive in explaining to a suspicious public the reasons for their previous reticence.
[417] Copy held as OA D68/8/17. The drafts of this paper survive as TNA ADM116/2324A.

- the inadequate treatment of the accusations of civilians being prevented from engaging in rescue work (p22) and of the involvement of Inspector Vance (p23);
- the failure to explain why the terms of reference of the Court of Enquiry were so narrow and why its findings could not be published (p23).

With the benefit of hindsight and of reading the files now available for public scrutiny it is now clear that although in fact the Admiralty staff had little substantive to hide, this was not clear to them in 1916 or even 1926, and they became mesmerised in the details and possible weaknesses in the planning of the voyage and the execution of the responses, and took refuge in their traditions of secrecy. Both the Admiralty and the government failed to recognise that the popularity and gravitas of Lord Kitchener and the prevalence of conspiracy theories from the outset meant that the fortunes of war and a combination of coincidences and ill-luck warranted a much more frank explanation that did not read like a "white-wash".

Despite these failings the Admiralty Narrative and the collapse of Freeman's campaign undermined the credibility of most of the conspiracy theorists. Useful accounts by Phillips, Wesson, Farnden and Cashman became available during the 1930s.[418] But populist tales continued,[419] and the extent of the issues outstanding in the 1950s were such that there was still plenty to be challenged and loose ends to be tidied up.

The book *The Mystery of Lord Kitchener's Death* by Donald McCormick in 1959
Donald McCormick (1911-1998), aka Richard Deacon, was a London-based journalist and popular historian.[420] Born in Flintshire, he served as a Lieutenant in Naval Intelligence during World War II. From 1946 till 1973 he worked as a full time journalist for Kemsley Newspaper Group, latterly as foreign manager of *The Sunday Times*. Between 1955 and 1976 he wrote 34 books, and almost as many again in his retirement. His subjects included biographies of Sir Maurice Oldfield and Ian Fleming and histories of the British, Chinese, French, Israeli, Japanese and Russian secret services. He was also attracted to controversial topics on which verifiable evidence was scarce: he wrote extensively about spies, and his other subjects included *Identity of Jack the Ripper* and *Taken for a Ride: The History of Cons and Con-men*. One of his publications lead to an out-of-court settlement, another had to be withdrawn following a libel suit. His prose is flowery but plodding, yet when disguised as non-fiction it is gripping. Deriving much of his 'scholarly information' from the files of his employer and his own fertile imagination, he was suspiciously productive for a supposedly non-fiction writer. His eye for a good story and his reliance on an informal network of oral informants mean that it is often difficult to separate fact from fiction and to judge the reliability of his more controversial claims. His frauds largely escaped detection until shortly before his death. Robert Leeson claimed:[421]

> *From a social science perspective, 'Deacon' McCormick can be dismissed as a fraud. From a literary perspective, however, he was a sensation – perhaps 'History's Greatest Fraudster', who deceived highly regarded, and highly self-regarding, scholars. .... The unsensational parts [of his writings] are primarily a repetition of material already published. Any 'knowledge' that is original to him – most of it sensational – must, however be tested.*

The Mystery of Lord Kitchener's Death was one of McCormick's first books. It has long been accepted in Orkney as the seminal work on this subject, and hitherto has received little criticism.[422] And to be fair to him it would seem that his treatment of Kitchener's death was less fraudulent than his treatment of his later subjects, for he did pull together a lot of disparate sources into a very readable book that debunked most of the conspiracy theories of Frank Power. He was also correct in his final conclusion that it was "an extraordinary combination of ill luck and coincidence [that] mainly brought about the disaster."

---

[418] Phillips 1930; *Sunday Express* 8 July 1934; Hammerton 1938, 604-7.
[419] For example *John Blunt's Monthly* (15 Oct. 1929); Wood 1932.
[420] Not to be confused with the Scottish journalist and popular historian Donald MacCormick (1939-2009).
[421] Leeson 2015, viii, 8, 10, 30, 33, 49, 50. Leeson, an Australian, is a leading political economist and Visiting Professor of Economics, Stanford University. Leeson quotes the welsh historian Howard Kimberley: McCormick was "guilty of poor scholarship and misrepresentation of legitimate evidence ... [and] was a totally untrustworthy author who fabricated evidence to misrepresent history" (pp208, 9). Leeson's colleague Daniel Baldino at Notre Dame University wrote "McCormick was a journalist who was drawn to contentious subjects" and "the evidence that underpins [his] analysis of unusual, controversial events is often sketchy and difficult to substantiate; his research tended to give considerable weight to low-grade or vague information; he over-relied on threadbare and recycled single sources; he had an eye for a good story; he too often gathered evidence and recalled ambiguous information in a highly selective manner, regardless of whether the information was credible or certifiable; [his] track record points to a pattern of poorly researched and reckless scholarship connected to a strong deficiency in solid, corroborative evidence." (pp.208, 9, 215, 6, 221, 2, 6). Professor Richard Spence of Idaho University thought that McCormick "had a knack for telling people what they wanted to believe ... the biggest problem with McCormick, from a historian's point of view, is that his fictions have become widely disseminated and repeated. ... In the end, the greatest disservice McCormick did with his lies – and let's be honest, that's what they were – was to historical truth. His books contain many legitimate and interesting details .... it is a shame that such things are contaminated by his devious and dishonest habit of larding his works with fables." (pp.239, 254). Jeremy Duns, the British author and critic, described McCormick as "a tabloid hack [who] had a brilliant sense for what would sell, what would ring true, and how to present it. .... I have my suspicions why he did what he did. I think it was essentially to sell books and make money, fast. ... [He] was aided in his deceptions by the fact that he flew under the radar. If he had been writing on academic subjects then he would have been put through the combine harvester almost immediately: but Prince Madog, the death of Lord Kitchener and Jack the Ripper were side disciplines run, at least in earlier times, by talented dilettantes. It also worked in his favour that he did not write more than one book in any field, apart from espionage where secret sources are the norm." (pp238, 9, 40).
[422] McCormick's book has even been described as "excellent" (Pickford 1999, 88; Hazell 2000, 51).

IV – Reliability and Availability of Relevant Accounts 103

However in his 1985 biography of Kitchener, Trevor Royle avoided quoting McCormick, his only reference being that "The more vivid of these fabrications are collected in Donald McCormick *The Mystery of Lord Kitchener's Death*".[423] In 1998 Melvin Harris[424] found that McCormick's account of the Frank Power story was "badly flawed". Harris then checked "the other 'evidence' in this book and ultimately reached this firm conclusion that the only new evidence (telling first-person 'revelations') was simply manufactured."[425] In 2013 Jeremy Paxman described McCormick as "a cheap journalist", offering "little that might be called evidence."[426]

So what were the weaknesses of McCormick's treatment of the *Hampshire* disaster? I can find no evidence that McCormick ever visited Orkney. He obtained some of his fresh "evidence" by writing to Ernest Marwick, part of whose verbatim reply McCormick wrongly attributed to JG Sinclair.[427] Several passages in his book are probably fictional, such as his unverifiable version of Mr Thomson having been told "if you attempt to launch the lifeboat, it's mutiny ... and I'll have the whole lot of you locked up" and being "very bitter about the chinking of glasses of pink gin in an adjacent room while I put my case to the Naval Commander", his insinuation that lassoo marks around the neck of the body of Fitzgerald were due to foul play, his chapter on "Espionage in a Turkish Bath", and his conversation with the Irish Republican Frankie Ryan in 1936.[428] McCormick's more tangible failings include:
- his claim that German interception of British signals led to the mining of the waters off Marwick Head;[429]
- his claim that only six people in Birsay actually saw the disaster;[430]
- his claim that the authorities' rescue efforts led to a "far greater" loss of life than need have occurred;[431]
- his fostering of the tradition that civilians were ordered not to help in rescue efforts (see Chapter 6 above);
- his claim that restrictions of travel to/from Orkney were triggered by the *Hampshire* disaster;[432]
- his claims concerning the alleged Secret Report of Detective Inspector Vance;[433]
- his incomplete analysis of some of the evidence then available;[434]
- his championing of the IRA plot conspiracy theory;[435]
- his insinuation that there was some mystery as to why Power was not arrested in August 1926: "perhaps the biggest puzzle of all is why no action was taken by the authorities against Frank Power",[436] when it is quite clear that the government, the Admiralty and the Kitchener family all wanted him and his campaign to disappear from public view as quickly and quietly as possible.

Accounts released by the National Archives
What was formerly the Public Record Office and is now The National Archives at Kew released most of the official records relating to the loss of HMS *Hampshire* and the death of Lord Kitchener in 1967, and the remainder between 1970 and 2014.[437] These records comprise some forty files, five of which are 5-10cm thick; they include contemporary details of Kitchener's mission, German mining and British minesweeping operations, copies of the original signals, telegrams and reports of June 1916 and correspondence, draft reports, hoax/conspiracy correspondence, and Parliamentary Questions and extensive enquiries by the Admiralty in 1926 arising from Frank Power's campaign. Particularly noteworthy are accounts by:[438]

Vice Admiral F Brock, ACOS, 5 June 1916, 2200 hours, and 15 June 1916, the latter including reports of Corporal Drever and Gunners Angus and Norn;
Lieut. Col. GNA Harris RMA, O/C Troops Orkneys, including précis of interviews with survivors on 6 June;
Capt. H Blackett RN, 7 June 1916, including Report of Court of Enquiry of that date;
Capt. FM Walker RN, 7 June 1916;
Lieut. Col. CL Brooke RMA, 8 June 1916, 21 Feb., 8 June 1926;
Lieut A Ruddell RN, HM Trawler *Brutus*, 17 June 1916 (Minesweeping report TNA ADM 137/1209);
GPO Staff in Birsay & Kirkwall: Miss JA Cumloquoy, 28 June 1916, J MacKay, JP Meason, 26 June 1916;

---
[423] Royle 1985, 413.
[424] Melvin Harris (1930-2004) was a British author, broadcaster, researcher and skeptic.
[425] http://www.casebook.org/dissertations/maybrick_diary/mb-mc.html. In a similar study of McCormick's book on Jack the Ripper, Royle "began to see that many Ripper studies were crippled by hoaxes, or were hoaxes in their own right. One of the prominent hoaxers turned out to be McCormick."
[426] Paxman, 2014a.
[427] OA D31/36/1/2; McCormick 1959, 57-8.
[428] McCormick 1959, 57, 60, 73, 104-121, 175.
[429] McCormick 1959, 143-7.
[430] McCormick 1959, 54.
[431] McCormick 1959, 206.
[432] McCormick 1959, 197. See also page 37 above.
[433] McCormick 1959, 191-204, 207, 214. This despite his claim on p130 that Vance did not exist!
[434] For example McCormick's claim that 78 branches of the British Legion supported Power, whereas more careful reading shows this figure later increased to 120 branches (*Referee* 28 Mar., 28 Apr. 1926). On the other hand McCormick seems to have had access to the contents of file ADM116/2324B which was not released by the Public Record Office until 1977!
[435] McCormick 1959, 206.
[436] McCormick 1959, 139.
[437] The last two files, TNA PC12/202 (Lord Kitchener National Memorial Fund – Supplemental Charter 1939) and TNA IR59/49 (Lord Kitchener's Will), were to remain closed to the public until 2015 and 2025 respectively. However Paxman had them declassified in Aug. 2014 under a Freedom of Information Act request and found both to be "dull as dishwater" (Paxman 2014a, 2014b).
[438] Except where indicated, all these accounts are filed in TNA ADM116/2323, 116/2324A, 116/2324B and 116/3621.

Mrs M Watt at Skaill House, 16 July 1916 (ADM1/8468/226); part factual, part hearsay;

Sub-Lieut. J Spence RNR in Birsay, 6 Apr. 1917 (ADM116/2323); factual, very detailed;

Anon, Birsay, n.d. (1917): letter alleging threat of shooting, lifeboat refused (TNA ADM 116/2323);

Capt. TE Davies *Flying Kestrel,* 23 Feb 1926; inconsistencies: claimed *Flying Kestrel* was an ocean going tug, which photographs show she clearly wasn't, and to have recovered 56 bodies!;

Shipwright WC Phillips, 26 Feb., 9 and 10 March 1926, including account written 4-5 weeks after accident, later embellished as the 56 page booklet he published in 1930;

Mr W Wesson, 15 May 1926: factual;

Capt. JW Jones RMA, 24 May 1926; this includes several callous comments;

Cdr. W Forbes RN steam yacht *Jason II,* 2 and 6 June 1926;

Lieut. J Vance, City of Glasgow Police, 16 June 1926: written denial that he had made any investigation or report concerning *Hampshire*;

Mr WE Bennett, 10 and 12 July 1926; denied speaking to press; factual;

Stoker FL Sims, 19 July 1926; denied making the statements attributed to him by the press.

The Naval Staff Monographs "Mining Operations of German Submarines around the British Isles 1915-1918"[439] and Chapter 3 of "The Loss of the Hampshire", in "Home Waters – Part VI"[440] offer valuable analyses.[441]

These accounts are largely consistent on the main issues, albeit none can be considered 100% reliable – for example, there remain the possibilities of the use of selective wording and of memory loss. There has been some editing of 1916 material into 1926 files, but no redaction or expurgation from the collection is readily apparent. The files are thus clearly much more reliable than the accounts that appeared in the press in the 1920s and those later promoted by McCormick and the many subsequent quotes thereof. Together the files constitute, in effect, "the secret dossier" that Power frequently referred to, but reveal no hint of truth in any of the conspiracy theories he advanced.[442] Indeed the internal notes, often candid, show clearly that Admiralty staff had nothing substantive to hide, and their secrecy, albeit intuitive, can be accounted for by their concerns over matters relating to national security and legal precedent.

Other contemporary material that has only come to light in recent years include Margaret Tait's Journal[443], the letters of Simpson of 6th June and Sims of July & Aug. 1916 and Nov. 1917,[444] and the original account by MacKay.[445] There is also a wealth of material now available on other topics touched on in this volume, notably with respect to Chapter 2 above in particular and to German submarines in general.

Later Accounts

Later tape-recordings were made of the recollections of eyewitnesses Joe Angus (1964), James Gaudie (1966), Mrs Sabiston (1966, 1977), Reg Holloway (1974), Dave Firth (1977), Mrs Hunter (1981, n.d.), John Fraser (1982) and Willie Harvey and Peter Brass (1982, alas partly inaudible), and the written recollections of Fred Sims (1960, 1984, 1991), William Cashman (n.d.), Mrs Bain (1970), Surgeon CJG Taylor (n.d. 1980s?)[446] and Winkie Cumming (n.d., published 1990).[447] All these oral histories offer colourful insights, but alas some significant inconsistencies and references to McCormick mean their reliability has to be questioned.[448]

In 1966 Ernest Marwick marked the 50th anniversary with a summary in the *Orcadian* (OA D31/48/13). This unfortunately added weight to McCormick's interpretation. In 1985 Royle published a comprehensive and freshly researched summary and added new information, though this volume has shown he was overly critical of both Jellicoe and Brock. Other publications adding minor "new" details include Warner 1985, Wylie 1996, Brown 2008, Hazell 2010, MacDonald 2011, 2012, Spence 2013, Paxman 2014a, 2014b and Storer 2014. Authors giving able and comprehensive summaries but apparently adding nothing new include Cassar 1977, Hewison 1985, Pickford 1999, Hazell 2000, Stell 2010 and Paxman 2013. Briefer summaries appear in OA D70/4/25, Royle 2006, Konstam 2009 and McCutcheon 2013. Examples of ill-founded, albeit no doubt sincere, "hearsay" accounts include Ritson 1983 and Brown 2016.

Several websites with relevant information not to be found elsewhere are listed in the Bibliography below.

---

[439] TNA ADM186/629.

[440] TNA ADM186/628.

[441] It is curious that subsequent authors, even MacDonald and Royle, have made so little use of this original material, much of which has been available since 1967; perhaps the sheer quantity of the records have been a deterrent, perhaps it was thought not worthwhile as what was presumably the most controversial material would be contained in files were still not open to the public.

[442] Apart from some evidence that the "secret" of Kitchener's visit had been leaked in London, in Russia and probably even in Germany.

[443] OA D1/825. Margaret Tait, then aged 44, was the sister of cabinet maker James Tait of 6, Broad St., Kirkwall.

[444] *Orcadian* 17 May 2012; Orkney Fossil and Heritage Centre, Burray.

[445] OA D1/1204/45.

[446] IWM Docs. 12018.

[447] Holloway: OA D1/933/2; Gaudie: OA D31/TR111; Angus: OA D31/TR113; Mrs Sabiston: OA D31/TR115, TA26/2; Firth OA TA26/1; Hunter OA TA26/3, OA RO7/131; Fraser OA TA26/4; Harvey and Brass: OA TA401, TA402; Sims: London Country Buses Magazine 1960, Royle 1985, 372, *Hemel Hempstead Gazette* 1991; Mrs Bain: OA D31/1/4/17; Cumming: *Orcadian* 30 Aug. 1990. Several of these recollections clearly refer to events and opinions recounted in McCormick 1959 rather than to their own memories: in TA402 the narrator even explicitly refers to "the book".

[448] This reservation on bias in oral "memories" of World War I events is not unique to Orcadians (Reynolds 2013, 370).

Acknowledgements

The authors wish to thank the following for their assistance:

Alison Aitken, Phil Astley, Wendy Barker, Mary Benjamin, Joanna Bourke, Graham Brown, Leslie Burgher, Lynn Campbell, Elizabeth Corsie, Anthony Denton, Jillian Donnachie, Karen Esson, Howie Firth, Tom Flett, Barbara Foulkes, Alice Garson, Sheila Garson, Pete Glazier, George Gray, Brett Green, Lucy Gibbon, Kenny Harcus, Winnie Harvey, Philip Hayes, Roger Holt, Bill Lawford, John Liptrot, Rod MacDonald, Eleanor MacLeod, Juliet Mann, Alan Manzie, Ann Marwick, Ron Marwick, James Miller, John Moar, Fiona Morris, David Murdoch, Hugh Pinchin, Spencer Rosie, Ken Ross, John Ryder, Alice Sabiston, Lesley Scarth, the late Jim Sabiston, Albert Spence, Bill Spence, Geoffrey Stell, Bertrand Taylor, Ivan Watt, Bryce Wilson, and Frank and Sarah Zabriskie.

Also the staff of Aberdeen Central Library, the British Library, London, the Burray Fossil and Heritage Centre, Burray, the Hydrographic Office, Taunton, the Imperial War Museum, London, the Orkney Library and Archive, Kirkwall, the Postal Museum, London, the National Archives, Kew, the National Museum of the Royal Navy, Portsmouth, the New York Public Library, New York, the Orkney Islands Council, Kirkwall, the Stromness Museum, Stromness, and the University of the Highlands and Islands Archaeology Institute, Kirkwall.

The following individuals and organisations have kindly given their permission to reproduce images from their records: Alice Garson, Scott McIvor, Frankie Tait, Craig Taylor, Marjo Tykken, the Imperial War Museum, the Mary Evans Illustrated London News Picture Library, Colin Keldie K4 Graphics, the Ministry of Defence, the National Archives, the National Collection of Aerial Photography, *The Orcadian*, the Orkney Library and Archive, Orkney Photographic, Peedie Models, the Stena Line Group, Gothenburg, and The University of the Highlands and Islands Archaeology Institute. Provenance is given under each illustration. Illustrations not credited have been supplied by the relevant authors. Best endeavours have been used to contact other copyright holders; the publishers apologise in advance if any copyright credits that have been overlooked and will ensure these are included in any subsequent editions.

Finally the editor wishes to thank the Orkney Heritage Society for taking on the role of publisher, and the staff of *The Orcadian* for once again providing much more advice and support than the simple words "Printed by" can imply. Without the support of these two organisations, and of course the knowledge, diligence, time, patience and encouragement of the other authors, this publication would not have been possible.

Bibliography

Manuscripts

Abbreviations:
- BFHC: Burray Fossil and Heritage Centre, Burray.
- BM: Bundesarchiv Militärarchiv, Freiburg, Germany.
- IWM: Imperial War Museum, London.
- OA: Orkney Archive, Kirkwall.
- POST: The Postal Museum, London.
- TNA: The National Archives, Kew.
  - NB: All TNA files below were closed till 1967, except where shown otherwise.
- UKHO: UK Hydrographic Office, Taunton.

BFHC	Hourie papers (photocopies of originals deposited by late Mrs. A Hourie).
	1916, June 29 Letter from Admiralty to Mr Harvey, Stockan.
	1916, n.d Letter by Mrs Sims to Mrs Harvey (quoted by Willie Harvey in TA/401).
	1916, Aug. 31 Letter by Fred Sims to Mrs Harvey.
	1917, Nov. 22 Letter by Fred Sims to Mrs Harvey.
BM KTB *U 75*	*Kriegstagebuch* (War Diary) of *U 75*; copied by U.S. National Archives and Record Administration microfilm series T-1022, roll 20 ref. PG 61653.
HO WS *Hampshire*	(n.d.) Wreck Sheet for HMS *Hampshire.*
IWM Docs.4098	1916 Yeoman G Reeve papers, press cutting.
IWM Docs.10730	1916, July 18 Mrs Hankey, letter from Frances Parker.
IWM Docs.10969	1916 Midshipman E Fellowes RNR, 14 letters, 2 photographs, obituary notice.
IWM Docs.12018	1916, Jan.-Dec. Surgeon CJG Taylor RNVR, m.film diary of service on HMHS *Soudan*.
OA D1/404/1	1916-1947 Bundle of printed papers involving Sir George T Arthur. Gifted Jan. 1994 by Margaret Flaws, née Arthur.
OA D1/525	1911-1918 Photocopy of journal kept by Margret Tait (c.1859-1939) of daily life in Kirkwall mentioning sinking of HMS Hampshire (35pp., gifted c.1980).
OA D1/768	2001 Photocopies of mss. ré loss of HMS *Hampshire*. Gifted by Brian Budge.
OA D1/843	n.d. (c. July1926) "The Loss of HMS *Hampshire* and Lord Kitchener 1916": Personal papers of Fleet Paymaster Victor HT Weekes, former Secretary to Admiral Jellicoe (copy of the typescript "Worked up" draft of the Narrative in TNA ADM116/2324A).
OA D1/933	1916 Sinking of the HMS *Hampshire*: Accounts of the Rescue of Survivors.
OA D1/933/1	2005, Aug. 25 Covering letter by AE Barker.
OA D1/933/3	Cuttings from *Daily Mail* 1916 June 11 and *Daily Sketch* June 12.
OA D1/933/4	1916 Postcards of HMS *Hampshire* and Royal Marines Rescue Party.
OA D1/939/2	1901-1933 Tom Kent Scrapbooks of photographs and newspaper cuttings of farmhouses where *Hampshire* survivors were given hospitality.
OA D1/1204/45	n.d. (c.1925) Major John MacKay typescript "HMS *Hampshire*".
OA D31	Ernest Marwick Papers.
OA D31/1/4/17	1970, Feb. 2. Xerox copy of letter from a Mrs. Bain, Hopeman, ré events of June 1916.
OA D31/36/1/1	1975-1976 Correspondence with William M. Grant, Edinburgh, ré proposed book.
OA D31/36/1/2	1957-1959 Correspondence with Donald McCormick, Tunbridge Wells, ré his book.
OA D31/36/1/3	1926, July 7 'The Tower of Remembrance opening of the Kitchener Memorial, Marwick Head, Birsay' in *The Orkney Herald Supplement*.
OA D31/48/13/4	1966, June 2 'The Day That Kitchener Died' in *The Orcadian*.
OA D68/8/17	1926 *The Loss of H.M.S. Hampshire on 5th June, 1916* – Official narrative.
OA D70/4/25	1997 Fereday Prize Essay. *Lord Kitchener and the HMS Hampshire*, Melissa Spence.
OA D70/16/29	2013 Fereday Prize Essay. *What really happened the night HMS Hampshire sunk*, Tom Flett.
POST 33/1821A	1926 Loss of HMS *Hampshire*: original telegrams to Admiralty, etc., official narrative.
Stromness Museum	1926 *The Kitchener Mystery* Scrapbook of George Ellison containing pp100 of newspaper cuttings, mainly by/concerning Frank Power.
TNA ADM1/8468/226	HMS *Hampshire*, Loss of. Allegations concerning delay in sending help.
TNA ADM1/8470/238	HMS *Hampshire*, Loss of. Précis of enquiry.
TNA ADM1/8960	HMS *Hampshire*, Loss of. Stray papers, 1926.
TNA ADM1/22774	Wreck of HMS *Hampshire* – requests re salvage, 1948, 1951 (released 1982).
TNA ADM53/53040	HMS *Menace*, Ship's log June 1916.
TNA ADM53/49310	HMS *Midge*, Ship's log June 1916.
TNA ADM53/50165	HMS *Minster*, Ship's log June 1916.
TNA ADM53/52211	HMS *Napier*, Ship's log June 1916.
TNA ADM53/53045	HMS *Oak*, Ship's log June 1916.
TNA ADM53/54247	HMS *Owl*, Ship's log June 1916.
TNA ADM53/66480	HMS *Unity*, Ship's log June 1916.
TNA ADM53/67364	HMS *Victor*, Ship's log June 1916.
TNA ADM116/1515	Bi-Monthly Minesweeping Statement, #96 15 June - #98 15 July 1916.

TNA ADM116/1526   HMS *Hampshire*, Loss of, Casualties, survivors, correspondence.
TNA ADM116/2323   HMS *Hampshire*, Loss of, Case 1893, v.I, Summary of Jellicoe's report on sinking; court of enquiry minutes; notices to press; services rendered to survivors (released 1977).
TNA ADM116/2324A HMS *Hampshire*, Loss of, Case 1893, v.II, Frank Power; conspiracies; signal records; *Flying Kestrel*; reports from officers involved in rescue attempts (released 1980).
TNA ADM116/2324B HMS *Hampshire*, Loss of, Case 1893, v.III, 250 Parliamentary questions and responses; conspiracies; F. Power hysteria (released 1977).
TNA ADM137/302   Jutland – Reports of Proceedings, 1916 (including that of HMS *Hampshire*).
TNA ADM137/1167   Records used for Official History Orkney Jan-June 1916: Summary of Case 1893.
TNA ADM137/1209   Records used for Official History Orkney July-Nov. 1916: Mines swept, by Lieut. Ruddell.
TNA ADM137/1992   Grand Fleet Intelligence Office Pack v.XXI (released 1968).
TNA ADM137/3056   Records of Director of Minesweeping – Demobilising of Auxiliary Patrol 1918-1919.
TNA ADM137/3138   HM Drifter *Laurel Crown*, Loss of. Court of Enquiry 23 Aug. 1916.
TNA ADM137/3621   HMS *Hampshire*, Loss of, Records used for official history.
TNA ADM137/3903   Papers concerning German Submarines *U 60 - U 90*.
TNA ADM139/3913   Original History Sheets *U 41 - U 80*.
TNA ADM137/4069   Intercepted German Messages.
TNA ADM137/4105   Reports of Enemy Submarine Activities received by NID.
TNA ADM186/624   Naval Staff Monograph Vol. XVI, Home Waters Part VI Oct. 1915 - June 1916.
TNA ADM186/628   Naval Staff Monograph Vol. XVII, Home Waters, Part VII, June-Nov. 1916; copied at http://www.navy.gov.au/media-room/publications/world-war-i-naval-staff-monographs.
TNA ADM186/629   Mining Operations of German Submarines around the British Isles 1915-1918.
TNA CAB45/276   HMS *Hampshire*, Loss of, Summary 1926.
TNA HO144/6029   Film *The Betrayal of Lord Kitchener*: Steps to ban exhibition 1921-26 (released 2000).
TNA HW7/23   Paper prepared for Jellicoe.
TNA IR59/49   Lord Kitchener's Will (closed till 2025, but released 2014).
TNA MEPO2/2469   Metropolitan Police file on Frank Power 1926-32 (released 1983).
TNA MT23/601/2   *Flying Kestrel*.
TNA PC12/202   Lord Kitchener National Memorial – Supplemental Charter 1939 (released early, 2014).
TNA PRO30/57   Horatio Herbert Kitchener, 1st Earl Kitchener of Khartoum: Papers on microfilm.
TNA PRO30/57/67   Russia: correspondence: Major-General Sir John Hanbury-Williams and others.
TNA PRO30/57/82   Munitions: correspondence and reports: Cabinet members and others.
TNA PRO30/57/85   Lord Kitchener's journey to Russia: correspondence and report of sinking of HMS *Hampshire*. Includes copy of invitation from Tsar.
TNA PRO30/57/119 HMS *Hampshire*: newspaper reports, 6-10 June 1916.
TNA TS27/42   HMS *Hampshire*: issue of whether civilians attached to Kitchener's staff were covered by the Injuries in War Compensation Act 1914 and Order in Council of 27 May 1915.
TNA WO138/44   Field Marshal The Earl Kitchener of Khartoum [Personal] No.1 file 1896-1916; No.2 file 1916-1926; Duquesne claims; Winnipeg Free Press 'I Killed Lord Kitchener ' etc.
TNA WO159   Field Marshal Lord Kitchener, Secretary of State for War: Private Office Papers, 5 Aug. 1914 to 5 June, 1916, assembled by private secretary HJ Creedy, "Creedy Papers".
TNA WO159/5   1916 Feb-May Strategic and political papers; Casualties, arms for Russia, munitions.
TNA WO339/45565   2nd Lieut. RD Macpherson.

Tape recordings by eyewitnesses
OA D1/933/2   Reg Holloway of the Mansfield Society of Artists, interviewed by Ann Morris, 1974 (2m 38s).
OA D31/TR111   James Gaudie of Netherskaill, Marwick, interviewed by EW Marwick, 1966 (5m07s).
OA D31/TR113   Territorial Joe Angus of Stromness, interviewed by EW Marwick, 1964 (8m 13s).
OA D31/TR115   Mina Sabiston, née Phillips, of Skidge, Birsay, interviewed by EW Marwick, 1966 (3m 09s).
OA RO5/255   "Lord Kitchener": Interview of 3rd Earl Kitchener (n.d., July 1986) (6m 50s).
OA RO7/131   Jeannie Hunter, interviewed by Ann Manson (n.d., post Dec. 1981) (11m 33s).
OA RO7/315   "*Hampshire*": report of 70th anniv. service, July 1986; 1983 salvage expedition (8m 35s).
OA TA/26/1   Dave Firth, interviewed by Howie Firth for Radio Orkney, 31 Aug. 1977 (5m 06s).
OA TA/26/2   Mina Sabiston, interviewed by Howie Firth for Radio Orkney, 17 Sept. 1977 (3m 13s).
OA TA/26/3   Jane Hunter, née Byas, of Flaws, Birsay be-north, interviewed by Brian Flett and Ann Manson née Marwick for Radio Orkney, 23 Dec. 1981 (14m 45s).
OA TA/26/4   John Fraser of Feaval, Birsay, interviewed by Ann Manson, 20 March 1982 (7m 59s).
OA TA/401   Willie Harvey, Garson & Peter Brass, Stockan, interviewed by Ann Manson, 1982 (27m 38s).
OA TA/402   (as TA/401, continued) (22m 10s).
Private   Brian Budge interview transcribed by Jim Sabiston, 2015.

Films
How Kitchener was betrayed   1921 – banned by London County Council.
The Tragedy of the *Hampshire*   1926 – shown privately by Frank Power (*Orcadian* 18 Mar. 1926).
Fraulein Doktor   1968 – controversial espionage/romance film.
Scotland's War at Sea II (BBC)   2015 – includes interview of Brian Budge & Jim Sabiston by David Hayman.

Newspapers and Journals

Aberdeen Press & Journal	Daily News	Liverpool Courier	Sunday Chronicle
Childrens' Newspaper	Daily Observer	Liverpool Post	Sunday Express
Daily Chronicle	Daily Sketch	Living Orkney	Sunday Referee
Daily Dispatch	Evening News	Lloyds List	Sunday Times
Daily Express	Financial Times	Newcastle Daily Journal	Sunday Times, Perth
Daily Herald	Glasgow Herald	News of the World	Times
Daily Mail	Hansard	Orcadian	Weekly Dispatch
Daily Mirror	Hemel Hempstead Gazette	Orkney Herald	

Published

Admiralty 1926	Admiralty *The Loss of H.M.S. Hampshire on 5 June, 1916 – Official narrative.*
Ala Mana 1922	Ala Mana (pseudonym for Margaret M O'Brien) *The Message: Lord Kitchener Lives.*
Arthur 1920	Sir George Arthur *Life of Lord Kitchener.* 3 volumes.
Ballard 1930	Colin Robert Ballard *Kitchener.*
Brown 2008	Malcolm Brown and Patricia Meehan *Scapa Flow.*
Brown 2016	Jackie Brown 'Truth comes but once in a lifetime' in *Sib Folk News* No. 77 March, 5.
Campbell 1986	NJM Campbell *Jutland: An Analysis of the Fighting.*
Carl 1935	Ernst Carl *One Against England.*
Cassar 1977	George H Cassar *Kitchener: Architect of Victory.*
Chase 2010	Sean Chase 'The Loss of HMS *Hampshire*: Act of War or Murder', *Daily Observer* 25 Nov.
Colledge 2006	JJ Colledge, Ben Warlow *The Complete Record of all Fighting Ships of the Royal Navy.*
Conway 1979	Robert Gardiner (ed.) *Conway's All the World's Fighting Ships 1860-1905.*
Courteney 1951	Charles Courteney *Unlocking Adventure.*
Dittmar 1972	FJ Dittmar and JJ Colledge *British Warships 1914-1919.*
Douglas 1923	Lord Alfred Bruce Douglas *The Murder of Lord Kitchener: and the truth about the Battle of Jutland and the Jews.*
Eunson 2005	Mabel Eunson, Isobel Clouston, Moira Eunston Hazel Foubister *Almost an Island.*
Freeman 1924	Arthur V Freeman *Great Eastern Railway (Suburban System) Scandals.*
Groos 1925	Admiral Otto Groos *Der Krieg zur See 1914-1918: Der Krieg in der Nordsee*, Vol. V.
Hammerton 1938	Sir John A Hammerton (ed.) *The Great War – I was there* pp604-7, copied www.hmsampshire.co.uk.
Harris 1990	John Harris *Lost at Sea.*
Hazell 2000	Howard Hazell (ed.) *The Orcadian Book of the 20th Century* Vol.1.
Hazell 2010	Howard Hazell (ed.) *The Orcadian Book of the 20th Century* Vol.2.
Hewison 1990	WS Hewison *The Great Harbour of Scapa Flow.*
Hewison 2005	WS Hewison *Who was who in Orkney.*
Hodges 1936	Arthur Hodges *Lord Kitchener.*
Leeson 2015	Robert Leeson *Hayek: A Collaborative Biography Part III.*
Irvine 2009	James M Irvine *The Breckness Estate.*
Jane's 2011	*Jane's Fighting Ships of World War I.*
Jellicoe 1919	Viscount Admiral Sir John Jellicoe *The Grand Fleet 1914-1916.*
Jessop 2002	Keith Jessop *Goldfinder.*
Kellett 1984	Richard Kellett *The King's Shilling.*
Konstam 2009	Angus Konstam *Scapa Flow: The Defences of Britain's great fleet anchorage 1914-45.*
Lake 2002	Deborah Lake *The Zeebrugge and Ostend Raids 1918.*
Le Bas 1916	Sir Hedley Le Bas *The Lord Kitchener Memorial Book.*
Leach 2007	Nicholas Leach *Orkney's Lifeboat Heritage.*
Leeson 2015	Robert Leeson *Hayek: A Collaborative Biography Part III Fraud, Fascism and Free Market Religion.*
Liddle 1985	Peter H Liddle *The Sailor's War 1914-18.*
Littlejohn 2015	LC Littlejohn 'The Kitchener Memorial and the *Hampshire* Wall' in *Living Orkney* Aug.
MacDonald 1990	Rod MacDonald *Dive Scapa Flow.*
MacDonald 2003	Rod MacDonald *Into the Abyss.*
MacDonald 2011	Rod MacDonald *The Darkness Below.*
MacDonald 2012	Rod MacDonald *Great British Shipwrecks.*
McAdie 1923	Alexander George McAdie 'Fate and a Forecast' in *Harvard Graduate Magazine* Sept.
McAdie 1925	Alexander George McAdie *War Weather Vignettes.*
McBride 2012	Keith McBride 'The Cruiser Family Talbot' in John Jordan *Warship.*
McCutcheon 2014	Campbell McCutcheon *The Ships of Scapa Flow.*
Magnus 1958	Sir Philip Montefiore Magnus-Allcroft *Kitchener, Portrait of an Imperialist.*
Marder 2014	Arthur J. Marder *From the Dreadnought to Scapa Flow*, Vol. IV, 1917: Year of Crisis.
Marwick 1966	Ernest W Marwick 'The Day that Kitchener died' in *The Orcadian* 2 June 1966, reprinted Robertson 1991.

Bibliography

Marwick 1967	Ernest W Marwick 'The Stromness Lifeboats' in *The Orcadian* 1967, reprinted Robertson 1991.
McCormick 1959	Donald McCormick *The Mystery of Lord Kitchener's Death*.
McCutcheon 2013	Campbell McCutcheon *The Ships of Scapa Flow*.
McKie 2008	David McKie *McKie's Gazetteer*.
Miller 2001	James Miller *Scapa*.
Morris, 1999	Jeff Morris *A History of the Stromness Lifeboats*.
Neilson 1982	K Neilson 'Russian Foreign Purchasing in the Great War: A Test Case' in *The Slavonic and East European Review*, Vol. 60, No. 4 (Oct. 1982), 572-590. http://www.jstor.org/stable/4208582, accessed 19 Feb. 2016.
Newbolt 1928	Henry Newbolt *Naval Operations*, Vol. IV.
Nock, 1972	Oswald S Nock *Speed records on British Railways: A Chronicle of the Steam Era*
ODNB 2004	*Oxford Dictionary of National Biography*.
Oliver 1915	FS Oliver *Ordeal by Battle*.
Paxman 2013	Jeremy Paxman *Great Britain's Great War*.
Paxman 2014a	Jeremy Paxman *The Strange Death of Lord Kitchener* Financial Times Magazine, 7 Nov.
Paxman 2014b	Jeremy Paxman *A Great British Hero* MailOnline, 15 Nov.
Phillips 1930	WC Phillips *The Loss of H.M.S. Hampshire and the Death of Lord Kitchener*.
Pickford 1999	Nigel Pickford *Lost treasure Ships of the 20th Century*.
Pollock 2001	John Pollock *Kitchener* (combines his two vol. biography *The Road to Omdurman* and *Saviour of the Nation*).'
Power 1885	Arnold Power *Letters from Khartoum*.
Power 1926a	Frank Power *The Kitchener Mystery (Reprinted by permission from "The Referee")*.
Power 1926b	Frank Power *Who Killed Kitchener?*
Raafat 2001	Sarrir Raffat 'The Sirdaria' in *Cairo Times*, 15 Feb. 2001, via http://www.egy.com/zamalek/01-02-15.php, accessed 1 March 2016.
Rangliste, v.d.	Marine-Kabinett (ed.) *Rangliste der Kaiserlich Deutschen Marine*.
Rendall 2012	Robert Rendall *Collected Poems*.
Reynolds 2014	David Reynolds *The Long Shadow: The Great War and the Twentieth Century*.
Ritson 1983	WC Ritson letter "HMS *Hampshire*" in *Orcadian* 25 August.
Robertson 1991	John DM Roberston *An Orkney Anthology* Vol. 2.
Rössler 1981	Eberhard Rössler *The U-Boat: The evolution and technical history of German submarines*.
Rössler 1997	Eberhard Rössler *Die Unterseeboote der Kaiserlichen Marine*.
Royle 1985	Trevor Royle *The Kitchener Enigma*.
Royle 2006	Trevor Royle *The Flowers of the Forest: Scotland and the First World War*.
Spence 2013	Albert Spence 'A Memorial and a Lighthouse' in *Orkney Vintage Club Newsletter* Aug.
Spindler 1933	Kontreadmiral Arno Spindler *Der Krieg zur See 1914-1918: Der Handelskrieg mit U-Booten*, Vol. III.
Stell 2010	Geoffrey Stell *Orkney at War: Defending Scapa Flow*, Vol 1.
Stoelzel 1930	Kontreadmiral Albert Stoelzel *Ehrenrangliste der Kaiserlich Deutschen Marine*.
Storer 2014	Jackie Storer *Hidden Stories of the First World War*.
Warner 1985	Philip Warner *Kitchener*.
Wood 1932	Clement Wood *The Man who Killed Kitchener*.
Wylie 1996	Andrew B Wylie *Orkney's Legionnaires*.

Websites
http://uboat.net/wwi/
http://www.navy.gov.au/media-room/publications/world-war-i-naval-staff-monographs
http://www.casebook.org/dissertations/maybrick_diary/mb-mc.html
http://www.hmshampshire.co.uk
http://www.submerged.co.uk/the-kitchener-memorial-orkney-php
http://www.usps.org/national/ensign/uspscompass/compassarchive/compassv1n1/hypothermia.htm
https://en.www.wikipedia.org/wiki/HMS_Hampshire_(1903)
https://www.westsussex.gov.uk/learning/learning_resources/great_war_west_sussex_1914-18/people_at_war.aspx (Themed Studies #20, People Studies #21)
https://kitchenerhampshire.wordpress.com/ and associated social media sites.

Otter, Gnr. J 25
Outshore Point, Sandwick 25
Page, W 9
Palestine 6
Pallast, Sandwick 30-32
Parker, Mrs. F 47
Parliament 34, 37, 70, 99, 100
Patterson, T 51
Paxman, Jeremy 103
Payne, LS F 61, 80
Peace, D 54
Pears, Charles 18, 19
Pentland Firth 12, 48
Peterborough 50, 44
Peterhead 40, 47, 50, 71
Petrie, George 50
Petrograd 10, 11
Pharos 82, 83
Phillips, Shipwright W 1, 15, 20, 22-24, 30-32, 62, 65, 100, 101, 104
Phillips, W, of Garson 20, 23, 29-31, 34, 35, 40, 41
Pickford, Nigel 15
Pickup, Surgeon W 23, 25-27, 30, 31, 62
Piper, Tom 78
Plymouth RN Memorial 58
Pollock, John 14, 15
Portsmouth 1, 63-68
Portsmouth RN Memorial 58
Potter, Boy F 61
Power, Arnold 100
Power, F, alias Freeman, A 12, 16, 17, 19, 20, 23, 24, 26, 27, 32-37, 44-46, 62, 63, 70, 84, 99-104
Power, Frank Le P 100
Prendergast, Rear Adm. 12
Point of Howana Geo 25
Quockquoy, Birsay 17
Quoybellock, Deerness 97
Rackwick, Hoy 53
Rasputin 44, 100
Read, L Stkr. Alfred 15, 22, 23, 31, 32, 62, 65, 99
Read, Mrs. Christina 66
Read, Pte. J 25
Rendall, Sgt. Maj. J 53, 54
Renshaw, J 54
Revell, G 62
Rivna Geo 23, 25, 26, 28, 31, 32, 35
Rix, Leonard 10-13
Roberts, Field Marshall Lord F 7
Robertson, James 17, 29
Robertson, Lieut. Col. Leslie 10, 11, 13, 80
Rogerson, LS, 62, 66, 99, 101
Romanov, Grand Duke Nicholas 10
Roosevelt, President T 46
Rosie, Spencer 55, 81
Ross, Eddy 83
Royal British Legion 53, 82, 83, 99, 101
Royal Engineers, Corps of 6
Royal Maritime Museum, Greenwich 79
Royal National Lifeboat Institution 21
Royal Naval Association 51, 82

Royal Society for the Protection of Birds 51, 55, 56
Royle, Trevor 14, 15, 34, 103, 104
Ruddle, Lieut. A 103
Rugby 5
Russia 9-13, 15, 36, 43-47, 84, 101
Ryan, Frankie 103
Sabiston, G 29
Sabiston, Jim 35
Sabiston, Mina née Phillips 29-31, 40, 64, 66, 80, 81, 104
Salvage 1983 – see *Stena Workhorse*
Sand Geo, Marwick 38
Sandom, Pte. G 61, 80
Sandwick 24, 29, 31, 33-36, 38, 41, 84, 97
Savill, Capt. J 1, 15, 16
Scapa 28
Scapa Flow 1, 3, 12, 14, 15, 19, 20, 46, 50, 57, 61-63, 69, 71, 72, 102
Scapa Flow Visitor Centre and Museum, Lyness 47, 59, 71, 72, 77
Scarth, George 51
Scarth, Miss C 51
Scheer, V. Adm 3
Scott and Yule, Fraserburgh 47
Scott, Lieut. W 54
Scrabster 12, 13
Searchlights 20
Sexton, Boy R 22, 61
Shanks, Stkr. J 80
Sharp, Ch. Ck. W 61
Shearer, Co. Sgt. Mjr. R 28, 29
Shearer, John 54, 100
Shearers, Kirkwall 30
Shearers, Stromness 34
Shields, William 10, 11, 13
Sidebottom, LC W 61
Simpson, AB Richard 15, 16, 22, 23, 29, 31, 32, 62, 66, 104
Simpson, Christina 66, 81
Sims, Stkr. Frederick 15, 22, 23, 30-32, 62, 67, 68, 101, 104
Sinai 6
Sinclair, JG 103
Sinclair, John 34
Sirdar of Egyptian Army 6, 7
Skaill House 24
Skaill, Bay of 20, 21, 24, 26, 28-32, 41, 97
Skaill, Mill of 24, 30
Slater, Adml. Sir John 83
Slater, Col. J 28, 101
Slater, R, Burray 51
Slater, Robert 50
Smith, AB E 61
Smith, Pte. S 25
SMS *Emden* 1, 61
SMS *Königsberg* 1
SMS *Möwe* 14
SMS *Thüringen* 2
Somme, Battle of 8, 32
Sophia 11
Souter, Rev R 51
South Africa, Union of 7, 43

Southampton 100
Spence, D 29
Spence, Lord-Lieutenant Bill 82, 83
Spence, Magnus 97
Spence, Sub-Lieut. J 16, 17, 25, 28, 34, 41, 51, 104
Spionkop 7
St.Magnus Bay, Shetland 3
St.Magnus Cathedral 52, 54, 78, 80, 81
St.Magnus Players 79, 80
St.Ola 33
St.Olaf's Cemetery 32
Stalin, Joseph 47
Stallard, Carp. G 61
Stanger, J 39, 51
Stanger, Miss M 51
Stanger's Yard, Stromness 24
Stavanger 100
Stena Workhorse 40, 42, 47, 71, 72, 75
Stewart, Col. 6
Stewart, Lieut. Cdr. F 20, 27
Stockan, Sandwick 30-32
Stout, Denise 82, 83
Stromness 16, 17, 24, 25, 27-29, 32, 35, 52, 62, 72, 74, 81, 97
Stromness Boys Brigade 54
Stromness life-boat 20, 21, 32, 33, 84, 101, 103
Stromness Museum 61, 78, 98
Stromness Rocket Brigade 21, 32, 101
Stromness Royal British Legion Pipe Band 81, 82
Stronsay 4
Suakin 6, 7
Sudan 5-7,
Suez Canal 6
Sule Skerry 48
Surguy, Henry 10, 11, 13
Swanson, Capt. 33
Sweeney, PO Samuel 15, 16, 22, 23, 31, 32, 62, 67
Swidler, James 30
Tait, Margaret 34, 36, 104
Tatchell, Peter 46
Tatton-Brown, Lady Kenya 55
Taylor, James 40
Taylor, Jenny 78
Taylor, Mrs, of Steddaquoy 52
Taylor, Surgeon C 20, 104
Terschelling 4
Thames 66
Thomas-Johnson, Hudson 82
Thomson, George 20, 21
Thomson, J 27
Thomson, Pte. R 80
Thurso 12, 13, 24, 29, 33
Tipping, Stkr. E 61
Torness, Hoy 15
Toski 7
Trafalgar Institute 68
Traill, WH 51
Tuck, OS C 61
Tucker, Mid. C 1, 61
Tullock, Duncan 81
Turkey 6, 11
Turton, Emily 73, 74
Twatt, Birsay 51
Tyler, Paul 79

U 25 1
U 71 2
U 72 2, 3
U 74 3
U 75 2-4, 13-15, 48-49, 84, 104
U 77 3
U 102 4
UC 65 14
UK Hydrographic Office 97
UK Meteorological Office 96, 97
University of the Highlands and Islands Archaeology Institute 73
USA 9-11, 38, 45-47, 56
Uxbridge 99
Van Winkle, Rip 47
Vance, Det. Insp. Lieut. 37, 46, 77, 103, 104
Vernon, Sub-Lieut. H 61
Versailles, Treaty of 47
Victoria, Queen 6
Wade, Ben 73, 74
Waight, PO E 61, 80
Walden, AB E 61
Walker, Capt. F 17, 19-21, 25, 34, 62, 103, 104
Walker, George 49
War Memorials Trust 55
Wart, Burray 50
Watt, Miss Robina 24
Watt, Mrs Mary 24, 36, 104
Watts, OS A 61
Weeks, Flt. Paymstr V 14, 101
Wei-hei-wei 1
Welbon, Keith 78, 83
Welsby, Boy W 80
Wesson, PO Wilfred 15, 19, 22, 23, 26, 31, 32, 36, 60-62, 68, 99, 101, 104
West, Francis 10, 11, 13
Westminster Coroner 45
Wharton Williams, Aberdeen 71
White Sea 1, 44, 72
Whitefield, Mr 70
Whitelaw, James 30, 31
Whiten Head Bank 14
Wilde, Oscar 43, 46
Wileman, Pte. J 25
Williams, AB W 61
Williams, Surgeon P 20,
Wood, Sir Evelyn 6
Wood, Stkr. W 61
Woods, Supt. 53
Wooldrage, D 54
Woolwich Arsenal 11
Woolwich, RM Academy 5, 6, 11
Worrell, Gnr. J 25
Wylie, Andrew 51
Yesnaby 27, 28
Younger, Maj. Gen. T 55
Yap 1
Ypres 11
Zaharoff, Sir Basil 70
Zakrevsky, Duke of 46
Zanzibar, Sultan of 6
Zaza 19, 97
Zeebrugge Raid 63